America's Great Loop
And Beyond

A BYOB "Bring Your Own Boat" Award Winner

By
Capt. John

Author of

America's Great Loop & Beyond
Caribbean Island Hopping
The Frugal Voyager

An informative, educational and encouraging narrative on the procedures and methods of living aboard and cruising America's Great Loop and beyond.

The sale of this book without a front cover is strictly prohibited. If this book is without a cover, it may have been reported to the publisher as "unsold and destroyed" and neither the author nor the publisher has received payment.

2013 BJR Publishing LLC, Mass Market Edition
"America's Great Loop and Beyond"

Copyright © 2013 by BJR Publishing LLC
Text Copyright © by author: John C. Wright AKA Capt. John
Allison Thibos Editor
All rights reserved.

Capt. John's "Bring Your Own Boat Series"
First edition published in the United States 2013
Second Edition published in the United States 2014 by:

BJR Publishing LLC
Titusville, Florida 32780

All rights reserved. No part of this book may be reproduced or utilized in any form, or by any means, electronic or mechanical, without the prior written permission by the author and or publisher.

Disclaimer: This book is intended for information and education only. It is not a cruising guide and not intended for navigation.

ISBN-13: 978-1492350941
ISBN-10: 149235094X

Library of Congress Cataloging-in-Publication Data Available.

Printed and bound in the United States of America.

America's Great Loop and Beyond

From the current Best Selling author in the nautical markets, BJR Publishing is pleased to announce the Second Edition of Capt. John's *America's Great Loop and Beyond. In its first release, "America's Great Loop & Beyond" soared to become the* 2013 #1 Best Selling Book in the nautical market. It won "Best Book" and "Best Book in a Series" Awards from our National Publishers' Best Sellers in a Niche Market.

Packed with useful information and written specifically for those with little or no experience. It provides encouraging narratives filled with all the right kind of information a frugal voyager needs to cruise America's Great Loop.

While Cruising Guides and Navigational maps give you the route, Capt. John gives you the reality like no one else. From required boat restrictions, fuel range requirements, distances for each leg of your voyage, anchorages and marinas, he provides all the information you need to make this voyage safely and comfortably on an affordable boat and budget.

If you are dreaming and planning to cruise America's Great Loop on a frugal budget, Capt. John's *"America's Great Loop and Beyond"* promises to be the most valuable book in your Great Loop library.

B.A, Ruisi, Ph.D.

Table of Contents

PREFACE	7
FORWARD	8
America's Great Loop	12
The Great Loop Route	20
The Atlantic Intracoastal Waterway	25
Atlantic & Gulf Intracoastal Waterway Tips	34
The Florida ICW	46
Georgia & The Carolinas	49
The Chesapeake and C&D Canal	56
The New Jersey Intracoastal Waterway	59
The Hudson River	65
The Erie Canal	71
Erie Canal Locks	78
The Great Lakes	82
Lake Erie	85
Lake St. Clair	88
Lake Huron	91
Lake Michigan	94
The Illinois River	99
THE MISSISSIPPI RIVER	104
The Upper Mississippi River	110
The Lower Mississippi River	114
The Ohio River	118
The Tennessee River	121
The Tennessee-Tombigbee Waterway	124
THE GULF ICW	129
Crossing the GULF OF MEXICO	137
THE OKEECHOBEE WATERWAY	143
BEYOND THE LOOP	147
Lake Superior	149

The Potomac River	157
The Ohio River	162
The Tennessee River	163
The Cumberland River	165
The Missouri River	168
The Alabama River	170
The Arkansas River	171
Cruising Canada	173
Inland Islands and More	182
Caribbean Island Hopping	190
The Great Loop Boat	193
Great Loop boat restrictions	195
Should your boat be NEW or USED?	213
What type of boat is best for you?	215
Provisioning your Boat	218
Equipping your Great Loop Boat	221
Cruising on a frugal budget	227
A $12.29 per day voyage around the Loop	235
Your Great Loop Adventure	239
Living Aboard	245
Great Loop Musing	252
Top Twenty Great Loop Questions - Answered	267
Making the Dream a Reality	275

DEDICATION

<u>To the Old Salts</u> that encouraged me, the storytellers of sailor's yarns that excited me, and the brave voyagers who went before me, lighting my way and inspiring the fantasies of my youth.

<u>To my Dad</u> who not only adopted me, taught me right from wrong, and encouraged me to live my dream. A missionary himself, who demonstrated his love for God by living a life of Christian example. Never complaining, and always eager to lend a helping hand to those in need, and God's greatest blessing in my life.

<u>To Allison Thibos</u> my valued and most deserving editor. It is she who wades through a sea of verbs to make my book float. A more precious and deserving individual you'll never find.

PREFACE

If you have ever passionately wanted anything for somebody else, you will understand how I feel about America's Great Loop. Cruising America's Great Loop is simply so special words just fail to describe its awesome greatness and pictures blunder at the attempt to capture its beauty.

As the Greeks, when they first referenced the seven natural Wonders of the World in 200 BC, they used the word "theamata" which translates most closely into English as: "must see and must experience."

The America's Great Loop is a "must see and must experience" boating adventure. It is the Mecca of boating, the "theamata" for every American Boater.

The purpose of this book is not meant to be all inclusive. It is to inform and encourage you to see and experience this incredible adventure for yourself. If I could, I would wrap it up and give it to you... boat, hook, line, sinker and PFD.

This book's true success cannot be measured in the number of sales, rather in the number of those inspired to take this incredible journey.

FORWARD

I often think how sad it is for most Americans that "the journey" has long been stripped of its romance and adventure by the methods of modern travel. Now everyone, it seems, wants to journey through life at warp speeds.

Today, the reality is that nearly half the world's population is perpetually on the move. It takes less than 16 hours to fly from Dallas, TX to Hong Kong. Where upon departure, one joins an overcrowded population of displaced humanity – herded like cattle from airport to airplane, only to end up making fixed stops on and off a tour bus with a tight schedule.

Yes, people travel for many reasons. Some travel because their career demands it. Soldiers travel because the Military orders them to. Missionaries travel because God calls them to do so.

I travel to satisfy a compelling yearning, conceived in youth long before I was able to travel anywhere at all. Now as an adult, I continue to be lured deeper and deeper by my own astonishing adventures. I am caught in the web of excitement as I voyage America's Great Loop. From one stop to another. Such powerful and potent motivation to me is the journey itself; seldom does the destination keep me in one place long enough.

From one stop to another, I chase that endless summer of breathtaking sunsets and meeting wonderful people from all over the world. My compass heading is always pointed toward destinations all too exotic to describe. I now live the imaginations of my youth and my heaven is measured in feet along the waterline of my boat.

For me, it's not the fast lane. It is the past lane. Travel takes me back to the fantasies of my boyhood when travel was an adventure and the writings of Twain worked its magic on me.

Now it is your turn.

INTRODUCTION

You will be glad to know this book is NOT about me. Nor is it about the things I have done. It is for you to look and see what you can do. In fact, this book has much more to do with "your" future encouragement than it has to do with anyone's past accomplishments.

Within these pages you will discover why America's Great Loop is beyond doubt the safest and most amazing long-distance voyage on the planet. Truly an adventure every American boater should take. You will also learn how you can experience this wonderful boating adventure without ever having to make a U-turn, and without ever facing the perils of a wide open sea.

Maybe the greatest aspect of cruising America's Great Loop is the fact that you can cruise all 5,600 (plus) miles of it and never leave sight of land, much less be more than a stone's throw from it. In addition, you will be boating in areas that are as readily accessible by the USCG, local EMT emergency medical personnel, and your voyage will be convenient to pharmacies, hospitals, banks, post offices, rental cars, airports, restaurants, movie theaters, museums, and endless amounts of historic places to see and experience. All things considered, the Great Loop is beyond doubt, the safest long-distance and most amazing voyage on the planet.

The American Great Loop offers many options and choices in the form of detours, side trips, and places to visit... some take longer than others, some require more money than others. Here you will learn about these options so you can choose the ones that best fit your philosophy, lifestyle, and pocket book.

Cruising the Great Loop is a dream voyage, an incredible adventure. It can be made in a small live-aboard size boat, in safety and comfort, and within most anyone's budget. Likewise, it can be made in a vessel that costs more than most upper middle income homes. Whichever situation fits your philosophy and pocket book, it promises to be the most talked about and treasured experience of your lifetime.

Right now you hold in your hand everything you need to discover how you can make this voyage in a relatively small and affordable live-aboard size vessel (sail or power) in complete safety and comfort. If you are in the upper income echelon – you will learn about the very best boat options available to cruise the Loop in style, comfort, and in the most accommodating and economical fashion.

You will learn why you do not need a ton of boating experience, but you do need a little. Why you don't need a big expensive "yacht," but rather a small and comfortable one. You will also learn you don't need any special training or education to make this voyage. Whether you are new to boating or have years of experience, your only critical requirement is to be a good safe boater with a good safe seaworthy boat.

Next, you will discover what to expect along the way. From boat size restrictions (yes, some boats are too big), to fuel range requirements (and some boats are too small). I will give you distances for each leg of your voyage and will help you determine what type and size of boat might be just right for you to make this incredible voyage.

Based on a "go small, go now, and stay out longer" cruising philosophy, you will get an honest look at the requirements for a smart sensible and affordable boat. Regardless the size of your pocketbook, I will point you in the direction of finding a boat that is not only economical to purchase, but to own and operate while cruising the Great Loop.

Inside this book, you will find the _entire_ Great Loop route including the many and most popular side trip and detour options with a complete narrative for each leg of your journey so you will know what to expect along the way. This includes many anchorages, marinas, waterfront restaurants and interesting sites, along with the required distance and fuel range for each leg of your voyage.

If one thing is true among long-distance live-aboard cruisers, it is that we all have our own boats, boat types and boat preferences. We all have our very own lifestyle, comfort zones and pocketbooks. I'm not here to say "do as I do". Nor am I saying my way is best. I'm here to give you the options so you will know what options are best for you.

From boat bums in the most humble of boats, to the most affluent cruisers in flagship vessels – we "Loopers" are that friendly group of boaters having all the fun.

And we can't wait for you to join us.

America's Great Loop

It's a dream worth living!

America's Great Loop

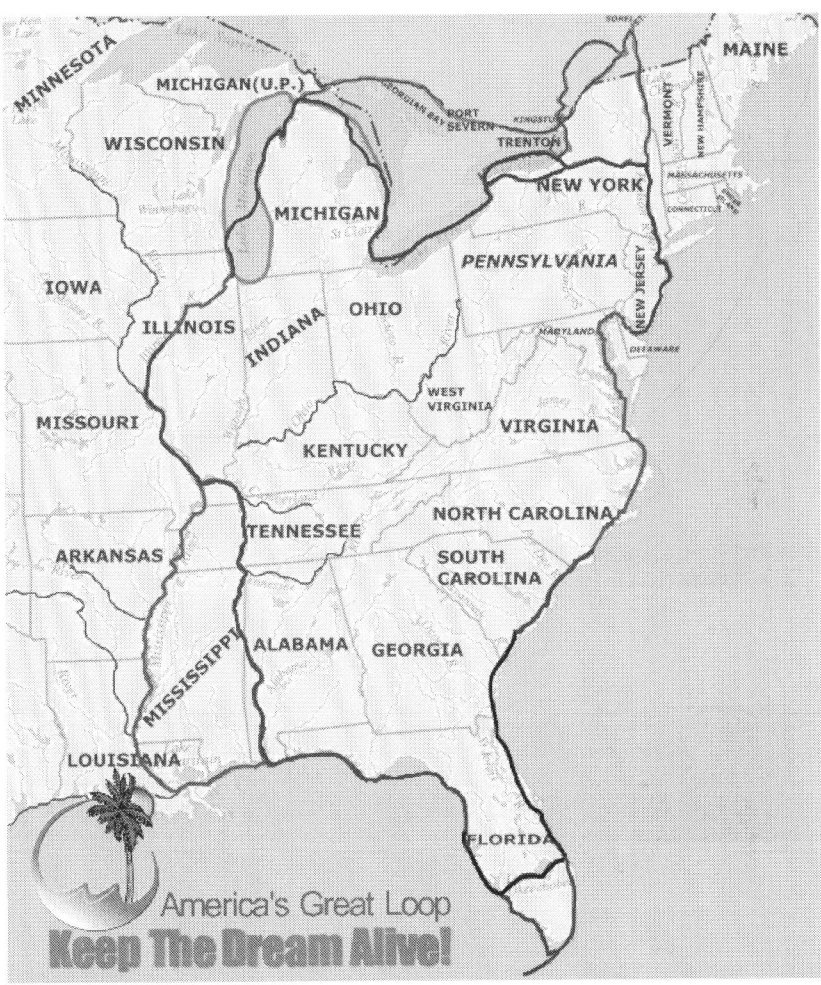

Just imagine... being a Looper... boating over 5,600 miles, through 25 states, along beautiful beaches, inland rivers, historic canals, across the Great Lakes, through downtown Chicago, and into the Illinois and Mississippi Rivers.

No matter which of the 25 states you start your journey from, in the end you will "cross your wake" at the same place you started, without ever having to make a U-turn, or face the perils of a wide open sea.

Sounds incredible, doesn't it? But that's not the half of it!

America's Great Loop

From the Washington Monument in D.C. to the Statue of Liberty, from the Erie Canal to Niagara Falls, you can take your very own boat through downtown Chicago to the St. Louis Arch, and from the Civil War battle fields of Shiloh, to the steel mills of Pittsburgh. Once you reach the beautiful inland rivers of America's Heartland, you can cruise to the home of Mark Twain on the Mississippi River and to the home of Reba McIntyre on the Cumberland. You can also take the Cumberland River to the Grand Ole Opry, and the Tennessee River to the Chattanooga Choo Choo.

Yes, from the "Big Easy" to the "Big Apple" and from Little Rock to Little River, which ever route you take, or detour you make, you have the option of voyaging the historic Louis and Clark trail west as far as South Dakota, and you can cruise east to the Wright brothers' Kitty Hawk. You can boat as far north as Quebec and south east into the Florida Keys or south west to Mexico… Even without taking any detours, America's Great Loop is an awe inspiring boating adventure that will take you as close to the Frozen Tundra as it does the Tropics of the Equator.

America's Great Loop is not only the finest, safest, navigable waterway system in the world; it is the longest "continuous" waterway system on the planet. Technically, America's Great Loop encompasses the entire eastern portion of North America. It includes the Atlantic and Gulf Intracoastal Waterways, the Great Lakes, and the inland rivers of America's Heartland. For the pleasure boater, the Great Loop offers over 5,600 plus miles of safe, scenic and friendly cruising without ever having to make a U-turn.

Realistically however, the Great Loop is your connecting gateway to cruising over 24,000 miles of navigable inland lakes and rivers for a total of more than 29,000 miles of boating pleasure. A distance of which is the same average distance for a sailor–sailing a qualified circumnavigation around the world – and that does not include your side trip or detour options of cruising into Canadian waters and voyaging along the hundreds of miles on the Canadian Heritage Canals.

Unlike crossing the open ocean, America's Great Loop is close to land and therefore seldom are you ever without cell-phone service, Internet, free Wi-Fi, or air digital TV. While the space on your boat may be small – you can still cruise with most all of the comforts of home.

Once you toss those lines that have been keeping you land-locked from freedom – you and your shipmate will quickly settle into your new life of cruising and living aboard. Soon enough, relieving each other at the wheel, and securing the lines when you dock or pass through one of more than a hundred locks... will be as routine as making the morning coffee.

On the coastal side, you will have to keep an eye on the tides and weather; but cruising the Great Loop is not fraught with the perils of the open sea. Unless you choose otherwise, you will always have land in sight and safe harbors at night. In fact, your biggest concern will be the water's depth – so be sure you stay between the channel markers, or you may run aground.

At night, you can "anchor out" or dock at a marina. You can dine on your boat or dine at a local waterfront or nearby restaurant. In the mornings you can have your coffee, read your e-mail, send some pictures, take care of your online banking, and get the boat ready to pull up anchor and shove off again.

You will most likely cruise at a leisurely 8 to 9 knots (about 10 mph) and you will average about 50 miles a day. You will often be stopping to see the sights, visit a museum, enjoy an ice cream, or take a stroll along the beach. There is simply so much to see and do along the way.

Yes! In the same 365 days it takes the Earth to travel around the Sun, you can travel around the Great Loop in your own boat. Most

Loopers take a year to complete this voyage even though they will have actually only cruised about 110 days. The rest of the time will be shared between enjoying a peaceful paradise cove and visiting one of the many famous historic or local sites along the way.

The very most economical way to cruise the Great Loop is in a counter clockwise direction, following the Atlantic ICW north to the Hudson River before passing though the Erie Canal en route to the Great Lakes. From Lake Michigan you will travel down the Illinois, Mississippi, Ohio, Cumberland, Tennessee and Tombigbee Rivers (herein after referred to as the Tenn-Tom) to the Gulf of Mexico. This way, you are boating with the current for more than 70% of your voyage. Time your journey correctly in tidal waters, so that you can "go with the flow" and you will be going with the current for over 80% of your journey.

On the Atlantic ICW you will boat through the beautiful blackwater of the Waccamaw River. You will pass crabbers in Chesapeake Bay, cruise and beneath the Statue of Liberty. On the Gulf ICW you will cruise past barges and watch divers harvesting scallops, oysters and sea sponges in the Gulf of Mexico. If so inclined, you can even dive for your own lobsters in the Florida Keys.

In the Everglades you will see egrets standing on cypress logs. Around Cumberland Island you will see wild horses that come to eat the exposed green marsh grasses at low tide. You will see hundreds of Bald Eagles on the Illinois River. The ever-changing scenery will keep you reaching for your camera –and you'll want to thank a geek for the technology of the "digital age" as you will want to take lots and lots of pictures and instantly send them wirelessly to your family and friends, or post them on your Blog or Facebook page.

When planning your voyage, remember: you don't want to get to the Erie Canal until mid-May because of snow and runoff, and you need to get off Lake Michigan by mid-September because of the winds and cold.

The most common live-aboard size boat used is live-aboard size between 26 and 36 feet long. Boats can't have more than a 6' draft and must be able to pass under a fixed 19'1" fixed bridge on the Chicago Ship Canal.

In the end, long before you cross your wake, this adventure will have changed your life. Not only will it have made you a better helmsman, it will have made you a better person. You will feel the change, and others will see the change in you. For no one can experience such absolute freedom as this… no one can be as blessed as this… and not have it remain within them for the rest of their days.

If you let it be, the Great Loop can also be a very religious experience. If you look for it, you can't help but see the Master's handy work. From beautiful sunsets and beaches to the tranquil sunrise, you will experience a landscaped water world of wonders. God, America, Geography, History, and Apple pie – until I cruised America's Great Loop – they were all just something I only thought I knew.

America's Great Loop

Not everyone is cut out to make an ocean passage.

Many of us dream of sailing off into the sunset –cruising through turquoise waters, walking on pristine sandy beaches, and having umbrella drinks under coconut trees. This dream in fact, is one of most popular dreams in America.

Sadly, however, not that many of us are cutout to make such a voyage. It takes a special kind of person to sail off into the sunset, leaving family and loved ones behind. When cruising the Great Loop, however, your options include having family or friends join you for a leg or portion of your journey. You can also rent a car or catch a flight home. In many cases, you can even boat right to (or very hear) a family member or friend's home – or at least their home town. Certainly, cruising America's Great Loop is a much safer, cheaper, and a more relaxing adventure than seeing America in an RV.

On the Great Loop, you are away from big-city traffic jams, noise and smog. Instead of anxiously cruising down the highway 70 miles an hour, you're relaxing on your boat enjoying the scenery at 70 *smiles an hour.*

In your own boat, you can voyage from Mexico to Massachusetts and on to Memphis. You can boat from Paducah to Padre Island and on to Pittsburgh, from Chicago to Chattanooga, from Nashville to New York, and from Waverly to Washington. You can boat from Tulsa to Titusville and on up to Tonawanda. You can even boat from the French Quarter in New Orleans to French Quebec in Canada…all without ever risking the perils of the open sea.

So you see… the Great Loop is much more than an alternative to crossing an ocean. This is an unbelievable adventure, and though different, it is absolutely second to none.

It is a boater's dream on a continuous series of beautiful waterways. It's been done in jet-skis, small boats, large boats, sailboats, powerboats, and even a few smaller yachts. In fact, whatever your lifestyle, philosophy, or pocketbook there is a boat waiting for you to take it on this incredible American journey.

Traveling in your own vessel, (bring your own boat, sail or power) and you will discover it to be an incredible way to see and experience the culture, diversity, and customs of life in the America. From big cities to the smallest of towns, villages, and the most wonderful countryside, you can travel at your own speed, stopping almost anywhere along the way to spend a night or a week. Yes, if you make some side trips, you can take your own little floating "portable motel room" to and through more than half the states in the US, and into the Canadian provinces of Ontario and Quebec.

The Great Loop Route

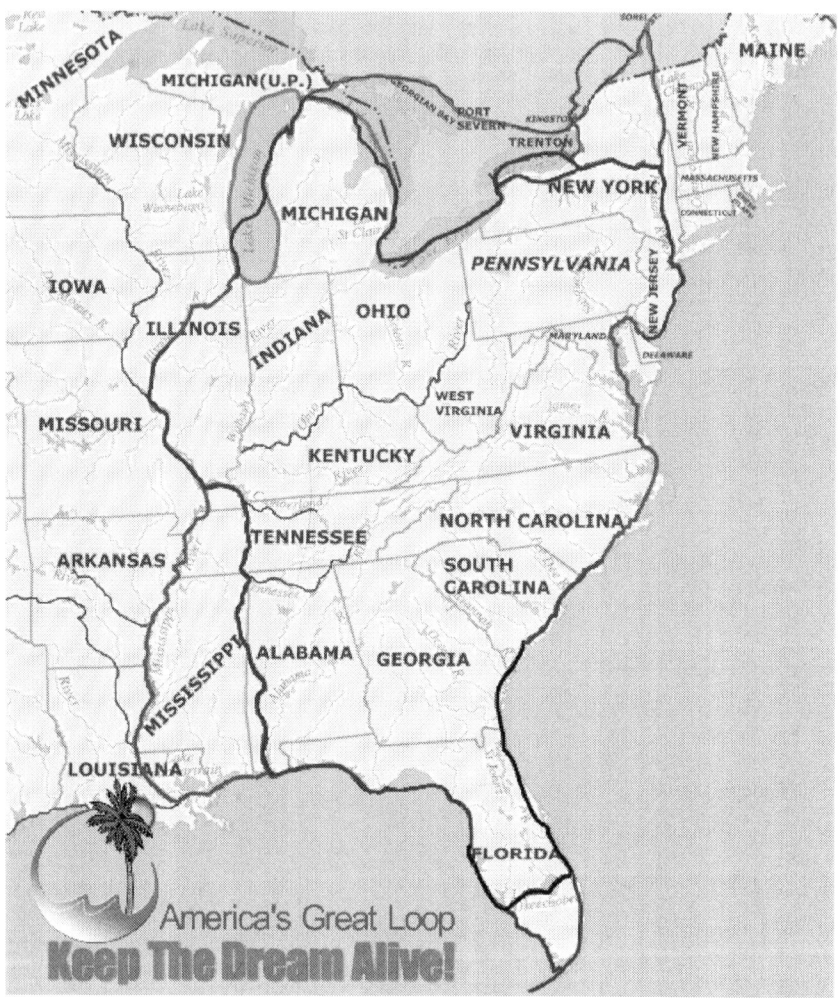

The short route: For your live-aboard and cruising pleasure, the short route around America's Great Loop provides you with 5,600 "statute" miles. Despite popular opinion, ALL miles on the Great Loop including the miles on the Gulf & Atlantic ICW, and inland rivers are "statute" miles. In summary, your route will include:

The Atlantic Intracoastal Waterway: Starting from the St Lucie Inlet on the east coast of Florida, your Great Loop distance on the Atlantic ICW is **987 miles to Norfolk**, VA. From Norfolk, it is another 279 miles to the Hudson River for a total of 1,266 miles. From Florida's east coast at St. Lucie heading north, the ICW will take you through the Waccamaw River to the Dismal Swamp, and lead you on up to the Chesapeake Bay, the C&D Canal, Delaware River, through the NJ ICW and across New York Harbor to the Hudson River. Remember, to plan your voyage so that you are at the entrance of the Erie Canal around mid-May. (A little sooner or later, depending on how harsh the winter has been.)

The Hudson River: This leg of your voyage is **154 miles** from the Statue of Liberty to the Troy Lock. The Hudson is deep, has a rocky bottom and gets lots of boat traffic. Fact is, the Hudson River Valley is home to many of the most famous historic and visited sites in America.

The Erie Canal: Your Great Loop distance on the Erie Canal is **338 miles**. It has 57 locks that lift your vessel 566 feet above sea level between Waterford, NY on the Hudson to the upper Niagara River between Buffalo and Niagara Falls in Tonawanda. If you take a left on the Niagara River, this will be your connection into Lake Erie. If you turn right on the Niagara River… you will have one exciting side trip over Niagara Falls, and all your friends will see you on the ten o'clock news.

The Great Lakes: Your most direct distance across the Great Lakes from **Buffalo, NY to Chicago is 892 statute miles**. This voyage (if you go non-stop on the direct route) will normally take between 10-15 days. However, beginning at Buffalo, there is simply a boater's world of stuff to see and do on your way to Chicago. You have plenty of time, as you really don't want to reach Chicago and be off the Great Lakes until mid-September. So take your time, see some sites, and visit with the local natives. They are friendly!

The Illinois River: Your Great Loop distance on this river is **334 miles**. This baby is the connection between the Great Lakes and the Mississippi River. At the entrance of the Illinois River you will encounter a 19' 1" fixed bridge you <u>must</u> go under. It is the lowest fixed bridge on the entire Great Loop which has no alternative waterway route around it. The Illinois River's close proximity to the Chicago River and the man-made Chicago Ship Canal is why we have a Great Loop and not a "Great U-turn." This leg of your journey takes you to the Mississippi River at Grafton, IL. You will see lots of Bald Eagles on your way.

The Upper Mississippi River: This leg of your journey is only **219 miles to Cairo** at the junction of the Ohio River and the Lower Mississippi. From Cairo, you may want to take the Ohio River to the Cumberland or Tennessee River and into Kentucky Lake on your way to the Tenn-Tom route to Mobile Bay. Or if you wish (and you have the fuel range), you may want to continue south on the Lower Mississippi route to New Orleans.

The Lower Mississippi River: This leg of your journey (if you choose to take it) is **871 miles from Cairo to the Harvey** Lock and Gulf ICW just south of New Orleans. The problem is that there are only two safe, convenient, stops for fuel and provisions along the way.

The Ohio River: If you take the Tenn-Tom route, your Great Loop distance on this river is only **46 miles**, but it's all against the current of the mighty Ohio River. From Cairo, IL this baby takes you to the Tennessee and Cumberland Rivers near Paducah, KY, and into what is referred to as the "Land between the Lakes," and the very "Heartland of America." For most Loopers, this is the entrance to some of the most enjoyable portions of the entire Great Loop. This river has 53 locks between Cairo and Pittsburgh. It also takes you to Cincinnati and

Louisville. In fact, if you are so inclined, you can cruise all the way into West Virginia.

The Cumberland River: You are now in the land of Daniel Boone and the key passageway (Cumberland Gap) through the lower central Appalachian Mountains. Here you can walk in the footsteps of early pioneers and Native Americans, visit the ruins of fortifications and battlefields of the Civil War, and experience the life of an early mountain community. Your Great Loop distance on the Cumberland River and Lake Barkley to the Tennessee River is an optional 33 miles. The Cumberland River is also your gateway for a beautiful side trip to Nashville.

The Tennessee River: Your Great Loop distance on this river is **215 miles**. It is 207 miles from the Ohio River to Pickwick Landing Lock and eight miles farther is the entrance of the Tenn-Tom Waterway. This river "side trip" also takes you to Chattanooga and Knoxville. Along the way you can stop at Birdsong Resort and Marina and visit North America's only fresh water pearl farm.

The Tennessee-Tombigbee: Your distance on the Tenn-Tom to Mobile Bay is **234 miles**. The Tenn-Tom Waterway has 10 locks and was a bigger man-made canal project than the Panama Canal. On your way to Mobile Bay, it is a <u>must</u> stop for fuel at Bobby's Fish Camp and Restaurant. It is my favorite stop for catfish. Umm good!

The Gulf Intracoastal Waterway: Your Great Loop route across this waterway is **218 miles from Mobile, AL to Carrabelle**, FL. The beaches you will cruise by are stunningly beautiful and the local shrimp, oysters at the "hole in the wall" seafood restaurants are absolutely the best you will find in the world.

Crossing the Gulf of Mexico: Your journey across the Gulf of Mexico offers some wonderful options. You can go **73 miles directly across to Steinhatchee**, or take the longer stretch to Tampa Bay. In the right boat, you can even hop-scotch your way around the coast. But believe it or not, while most Loopers are anxious over crossing the Gulf, it is not the most treacherous waters you will cross. If you started on the Atlantic ICW, compared to Albemarle Sound, this section of the Gulf will seem like a piece of cake.

The Lake Okeechobee Waterway: Your Great Loop route across this waterway is **154 miles**. Here, a series of five locks helps you through this inland waterway across the lower peninsula of Florida. The canal depth of the waterway is approximately eight feet, and the width of the canal varies from 80 to 100 feet. Most cruisers access the waterway from the Gulf ICW at Ft. Myers, shortening their trip to the east coast of Florida and bypassing the Florida Keys. You can also visit the Florida Keys from the Atlantic side, which offers a more protected waterway with much more to see and do along your way.

The Atlantic Intracoastal Waterway

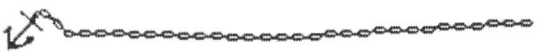

(The "ICW" or "The Ditch")

This leg of your voyage is 1,266 statute miles. It is 987 miles from the St. Lucie Inlet to Norfolk, VA. From Norfolk, it is another 279 miles to the mouth of the Hudson River for a total of 1,266 statute miles.

The Intracoastal Waterways consist of natural inlets, salt-water rivers, bays, and sounds; other parts are man-made canals. All together, they are a vital part of cruising America's Great Loop by providing a safe, navigable, "inside" route along the Eastern Seaboard. Except for crossing a few bays and sounds and a small section of New York Harbor, you never have to travel on the open sea. Additionally, you are never that far from land and most of the time no more than a stone's throw from it.

The Atlantic Intracoastal Waterway runs most of the length of the entire Atlantic Coast. It is toll-free for pleasure boats and serves ports from Atlantic City, NJ to Key West, FL. This route is linked by man-made canals including the Chesapeake and Delaware or C&D Canal, and Chesapeake-Albemarle Canal, and the lowest "controlled" depth is 6' in the Dismal Swamp Canal.

Technically, however, additional canals and bays extend the navigable ICW all the way north to Boston, MA. From which, many of the more than 4,000 "Snowbird" boaters make their annual south for the winter and north for the summer voyages. The ICW waterway is also used by boaters when the ocean is too rough for travel. Numerous inlets connect the ICW with the Atlantic Ocean.

Of course, you can start your Great Loop voyage from most anywhere. If you live in Texas, you would start on the Gulf ICW. If you live on the Great Lakes, you would start from there. In our case however, we are going to start near the St. Lucie Inlet at Stuart, Fl. Your AICW or Atlantic ICW Mile Marker will be 987. This means we are 987 statute miles from Norfolk, VA.

While the inland waterway continues north of Norfolk, VA, Norfolk is Mile 0 on the ICW.

If you look at the map on the following page, you will see Stuart, FL at the lower portion of the map. This is where you will be after you cruise through the Lake Okeechobee Waterway from Florida's West Coast from Ft. Meyers, FL.

In addition, using the map you will notice Vero Beach is mile marker 952. This means Vero Beach is 35 (statute) miles from Stuart. Which is most likely to be your next stop for the night.

America's Great Loop

- Troy, NY - Entrance to Erie Canal
- Sandy Hook Bay, NJ
- **C & D Canal**
- Delaware River
- Chesapeake Bay
- Norfolk, VA - ICW mile marker 0
- **Dismal Canal** - Elizabeth City
- Beaufort, NC - ICW mile marker 202
- Cape Fear, NC - ICW mile marker 310
- Charleston, SC - ICW mile marker 570
- Savannah, GA - ICW mile marker 583
- Jacksonville, FL - ICW mile marker 747
- Daytona Beach - ICW mile marker 829
- New Smyrna Beach - mile marker 847
- Titusville - mile marker 878
- Vero Beach - mile marker 952
- Stuart, FL - ICW mile marker 987
- Lake Okeechobee
- Gulf of Mexico
- America's Great Loop

Keep The Dream Alive!

Navigating the ICW is as easy as 1, 2, 3, (well, almost). The heaviest commercial traffic (oceangoing vessels and barges) will be concentrated around the industrial areas of Norfolk, VA. The heaviest pleasure boat traffic will be found south of Vero Beach, FL.

ICW waterway day markers and signs will mark the channel and point the way for an amazing, well-protected passage for all but a very few and small sections of its entire length. These in the water "day markers" are much like road signs on the highway that point you in the right direction and keep you in the channel. They make it <u>almost</u> impossible to get lost. (Notice, I emphasized "almost.") In some areas it is difficult, if not impossible, to spot the next ICW day marker if you don't know where it is (or is supposed to be) but that's where your GPS comes in really handy, as it also marks your way and tells you where the channel markers are located – so you know where to look for them.

Yes, you will share the ICW with other boats, tugs, bugs and barges, Navy ships, and at Kings Bay possibly even a submarine or two. In addition, you will encounter cruise ships, large freighters, container ships, all sorts of commercial fishing and shipping traffic, and a lot of Ferry boats. At times it will be hard to remember that you are the intruder here, as the entire ICW is free to recreational boaters. It is all those commercial vessels that not only pay their way – but ours. So be thankful when you see them, and be nice. Give them plenty of room – as they have the right of way.

Often referred to as "The Ditch," from St. Lucie Inlet to the Hudson River, you will discover some real cruising jewels along the way. By far, cruising the ICW is an adventure. In some areas, just when it really starts to bore you, along comes another jewel that makes the entire length of the ICW worth cruising all over again.

Atlantic Intracoastal Waterway
← South   Destination   North →

South		North	
COINJOCK	37	NORFOLK	12
ELIZABETH CITY	64	NEWPORT NEWS	24
BELHAVEN	126	CAPE CHARLES	50
BEAUFORT	182	RICHMOND	115
WILMINGTON	297	WASHINGTON	209
SOUTHPORT	310	BALTIMORE	210
GEORGETOWN	392	PHILADELPHIA	296
CHARLESTON	455	NEW YORK	452
SAVANNAH	575	BOSTON	717
JACKSONVILLE	734	EASTPORT	967
MIAMI	1084		
KEY WEST	1236		

Safe boaters can rest assured, however, that on your entire voyage around America's Great Loop it is all about safety. Experience doesn't matter (none of us had it, until we did it). Simply being a safe boater is your primary concern.

It is surprisingly difficult to get into any real trouble as long as you stay within the boundaries of the marked channels. For the most part, even if your boat sinks, it will be resting hard on the bottom long before it disappears under the water, as most of the ICW is shallower than your boat's hull height.

For a safe boater, probably the very worst that can happen is running aground and suffering a lot of temporary embarrassment until the tide rises again – a situation of which most every "experienced boater" has encountered at least once. So, if and when this happens to you – don't panic. Consider it your Graduation Ceremony from a novice to a pro.

If you are worried about crossing that 73 mile stretch between Carrabelle and Steinhatchee on the Gulf of Mexico – don't be. If you started on the Atlantic, by the time you get to the Gulf of Mexico, you will have cruised across Pamlico Sound, Albemarle Sound, Chesapeake Bay, the Delaware and the Great Lakes – all of which will make your eventual Gulf crossing seem like a piece of cake.

We Loopers all have our own experiences. We all have our best and worst parts of the ICW as well as the Great Loop. So don't let what you've heard or read prevent you from going. Instead, go and discover your own best and worst. As I've mentioned, and will mention again, if you are a safe boater in an appropriate and safe boat, about the worst "life threatening" thing that can possibly happen to you is a bit of embarrassment. Believe me... even the worst part of the Great Loop is worth doing again just to see and experience the rest. It is our <u>imagined</u> fear that always makes that big bad wolf bigger than he really is.

You are about to discover for yourself, the ICW is a great place to cruise.

The Atlantic ICW is really a great training course for the rest of your voyage. In addition to the sights and sounds, there are plenty of waterfront restaurants and marinas along the way. However, you have to make it all the way to St. Augustine, FL, before you reach Hurricane Patty's (next to the Marina on the San Sebastian River) which is one of our very favorite stops for eats on the entire Florida section of the ICW. If at all possible, don't pass it by.

Our very favorite stops along the Atlantic ICW include Hurricane Patties, the Isle of Palms, Myrtle Beach, Wacca Wache Marina, Washington City Docks, Ocracoke, Lady's Island Marina, and Elizabeth City. From Wacca Wache Marina, you can take your dinghy or rent a car and visit Pawley's Island. There, you will find the Hammock Shop Village, an eclectic mix of specialty stores and restaurants, such as the High Hammock Maverick Seaside Kitchen, which alone is worth the side trip.

On the Waccamaw River, you will find yourself on one of most unique and beautiful parts of the entire ICW. My last adventure through this wonderful display of nature presented me with dolphins swimming along the side of my vessel while a pair of Bald Eagles rested at their nest atop a huge moss covered cypress tree. This is one section on the ICW you will not mind at all that you are going so slowly.

At Beaufort, after you pass under Lady's Island Bridge and go to Lady's Island Marina, about 100 feet or so from the marina you will come to a real hole-in- the wall (dive looking) bar called the "Filling Station." This is one place where looks are deceiving. At happy hour every day, they serve up the best eats for the dollar of any place on the entire Great Loop. Here, you will find cheap drinks and a cheap meal that will absolutely blow your mind. The meal changes every day. In 2011, the last time my son and I were there, it was "hamburger and hot-dog" day. For $3.00, we had one of the best burgers in the world together with one mighty fine (big thick) hot-dog, both cooked on a wood grill. Both (yes, you get both) come with your choice of all the fixings plus potato salad and beans – and it's all for only $3.00. We stayed an extra day just to go back for "steak night."

The point is that there are many little "jewels" like these hidden along your route around the Great Loop. While I like to call your attention to the ones we find, the very best ones indeed will be the ones you find on your own and tell us about.

In addition to commercial traffic, the ICW is used extensively by recreational boaters, so you will (by far) not be alone most anywhere on either the Gulf or Atlantic ICW.

On the east coast, some of the traffic in fall and spring is by snowbirds that regularly move south in winter and north in summer. Numerous inlets connect the Atlantic Ocean with the Intracoastal Waterway.

If you are visiting the Florida Keys and take the Intracoastal Waterway from Ft. Myers, Longboat Key is a favorite destination of sailors and fishermen alike.

The waters from Ft. Myers through Pine Island Sound and Charlotte Harbor have to be one of the most beautiful boating locations on the Gulf side of Florida. Hundreds of islands dot the Sound; redfish, snook, pompano and speckled trout are the fishing favorites in the area. Pine Island's mangrove shorelines, tidal creeks, and oyster bars still resist the crush of development.

In Charlotte Harbor sits Cayo Costa State Park, a spectacular wild and scenic Gulf coast barrier island accessible only by boat. Nature trails, safe harbors, cabins, tent sites, hiking and biking trails and miles of deserted beaches make this a must-see location. The Intracoastal runs along the eastern shore of Cayo Costa before heading inland at Boca Grande Pass – the "Tarpon Capital of the World."

At the southern end of this section of the Intracoastal sailors pass through Card Sound before reaching Key Largo, the first island in the famous Florida Keys chain. The largest of the Keys, Key Largo is famous for its diving and fishing. The John Pennekamp Coral Reef State Park, the nation's first underwater park, is the crown jewel of the area and worth a visit.

America's Great Loop

Atlantic & Gulf Intracoastal Waterway Tips

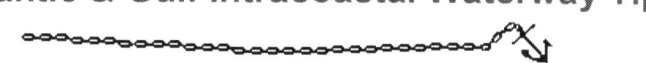

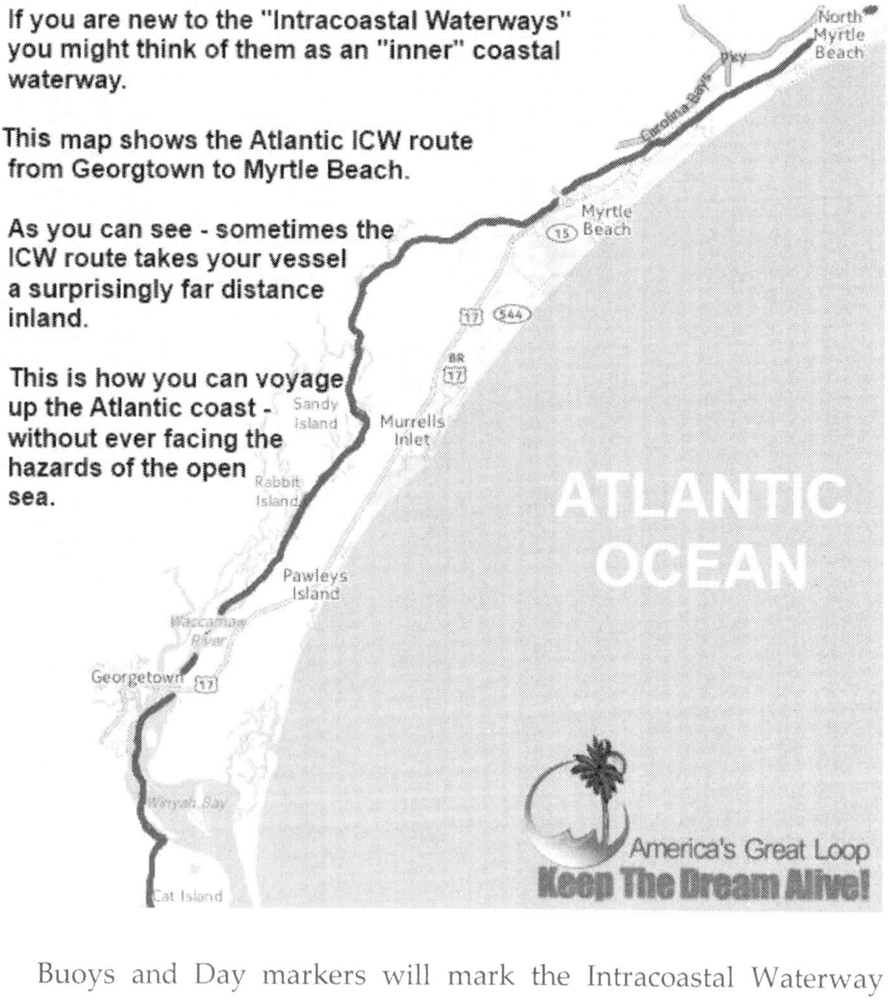

If you are new to the "Intracoastal Waterways" you might think of them as an "inner" coastal waterway.

This map shows the Atlantic ICW route from Georgtown to Myrtle Beach.

As you can see - sometimes the ICW route takes your vessel a surprisingly far distance inland.

This is how you can voyage up the Atlantic coast - without ever facing the hazards of the open sea.

Buoys and Day markers will mark the Intracoastal Waterway (ICW), which is a 3,000-mile inland passage that is made up of a chain of channels that are linked together and stretches from New Jersey to Brownsville, TX. This Inland Passage includes natural inlets, bays, saltwater rivers, sounds and man-made canals, all of whom have lateral and non-lateral buoys and markers as well as ICW markers to help boaters travel to their destination on the water.

Buoys and markers are used to identify the Intracoastal Waterway (ICW) and have yellow symbols on them. These buoys and markers serve two purposes: they serve the United States Navigation System and the ICW. Even though these buoys are dual purpose, anytime a boater is following the ICW they are to pay attention to the ICW symbols, which are either a yellow square or a yellow triangle. This is true regardless of the shape and color of the marker or buoy. So in some places, the ICW symbol (that little yellow sticker) may be on a buoy.

Most Intracoastal Waterway symbols are located on day markers or buoys which are permanently attached to posts or other structures that are located in (or sometimes near) the water. Also, a yellow horizontal strip on a buoy simply identifies the ICW.

Parts of the ICW are very shallow, and it is critical that you stay within the ICW Channel Markers. Some parts of it will take you an unbelievably far inland distance. You will see tugboats pushing barges, large ferry boats, and several large ships almost anywhere on the ICW. Many of these vessels draw ten feet. However, the Army Corps of Engineers is once again operating on a tight budget (aren't we all) and, in their case, lack of funds means they have to pick and choose where to dredge. Therefore, where the commercial traffic is located is where you will find the deepest water and better maintained waterways.

So, if a large tug, barge or ferry can make it, you can make it, but you need to stay within the channel markers.

Additionally, do NOT under any circumstances, cut the corners. When you see the ICW channel marker, normally make a huge long oval turn – don't hug the channel markers unless your updated Guide

Book or another boater making the pass tells you so. Taking the "short cut" is what gets most boaters into trouble.

Shoals drift and channel markers get moved. Your paper charts (if you use them) are not automatically updated. I have seen many boats religiously following the magenta line on their paper charts, some at high speeds, come to an abrupt stop as they pass on the wrong side (or too close) to a recently moved channel marker. Use the magenta line on your GPS as an indicator of the direction that the channel takes – but don't follow it as if you were on a railroad track. Keep one eye on the water in front and on both sides of you, and the other eye on your depth finder.

The best advice I can give you about navigating the ICW and the Inland Rivers, is to "think like a Tugboat captain." Keep in mind he runs deeper than you and he can't take those sharp turns, and you shouldn't either. His route is the dredged and deepest route.

Unless you have an updated "Guide Book" or USCG navigational report (VHF radio) stating otherwise, do not play tag with the channel markers. In most cases (not all) the deepest part of the channel will be the middle of the channel. The USCG gives water hazard and weather alerts on the VHF ever hour. Since your VHF has a relatively short range, you will only hear the ones for the waterways you are traveling in or near. They will keep you informed of shoaling and other water hazards in your area.

In some areas (Bogue Sound for example) long straight runs will have alternating red and green ICW markers spaced hundreds of yards apart. In these cases, the deepest portion of the channel is straight down the middle. Remember, boats passing the channel markers as if they were ski poles on a downhill racing slope are the ones most likely to run aground.

Crab pots and crab pot floats are everywhere... while at times, I know you will think "those stupid crab fishermen" have put their crab pots in the middle of the ICW channel. Fact is, they haven't. One, it is against the law, and two, if their floats get cut away by props, they will never find their crab pot. They are professional fishermen; they don't want to lose their catch, or their equipment. If you're in the center of the channel, you will avoid the crab pots. If you're running over crab pots, you're not in the channel – it is as simple as that.

Watch your depth, and make sure you know your vessels <u>fully loaded </u>draft – NOT the draft the manufacturer said it was – but its true fully loaded draft. Until you load your boat full with fuel, water, provisions, and crew – and physically measure it – you won't really know for sure what your full load draft is.

Most manufacturers list the "designed" draft at 50% fuel and water with no weight additions for additional provisions in their specifications. So often your vessel's fully loaded draft can be a foot deeper than what you think it is. (That's why I believe so many Trawlers run aground.)

It is unlikely that you will be able to maintain a constant vigil and keep yourself directly in the center of the channel for the entire length of the ICW. Occasionally, you will lose your concentration. You'll be watching an eagle, an alligator, a dolphin, or a bikini, and you'll drift off course. That's generally not a problem as long as you're still in the channel – but if there is a single instrument on your boat to keep a vigil watch on – it is your depth finder. When things start getting too shallow – slow down to a snail's pace until you find deep water again. In many cases, it requires backing out the same way you came in.

Set your depth sounder alarm for about a foot deeper than your full load draft. When the alarm sounds, if you haven't already slowed to a snail's space, you're likely to hit bottom. If you set your depth sounder alarm any deeper than that on the ICW, it will probably drive you nuts.

Don't speed..
Stay in the Channel..
Don't take short cuts..
Cruise on a rising tide..

And this won't happen to you . . .

When traveling on the Atlantic (or Gulf) ICW, always remember the red "ICW" marker is the one with the <u>little yellow sticker</u> on it. All of these stickers are small and many of them (which mark the ICW) are faded and hard to see at a distance– one of the best reasons to have a very good set of high powered binoculars.

On the ICW route – the red day (or channel) markers with the little yellow stickers <u>ALWAYS</u> mean "Red Right Return to Texas" – so traveling north, these red markers will always be on your left or port side. Red day or channel markers <u>WITHOUT</u> the little yellow stickers mark a channel – but **NOT** the ICW. Therefore don't follow the red or green markers without a yellow triangle sticker unless you want to leave the ICW. Normally, of course, "red right" markers mean return from the sea. But on the ICW – "red right" means return to Texas.

America's Great Loop

This is a waterway 'Day Marker'
The triangle ones are colored red
and have 'even' numbers.

The little yellow triangle sticker
above the number tells you it is an
ICW channel marker.

This is a waterway 'Day Marker'
The square ones are colored green
and have 'odd' numbers.

The little yellow colored sticker
is what tells you it is an
ICW channel marker.

A good reason for a great pair of binoculars!

The narrow ICW forces you to pay close attention to navigation and to steer constantly instead of relying on the auto pilot as most boaters can do offshore. Unless you are indeed a very brave soul, you should not attempt to navigate the twists and turns of the ICW at night, so plan on anchoring out or finding a slip at a marina each night.

Bridges are also a "timing" problem. Many of the lift bridges you encounter operate on a restricted schedule. While the bridge tenders are mostly very polite, helpful, and friendly, if you aren't in range to make an opening, they have little choice but hold you back for a half-hour or hour wait depending on their scheduled next opening.

But by far the biggest problem in navigating both the Atlantic and Gulf ICW is the water's depth. When the waterway was constructed, it was intended to be used by commercial barge traffic. That mandated depths of 10 feet or more. Now, however, in many areas with less barge traffic, depths are generally around nine feet, often six feet is found squarely between the channel markers. Add shoaling and silting, and you often cruise over four feet of water.

Additionally, power boaters don't really have too much advantage over sailboats. While shallow drafts can ruin the props on a power boat, they can also stop a sailboat in its tracks and even damage a keel.

I motor around the loop in my sailboat, and only raise her sails when sailing out to sea and crossing the Great Lakes. I'm often asked why I don't sail on the ICW. Because having your sails up when you go aground unexpectedly is like having a 150-horsepower engine in gear that you can't turn off, put into neutral, or put in reverse. The wind can just drive you harder and harder aground.

For power boats, of course, the danger is bending or breaking a propeller. In places, many of which are totally unexpected, the ICW is so shallow that I see 36 foot (and plus) trawlers more frequently hard aground. Tearing up the props or running gear on a 36 foot vessel is an expensive proposition. My advice? Doesn't matter how fast your vessel is capable of going – it is always best to go slow on the ICW.

The ICW route is not all just one skinny narrow canal of waterway. Its "marked channel" often takes you across bays and sounds. One such place, for example, is Albemarle Sound in North Carolina. The sound itself is a very wide expanse of very shallow water. It is easy to get the feeling you can put a little break-neck speed into your crossing. Albemarle Sound can also get very rough in the slightest bit of stronger winds, and the ICW channel is narrow. With my four foot draft it is, by far, my most dreaded area of the Loop. In comparison, it makes the Great Lakes and that little stretch across the Gulf seem like child's play.

The ICW has lots of navigational aids: day marks, buoys, and ranges. Most of the time, the navigation is straightforward, but there are areas where things can get confusing.

Some portions of the waterway cross wide bodies of water that are very shallow, in fact, too shallow for many boats. In these waters, it is imperative to stay within the marked channel. Often these areas have a very narrow dredged channel that is conspicuously marked by numerous day marks. It's important when traveling in these areas to stay in the channel, because outside the deeper narrow channel, the water can be very shallow (often just two or three feet). In these areas, you need to frequently look ahead and behind, and observe your boat's track with respect to the channel markers. If there's a crosswise wind or current, it can appear you are heading directly towards the next marker, but you may in fact be drifting sideways out of the channel. By looking at additional markers ahead and behind, you can keep yourself in line with the center of the channel.

Other portions of the waterway travel along wide rivers, or cross large bays or sounds. Rivers can have "points" along the shore, with shoals extending into the river. There are usually navigational aids present, but they may be hard to see from a distance, especially if it's hazy or foggy. In some areas you can easily spot a day marker, but it will be not so easy to tell if it is an "ICW" marker. (Those little yellow stickers can be impossible to see at a distance.)

This is where your GPS navigation system comes in real handy. If there's any difficulty seeing navigation aids your GPS will show you where they are supposed to be. Using GPS waypoints also helps a lot when crossing large bays and sounds (Albemarle Sound for example, has always been my personal most stressful crossing – not the Gulf or the Great Lakes). Aside from the fact I always manage to be there in the roughest of water, it's often difficult to follow the waterway so you end up where the channel resumes. I've never run aground in Albemarle Sound, but I always simply get caught in the rain or fog in rough water and no visibility.

We "Loopers" all have our favorite parts of the ICW and the Great Loop. Albemarle Sound just isn't mine. But that doesn't mean it won't be yours. What awaits you on the other side however, is about as wonderful as it gets.

NOTE: Here's a little "safety tip" for you: Never assume the guy in the bigger boat knows what he's doing – or in fact – is even at the helm or awake. Many larger vessels can seem a bit intimidating. That goes for pleasure boats as well as tugs and barges. Many of the commercial vessels travel 24 hours a day and their routes are very routine. They also get sleepy. So keep an eye out for all other boats. You have the smaller, more maneuverable vessel, and these larger vessels have the right of way. But if they are not paying attention, they may be, in fact, right over the top of your boat. So always be prepared. Until I see another boater approaching me, and wave at me, I always assume they have their radar off and are asleep at the wheel.

Bridges on the AICW

There are about 150 bridges between Miami and Norfolk on the ICW. All but two of them are 65' fixed highway bridges. The two that are not, one is 64 1/2 feet (twin highway bridges at Mile 720.9) and the other is 56 feet (Julia Tuttle Causeway Bridge at Mile 1087.2. The rest are a combination of lower "opening" bridges, a few swing bridges, and some railroad bridges. The railroad bridges are always open except for when a train is coming. The rest are divided between bascule, swing or lift bridges and most of them either open on a fixed schedule while some open as boat traffic demands.

As mentioned, it is very important to know your vessel's actual and true draft (depth) below the water when cruising the ICW. It is also important to know your exact height above the water. USCG regulations provide for a fine of $10,000 for unnecessary bridge openings. So you don't want get fined if you call for an opening on a 30' bridge and your vessel is only 24' above the water. In some cases you must lower your antennas to permit passage under the bridge without requesting an opening.

All bridges are either 'open on request' or they are on a restricted opening schedule. Your Skipper Bob's will have all this information in it, and it is in order as you approach the bridges.

When approaching a bridge, call the bridge tender and state your boats name, and what direction you are traveling (north or south on the ICW). After they acknowledge you, request an opening, or let them know you are on stand-by for their next scheduled opening.

Bridge openings are just another reason why the tortoise and the hare end up in the same anchorage or marina at night. Often speeding on your way in a fast boat, only results in a long wait at the next bridge. With a little planning ahead, you can time your arrival to be at the bridge just in time for the next opening.

Also, please, be nice to the Bridge and Lock operators. They are there to do their job, and their job benefits us. While no one should ever have to remind anyone to be nice and kind to another – sadly, I've heard boaters argue with Bridge Tenders and Lock Masters without mercy or good reason. When a bridge says it opens on the hour every hour – car traffic or no car traffic – that's when it opens. You won't change their schedule, and if you are but a minute away when it has to close, it is going to close. If you are on such a tight schedule, you shouldn't be on the water.

Also, it is common practice and courtesy to let vessels going with the current to pass thru the bridge first. If there is a commercial vessel or tug/barge coming the opposite way, it's best to call them on Ch. 13 and find out their intentions, and let them know yours. Many bridges have very swift currents and no extra space for additional maneuvering, so plan ahead and be aware of other boaters as well as your surroundings. Patience and planning ahead will make your journey carefree, stress-free and more enjoyable!

The Florida ICW

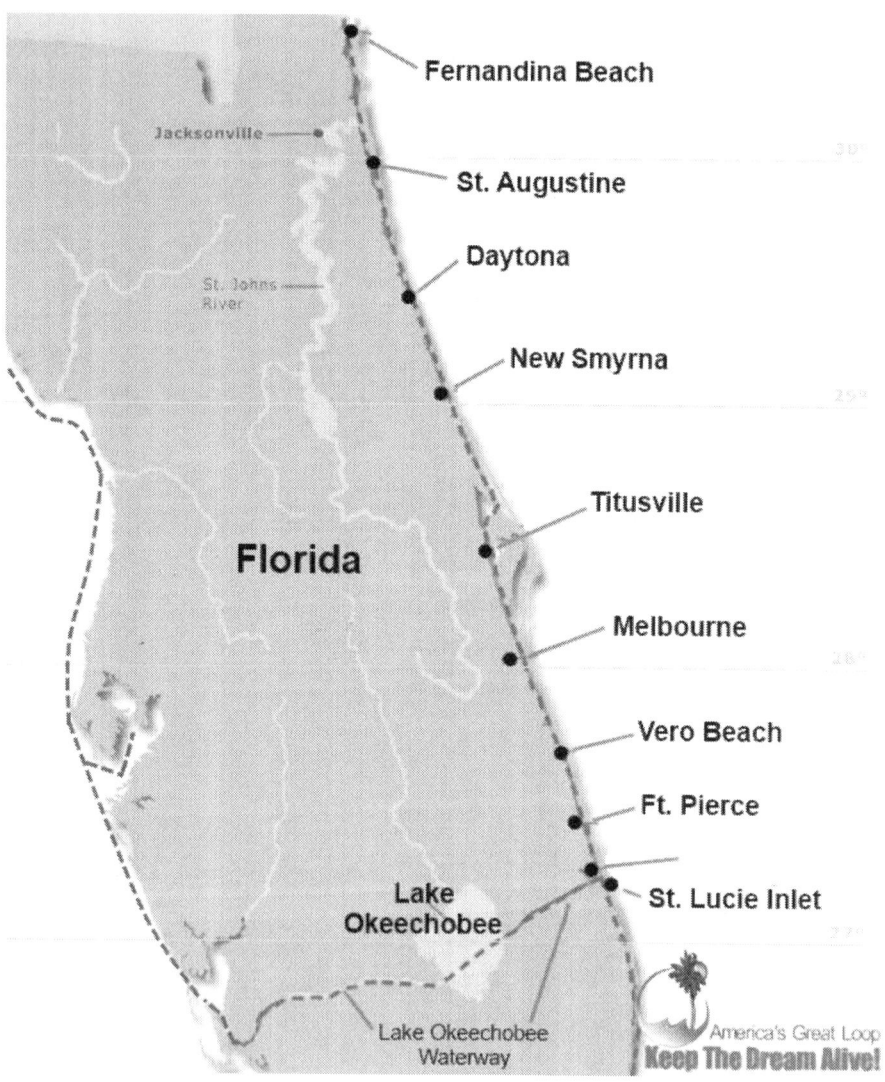

For sure you will want to visit Myrtle Beach, Amelia Island, and Fernandina Beach. New Smyrna and New Smyrna Beach are also worth a visit. You can anchor out just south of the bridge from the free city dinghy dock, visit the downtown area, and perhaps rent a car or take the bus over to New Smyrna Beach.

For Great Loopers, boaters will also get glimpses of the towering vehicle-assembly building at the John F. Kennedy Space Center in Titusville, and see some of the citrus groves that have made Indian River fruit world famous.

Kennedy Point Marina – Titusville, Florida

Kennedy Point Marina still makes for a nice stop. It is no longer the "Yacht Club" it once was. In fact, the Marina is for sale, and well, we all know (or can guess) what it means when the Marina's owners no longer have an interest. It no longer has fuel, ice, or a restaurant. However, it is in good shape, has some very friendly and helpful live-aboards, and it is in a nice location. It is directly adjacent to the Kennedy Space Launch Center, so if you are lucky, you might catch a rocket launch. It has to be the best seat for watching a launch in the area. Nice people, great pool, and right on a public bus route that can take you to a church, local shopping, movies, and even a Walmart.

Several cities, including Titusville, Cocoa, Melbourne, Vero Beach, Ft. Pierce, Port St. Lucie, and Jupiter also dot the Indian River area. All make for great stops.

Highlights heading south on the Florida ICW include the elegance of all the Palm Beaches, Boca Raton, Ft. Lauderdale, and everything that has made Miami and Miami Beach a hot destination for boaters and visitors from around the world. The large "yachts" will put your vessel in their shadow as you cruise by them and the condominiums will make your cruise feel more like walking in Manhattan, but it's an experience you will never forget.

At the southern end, the ICW runs right through the middle of downtown Miami – the departure point for Key Biscayne and Key West.

America's Great Loop

Georgia & The Carolinas

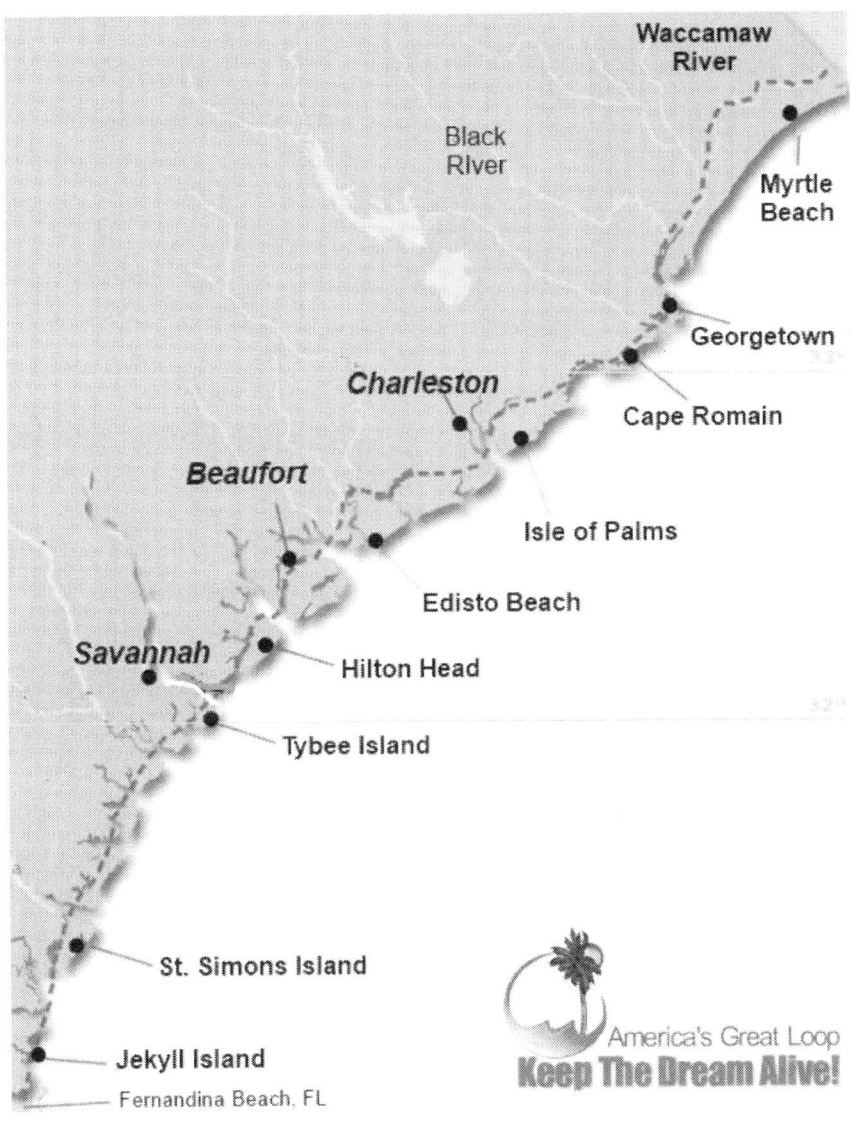

Where do I start, and what do I highlight? Fact is the miles from Fernandina Beach, Florida (mile marker 717) to Norfolk (mile marker

0) are simply the most beautiful and historic waterways you will ever travel in your own boat.

While my purpose is not to replace or duplicate information you will find in Waterway Guides or your Triple A trip packs, I do have to say, this portion of your trip on the Atlantic ICW will be one of the very most interesting and exciting. And in case you are wondering, Waterway Guides excel and giving you descriptive information on the areas you will be cruising through (you just have to scramble past the far too numerous amounts advertising). It you are cruising with an Internet WiFi equipped computer or smart phone (and you should be) then you will be able to search the Internet for local information in the areas you are cruising in.

Often, very often, what's just beyond the beach or the trees sometimes less than a few hundred yards away, a whole new world of adventure is yours to explore. However, when you can't see it from your boat, and you don't know it is there, you will miss out on some of the very best sites to see and places to visit all along your way.

From St. Marys, Jekyll Island, St. Simons Island to Thunderbolt, Charleston and Savannah, you will be rubber necking all the way. What can you expect?

You can expect your Skipper Bob's AICW anchorages guide to be worth its weight in gold from here to Norfolk. Marina fees for docking in the immediate Charleston area are expensive. Just north however is the Isle of Palms which is less cluttered and less expensive. Once you reach South Carolina, the Waccamaw River will take your breath away. The Wacca Wache Marina (mile 383.5) offers free showers and their Hanna Banana Restaurant has some great eats.

Wacca Wache Marina on the Waccamaw River

From here at Wacca Wache Marina, a road trip to Murrells Inlet, and a tour of Pawleys Island and the Pawleys Island

Hammock Shop is worth the effort. I highly recommend you take some time to see the sites in this area.

From the Waccamaw River to Norfolk, which ever route you take from Albemarle Sound to Norfolk, the scenery is constantly changing, and so do the waters.

For most of us, planning an over-night anchorage in Mile Hammock Basin at the edge of Camp Lejeune is a tradition. It can also be an interesting and sometime busy place. Between life fire exercises, helicopter training, and or drown practice, you just never know what you might see in the air. Additionally, amphibious and gun boat drills often make the sights on the water very interesting.

Once you cross Albemarle Sound, it's like cruising into a whole different world.

While many Loopers never mention it, I personally (bad timing or bad luck I guess) always have trouble crossing Albemarle Sound. It's not that the Sound itself is so bad, it's just that I always seem to get caught crossing it in bad weather. When the wind and weather kicks up, (and it always seems to do that when I'm crossing), Albemarle Sound can get really choppy and rough. In fact, I've sailed all around in the world including trips from the U.S. mainland to Venezuela but the only place I've ever been seasick is crossing Albemarle Sound.

Elizabeth City – NC

Two Day Free Docking – Makes Elizabeth City a favorite stop among many Loopers. This is your southern entrance to the Dismal Swamp Canal.

Elizabeth City – Harbor of Hospitality

It's a tough choice. A delicious Prime Rib dinner at the Coinjock Marina & Restaurant, or two days and nights of free dockage at Elizabeth City. Hmmm.

Actually, there are several wonderful restaurants within easy walking distance from the free City Dock at Elizabeth City. Located on the inside route, this is your "Dismal Swamp" entrance located just about 20 miles up the Pasquotank river after you cross Albemarle Sound. So if you plan to cruise the Dismal Swamp, this is the route to take and the stop to make.

The Dismal Swamp vs the Virginia Cut

The Dismal Swamp route is by far the route less traveled. I think that's mainly because it is slower. However, it is beautiful, and it is about as smooth and protected a route you will ever find. You will most likely see deer and even a bear or two along this route.

This is the route of Jane Adams's Floating Theater which inspired Edna Ferber to write "Showboat". If you remember that, then it will be easy for you to remember, this is the route for those that don't mind cruising on a "Slow boat".

I have cruised "The Carolina Loop" which involves cruising the Dismal Swamp and the Virginia Cut. Both these routes are safe and beautiful. The Virginia Cut is the most popular ICW route. It is faster. It also has greater traffic, and it is more susceptible to weather.

Which route do I prefer? Both are fantastic. For me, it depends on the mood and partly on where I have been. Usually, if I have detoured out to Ocracoke, I will then take the Dismal Swamp route. If I detour in to Washington on the Pamlico river (they offer free 2 night docking) I will then take the Coinjock route. This way I make the change between both big and small waters.

Mile Zero

Norfolk is home to many things nautical. One of them is the Atlantic ICW's Mile Marker Zero. It is actually marked by the lighted red buoy #36, which is located off Hospital Point. This is the official beginning (or end) of the Atlantic ICW and all its 1,243 miles are measured in "statute miles" not nautical miles.

There is much to see and do in Norfolk, I'm not even going to make an attempt as all this information is in your Waterway Guides. I will say however, the Elizabeth river west side offers the most free anchorages free dinghy docks, as well as easy to walk to places to see and do.

The Chesapeake and C&D Canal

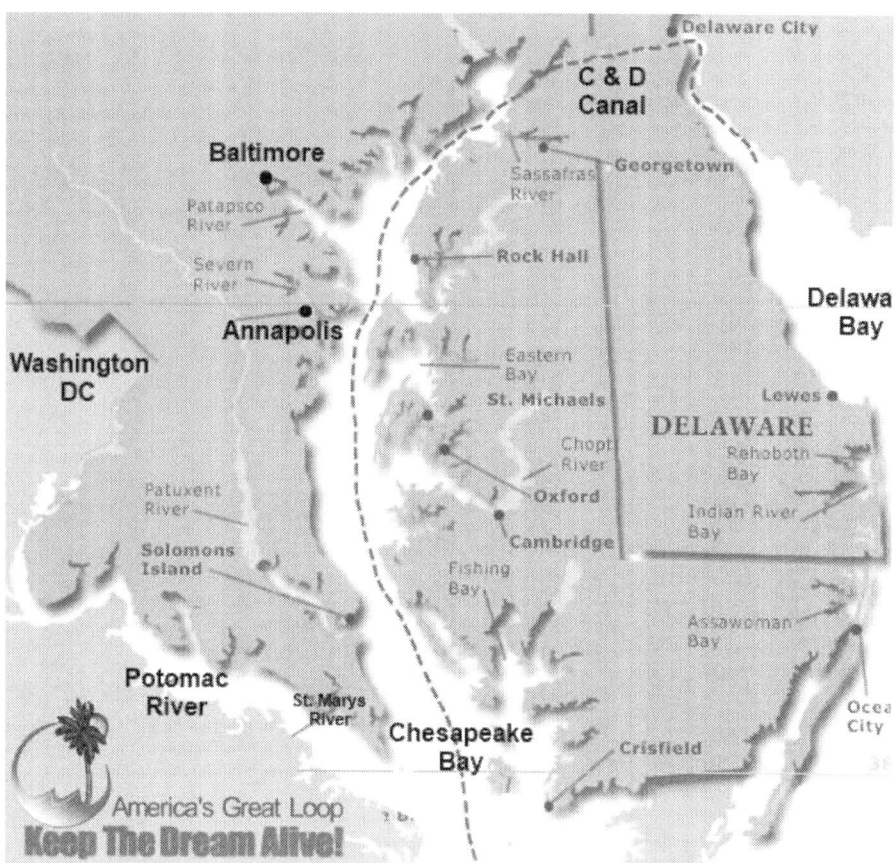

Spend a week or two... It could take a year or more just to explore all the wonderful reaches of the Chesapeake Bay. Did you ever want to see DC? The Washington Monument or George Washington's home on Mt Vernon? What about the National Archives? The Smithsonian? Or the White House? Well, why not take your boat?

Most people (even boaters) don't know you can take your boat to Annapolis, MD, Philadelphia, PA or Washington DC, but you can! Cruising America's Great Loop is the very best way to get there.

It is the Atlantic ICW that will take you past Norfolk and on into Chesapeake Bay. It is the Chesapeake Bay that will take you to Annapolis and to the Potomac River. From there, you can boat right straight into the hub of Washington DC.

From Colonial Beach your waterway tour of our nation's capital is a mere 62 miles farther up the Potomac River.

From your boat, Washington DC can be seen from any number of ways and perspectives. It is a place that was planned and created as the seat of government in a way that evokes strength. It is the treasury of our nation's heritage. At the same time it is home to hundreds of

Boating by the Washington Monument

thousands of people.

The Mall's formal structures, ceremonial spaces, and carefully planned vistas were designed after earlier European cities that were designed to showcase autocratic regimes. Here, however, these same places are where people come to play on weekends, to attend cultural events, or to petition the government. In a single day, the Mall is where it is easy to see Frisbees and footballs, picnic baskets and bicycles, protest signs and groups of people chanting statements of change.

In Washington DC you can see the magnificent buildings that house the three branches of government. It is also where the nation celebrates and commemorates the wars the country has fought and the men and women who served and gave their lives. The nation's great presidents – those to whom the nation is indebted for their leadership during the time the nation was formed, or those for whom the nation is grateful because of their leadership during times of crisis – are honored here: Washington, Jefferson, Lincoln, Kennedy and Roosevelt. Others of the nation's greatest leaders deserving of national historic sites are also commemorated.

Don't forget, Washington DC is the home to the National Archives, the Smithsonian Institution and other repositories, buildings, and monuments of which our nation holds significant.

Architecturally, the buildings and monuments of Washington can be powerful, as well as controversial. However, they are most important in what they say about us as Americans. Way beyond the events and people in Washington somewhere exists the truth it embodies: freedom, justice, equality, courage, and honor– the tools that built the foundation of our free America. If you've never been there, if you've never seen it, here is a wonderful opportunity to do so.

The New Jersey Intracoastal Waterway

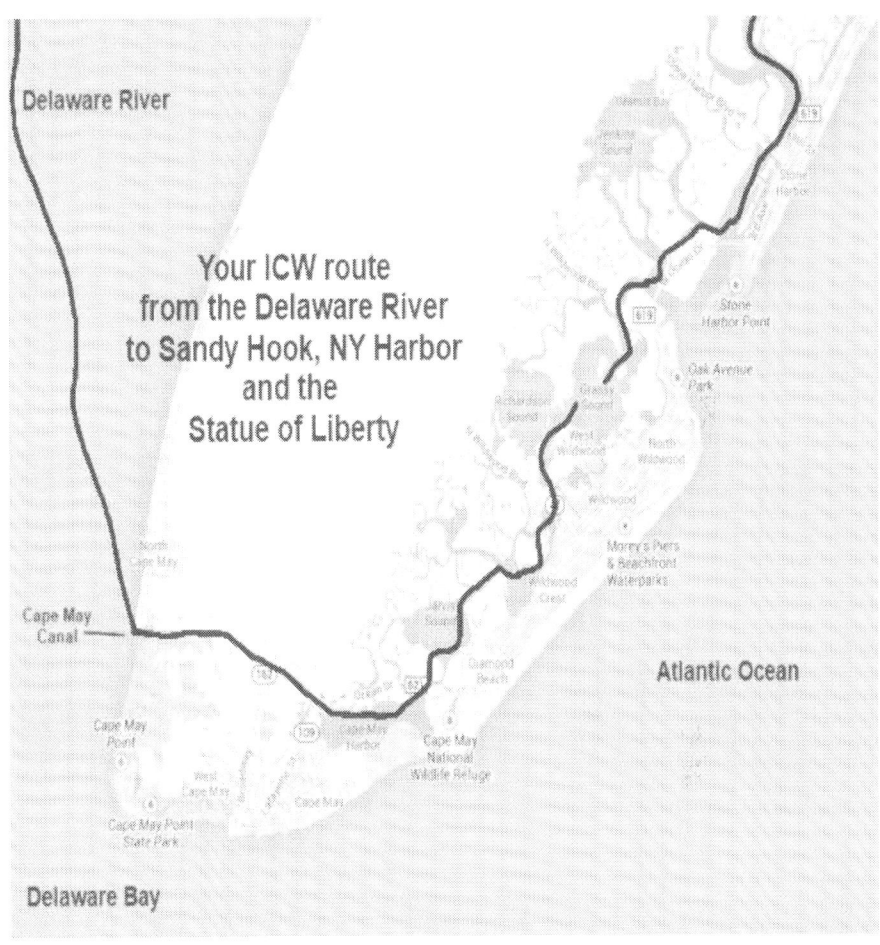

From Cape May Canal and Delaware Bay, to the Manasquan Inlet at Point Pleasant Beach, the Intracoastal Waterway in New Jersey winds 120 (statute) miles through bays, waterways and canals. It's a route traveled by snowbirds heading south in the fall, north in the spring; and it's a summer playground for millions of residents of NY, NJ, and Mid-Atlantic states. It's the home of thousands of fishing and charter boats.

"What?" you say..."A New Jersey Intracoastal Waterway?" You didn't know there was one? Well, there is. While I have included the mileage in your over-all Atlantic ICW route miles, this section of the ICW requires special attention.

For those familiar with the Great Loop, and those that have been reading Loopers' websites and blogs, seldom does the "New Jersey ICW" ever get a mention. That leaves most everyone wondering just how do you get from the Delaware River to New York harbor without going out to sea. Fact is – most everyone goes from Cape May to Manasquan Inlet. That leaves them with a 30-mile open ocean run to New York Harbor. However, if you have a 4' draft or less, and you travel with high tides, you can make it all the way without having to "go outside" into the sea. Even going outside, you have less time and distance here than you will crossing many sounds and bays, and it is half the minimum distance you will have crossing the Gulf of Mexico from Carrabelle to Steinhatchee.

Many cruisers do go out to sea, especially those in deeper draft vessels (usually four or more feet). However, there is a New Jersey ICW. While most cruisers either know or believe it to be shallow, winding, crowded, and topped off with low bridges... I say, "What's new?" That describes much of the Atlantic ICW.

If truth were known, I believe most Loopers that badmouth the Jersey ICW, have not cruised it; they've just heard how bad it is.

If you are cruising in a 4' draft or less, I'm here to tell you there is an amazing mix of scenery along this route. There is nothing more wrong with it than with other areas on the Loop. We are after all, cruising feet (maybe inches) above the bottom of an ever changing waterway – not on a concrete interstate highway. In my 4' draft sailboat, I've bumped bottom dozens of times cruising across Lake Okeechobee when the water was choppy.

The "crown rule" to cruising shallow tidal waters – is to ALWAYS cruise at high tide on a RISING tide. When the tide is going out – you need to have a safe deeper water area (anchorage) to stay put. Do this, and if and when you run aground it is just a short waiting game until you are afloat again. Otherwise, when the water drains from underneath your boat, you could be faced with a very expensive Sea Tow or BoatUS® rescue.

As a note here – you should be aware that the USCG's mission is to save <u>LIVES</u> not <u>BOATS</u>. They will come and rescue you (if need be) off your boat, but they will NOT rescue your boat. With your permission, of course, they will call Sea Tow to rescue your vessel, and you will get the bill.

Obviously, if your draft is 3 feet or even less, you can easily take the inside route from the Delaware to Sandy Hook and Raritan Bay. On your cruise along the New Jersey ICW you will see everything from Trump Plaza Casino to all kinds of wildlife and beautiful nature. You will also see lots of high rise condominiums and fisherman. Most of the fishermen are fishing for flounder – they love grassy shallow waters. So that alone should tell you something.

In this area, it should come as no surprise that the faster boats are the ones that end up in trouble. So, from the Cape May harbor to where the sea channel splits off from the ICW – it is wise to take your time, go slow, and go on a rising tide.

The New Jersey ICW winds around through wetlands and shallow sounds, behind the heavily developed barrier islands. Often the high rise buildings will come and go out of sight. Good news is there is lots of free Wi-Fi in the area.

<u>On Running Aground</u>: Don't panic! Don't rev up your engine and try to plow through it. In most cases that gets you stuck further. In these shallower waters, simply go slower than your normal slow. Cruise on a rising tide, and always be aware of your direction so you can "back out" the same way you came in. Be patient. If indeed you are cruising on the rising tide, it won't be long until you are floating again. Make your run through these areas at idle speed. Also, if you follow these rules, there is no reason to let the fear of running aground prevent you from going. The fact is I've run aground on several occasions. So have many others in deep draft (four or more feet) vessels. The key (or secret) is not to run aground and have to call Sea Tow (very expensive) to pull you off. So, in these shallow areas, just remember: go slow, go on a rising tide, and don't cut corners.

On the NJ ICW the trickiest area is in Grassy Sound (just west of North Wildwood) and in the area where the Hereford Inlet channel meets the ICW behind Stone Harbor.

Again, another reason to have a dinghy: If you do get stuck, you can always take your anchor out into deeper water, drop it, and heave your vessel off the shoal. In fact, I have seen some boaters "tow" their vessel off a shoal simply by using their dinghy.

Obviously, if you need to "heave" your vessel off a shoal with your anchor, it helps to have a good (power) anchor winch; in this case, a dinghy, a winch, a little anchor rod. The bow will then swing towards deep water. A little more winching and you'll be on your way again. This time, a little more carefully.

Sandy Hook, is a nine mile sandy beach at the top (north end) of New Jersey that extends into New York Harbor. West of Sandy Hook, you will discover a huge patch of harbors. This is your thoroughfare which runs between New Jersey, Long Island and New York City and the Hudson River.

Sandy Hook Bay - Raritan Bay

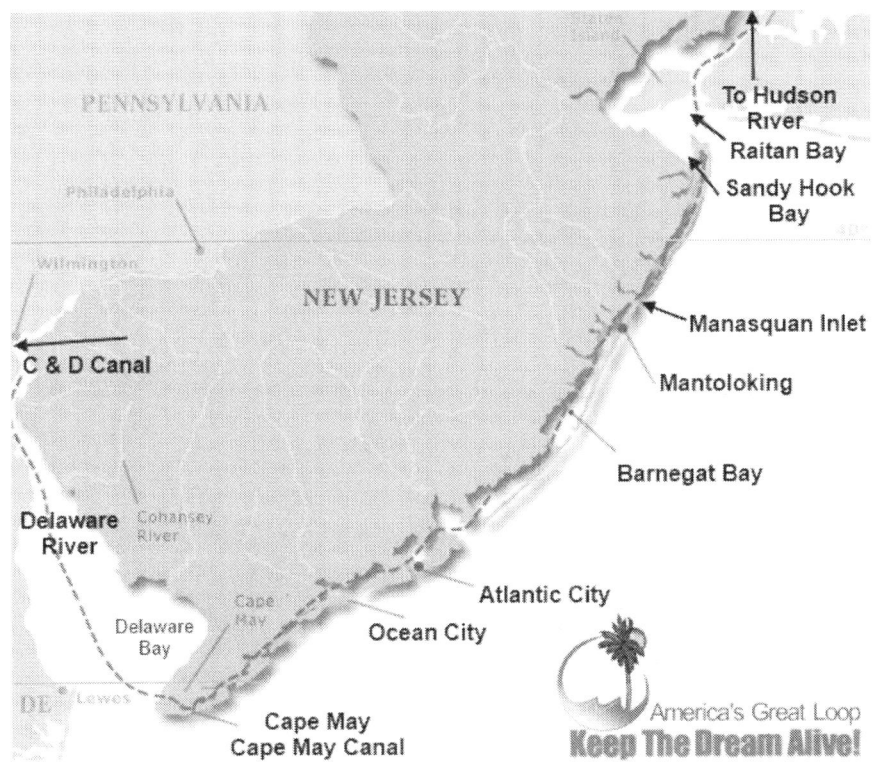

Sandy Hook Bay & Raritan Bay - Here you will find a well marked entry from the Atlantic which opens up about 18 miles of deep sheltered water. You will also find some great fishing along the New Jersey shoreline.

Raritan Bay is bordered by Staten Island to the north, Sandy Hook to the east Altantic Highlands in the south, and the port of Perth Amboy to the west. There are five lighthouses in the area and all sorts of yacht clubs, marinas, anchorages and gunk holes. If you want to take a few days and plan your agenda for cruising through this area, This is the time and the place to do it. You will find waterfront all sorts of seaside shopping and restaurants.

I always enter the area from the Sandy Hook channel and anchor out in Horseshoe Cove which is only about a mile or so south of Sandy Hook point. The Sandy Hook Lighthouse (by the way) is the first thing a sailor from across the ocean will see when approaching the area.

This entire area has a great maritime history. For those wishing to stay, explore and linger, anchoring out in the southern portion in the area known as the Atlantic Highlands, will put you just below the beautiful Navesink Heights. This is the highest natural point on the Atlantic Seaboard between Maine and Mexico's Yucatan Peninsula.

From Sandy Hook and Horseshoe Cove to Perth Amboy, dockage, moorings, anchorages, marinas, pump-out stations, fuel, ice, etc. are all abundant. Just be aware, the area has a 6 foot tidal range, so make sure you leave yourself with plenty of depth when anchoring out. There are lots of free dinghy docks, and good restaurants and shopping all in easy walking distance.

America's Great Loop
The Hudson River

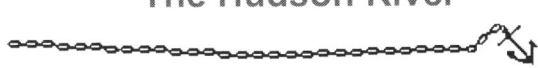

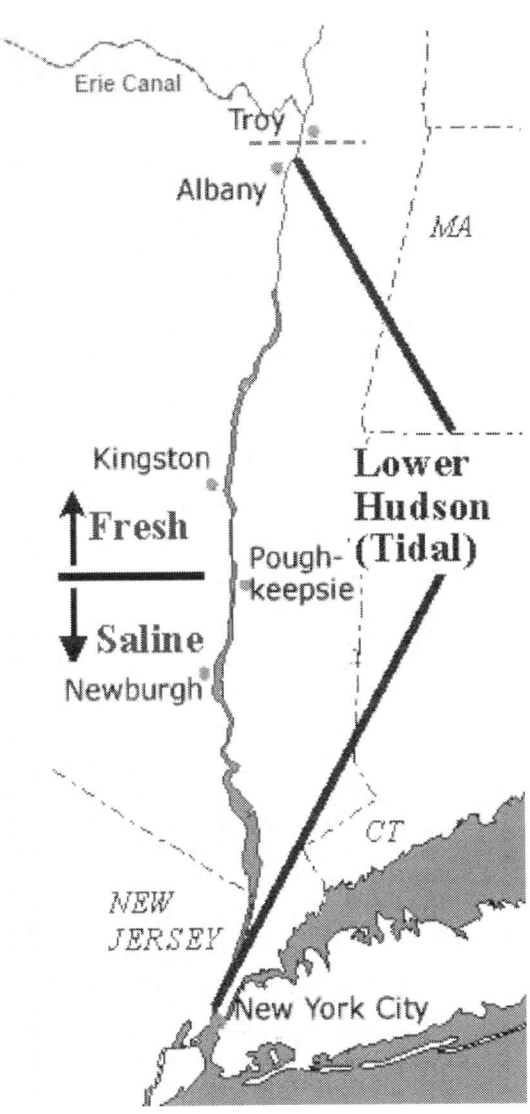

This leg of your voyage is 154 miles from the Statue of Liberty to the Troy Lock entrance to the Erie Canal.

The Hudson River seldom gets enough mention in many Great Loopers' blogs, or even Guide Books. However, the Hudson Valley is home to many of the most visited historic sites in America. From the US Military Academy at West Point,

The Mohonk House, the Culinary Institute of America, and many more.

Problem is, few take the time and effort to stop to explore the rich heritage and history of the Hudson Valley.

With Manhattan as a backdrop this unbeatable cruise extends through the Hudson Valley and past such legendary villages of Sleepy Hollow, the estates of Rockefeller, Vanderbilt, and Mills, and the mansions of Franklin Roosevelt, Martin Van Buren, Samuel Morse, and Washington Irving.

If you let it (don't be intimidated) this 154 mile leg of the Great Loop (from the Statue of Liberty to the entrance of the Erie Canal) can be most enjoyable. It is at the top of my list as one of the most beautiful and interesting areas on the Great Loop. It will also be yours – provided, of course, you take time to visit some sites. Lady Liberty is not on the Hudson River, but she is so close to it and welcomes you to this wonderful waterway through the Hudson Valley.

From Lady Liberty your cruise past Governors Island and past the East River will have you rubbernecking all the way to the Erie Canal. With over 60 marinas within a 154 mile stretch, it should give you an idea of just how popular boating on the Hudson River really is. For this reason, I suggest you find an anchorage behind Sandy Hook and wait out the weekend in order to make your voyage up the Hudson during the much less crowded weekdays.

Seriously, how much better can it get than taking a Hudson River excursion with the one you love and getting a firsthand view of this historic shoreline from the deck of your very own vessel? Annually, tourists spend millions of dollars for a ride on a charter boat – just to see what you are about to see for free. Not only can you visit the estates of Roosevelt, Martin Van Buren, Mills, Vanderbilt, Rockefeller, and Samuel F. B. Morse, you will boat right beside the Livingston's Clermont Estate – this is the location and namesake where Fulton's steamboat, "the Clermont" was built and demonstrated for the very first time. In addition, you will cruise past Dobb's Ferry, and West Point.

Entering NY Bay from the south, the first landmark you will see will be the Statue of Liberty…the statue with the equivalent height of a 22-story building. In 1886 it was the tallest structure in all of New

York. The Statue of Liberty faces southeast and as you cruise by with her on your port side, the Hudson River is just ahead.

If you cruise just east of Lady Liberty (between Liberty Island and Governors Island) then you will cruise past Ellis Island. It too will be on your port side as you approach the Hudson River. The Troy Lock and Dam, is 154 beautiful miles away, and you won't have any problems taking your time on this leg of your voyage. You can expect a lot of charter and ferryboat traffic between Liberty Island and on past the Hudson River's famous lighthouses.

The Hudson River south of Federal Lock 1 is technically not a river at all. It is a fiord which is subject to tidal changes of up to five feet. You will want to remember that tidal changes can be a real challenge when you are tied to a fixed (non-floating) dock or pier. Tides also have to be considered when you anchor since every five or six hours the tide will reverse sending the boat 180 degrees in the opposite direction. Keep in mind the current is roughly 2 knots, and it also changes direction every six hours or so until you reach the non-tidal waters past the first lock on the Erie Canal.

The tidal flow can work with you or against you, literally. Normally, on your voyage up the Hudson you will experience a tidal flow change as much as 2 knots. The Hudson River has very deep sections of water and very high cliff-like walls. At first, you are not likely to realize the depth of this canyon until you see the size of a freight train hugging the sheer wall on the shore, or see a commuter train racing along near the water, or start to notice some really huge buildings dwarfed by cliffs. There are many interesting places to stop see and do on this leg of your journey.

I always stop at the Striped Bass Restaurant in Tarrytown. It offers casual waterfront dining, plenty of free transient slips, and smooth wave free docking. You can also fuel up on your way out and you will have made the perfect stop. There is also Half Moon Bay Marina about

25 miles north of New York City, and Rondout Bay Marina and Restaurant, Kingston, NY.

If at all possible, I suggest you take some time off your boat and pay a visit to the America's Culinary Institute. Obviously, this is a great place to take a tour so that you are there for lunch.

The Hudson River is a popular getaway destination offering spectacular mountain views, historic estates, wine trails, shopping, outdoor adventures, river tour boats, lighthouse tours, and more. Literally, millions of visitors visit the Hudson River and Hudson Valley where all these bountiful choices are but a stone's throw away from where you are going to be cruising.

The New York Harbor Region includes the NJ side of the Hudson River. This is an extremely busy area. There are commercial ships, tour boats, ferry boats and, of course, recreational boaters on the water all the time during the boating season. The waters around the Statue of Liberty are especially busy. The river is usually quite choppy. However, the view and the voyage is more than worth the effort.

The good news is that the farther you cruise north, the less and less traffic you will see and the less expensive it gets. There are ample marinas and services along the river. Tugs and other commercial ships also run the river.

The tides under the Verrazano Narrows Bridge can be quite swift. Sail boaters will have a better time of it traveling with the tide. Liberty Island does not have public docking, and there are buoys designating a "do not enter" area around the Island.

If you have followed the seasonal plan, most likely you are here on the Hudson in May. That means you have plenty of time to spend time to enjoy the sites. Certainly, no other place in the world has the amount of (cheap) public transportation as NY and NJ. So, I suggest you stop and visit the area. Don't miss Times Square, Kingston, Sleepy Hollow, or The Culinary Institute.

Lighthouses and mansions: You are at one of the north east's most popular tourist areas. There is a lot to see and enjoy, and much of it is free.

Traveling north from Battery Park, there are numerous free courtesy docks for restaurant patrons and nearby shopping. Most every waterfront restaurant provides a free courtesy dock on the Hudson... another good reason for NOT voyaging the Hudson on weekends. It gets very crowded and free docks at restaurants are not always available. During the week, however, you can take your pick.

As a special note for sailors– The Castle on the Hudson Boat Club offers $5.00 moorings with showers and restrooms included. In addition, they offer a crane ($50.00 fee) for a DIY mast stepping. This is great, since you have to take your mast down to travel the Erie Canal which is just ahead.

At the far end, the Waterfront Harbor Visitor Center at the entrance of the Erie Canal has free docking for 48 hours (believe it or not). There is a huge floating dock that has complimentary electric and water, as well as showers and a nice Wi-Fi connection. Restaurants, post office, laundry, groceries, and shopping are within six blocks away. Price Choppers will let you take a grocery cart back to the waterfront. During season, a Farmers' Market at the pier is held on every Sunday.

The Erie Canal

This leg of your journey is 338 miles from Waterford, NY at the Hudson to Tonawanda, NY at the Niagara River and entrance to Lake Erie. In order to pass through the entire length of the Erie Canal your vessel must be able to clear a fixed bridge height of 15' 6". If you can't clear this height, you must exit at Oswego at Lake Ontario. There are 57 locks on the Erie Canal that lift your vessel a total of 566 feet above sea level. The Erie Canal is lined with dozens of canal towns offering all the services that a transient boater would need.

Today's canal runs an average of about nine feet deep. It has a vertical clearance of 2' between Waterford and Three Rivers (Oswego Canal junction), and 15' 6" feet between the Tonawanda and the Niagara River. The largest vessels that can make the entire journey must be under 300 feet long, 43' 6" feet wide, 9' draft, and a maximum 15' 6" height above the water.

Waterford, NY
Erie Canal
Welcome Center
and free dock

All recreational vessels passing through the Erie Canal System must purchase either a seasonal pass or a ten-day pass. For boats over 39 feet the toll is $50.00 for a ten-day pass. For 2013 the ten-day pass for my 27 footer was $37.50. Smaller vessels have a smaller fee.

The Erie Canal is open from May 1st to September 1st (weather permitting). Locks and lift bridges are operated daily from 7:00 a.m. to 10:00 p.m. So there is no cruising at night as you cannot go any farther than the next lock or lift bridge.

For sure, when voyaging the Erie Canal, you will come to see life from a different perspective. A solitary blue heron, flocks of geese, small herd of deer, and even an occasional pair of lovers are often in view as you slowly traverse from one end of the canal to the other. Between small towns and villages the journey is most often very quiet, peaceful, and relaxing. It can also be very thought provoking. It is a time when being on your boat –moving over the quiet, calm, still and relaxing waters of the canal – has a way of making you put your entire life in prospective. It is here, you will realize what is really important to you, and what energizes and excites your life.

If you have young kids, grand kids, nieces, nephews, etc., and any thoughts or desire whatsoever of having them join you on any portion of the Great Loop – this is the time and the place. The Erie Canal offers not only an enjoyable trip but an incredible educational experience. The slow, easy-going pace of the canal makes it very safe, and provides ample opportunities to stop almost anywhere along the way. There are museums, nature trails, bike trails, caves, and waterfalls…even an underground boat tour. Along with the fish, deer, geese, and ducks, you will even see a few "Golden Arches" along the way.

Cruising the Erie Canal is a long (six or seven days) and a very slow cruise. Between moments of sheer excitement and reaching for your camera, there are long stretches of the canal where your own personal thoughts will seem to be the only thing that changes.

The Basket Factory – on the Erie Canal

The Basket Factory in Middleport, NY is my favorite restaurant stop on the Erie Canal. It has a history dating to the very beginning of the canal. Plan your day to arrive in the evening, and after passing under the Middleport lift bridge, you can dock right on the wall for the night. Enjoy a fun relaxing evening of great food, drinks, and friendly people and then shuffle off to Buffalo in the morning.

Navigating the Erie Canal

When it comes to navigation, there isn't anything to worry about on your cruise along the Erie Canal – as long as you are going forward, you cannot possibly get lost.

If you time your entry into the Canal for mid-May, occasional floating debris is likely to be your only hazard for the entire voyage, and the depth remains constantly at eight to ten feet.

I always get the $50 ten-day pass and use every bit of it for the 338 miles between Waterford, NY and Buffalo on the Erie Canal. The Canal begins at the Hudson River, just north of Albany, and meets the Niagara River in Tonawanda, NY just north of Buffalo (and just south, and upstream – by the way – of Niagara Falls).

Provided, of course, you can clear that 19' 1" bridge just south of Chicago, the only restriction for a Great Looper wanting to cruise the entire Erie Canal is a fixed 15' 6" overhead bridge at the west end of the Canal at Tonawanda. Your vessel's super structure height above the water must be able to clear 15' 6" to make it under this bridge. Otherwise, you will have to turn around and cruise all the way back to exit via the Oswego Canal into Lake Ontario.

Depth of the Erie Canal varies based on the amount of rainfall and although its intended depth is 12 feet; its actual depth is usually closer to nine feet. With two exceptions, the clearances for navigating under bridges on the Erie Canal are all greater than 19' 1" (the height you will have to clear in Chicago). Only one of these exceptions (the 15' 6" fixed bridge in Tonawanda) prevents your voyage through the entire length of the Canal. The other exception is an alternate (side trip) route off the canal at the entrance of the Syracuse Inner Harbor which is 16' 6" above the water.

If you exit the Erie Canal at Oswego and go into Lake Ontario, you can visit the Thousand Islands (which I highly recommend) and visit Toronto. You can go through the Welland Canal to Lake Erie, or travel through Canada's Heritage Canal System (Trent-Severn Waterway) to Lake Huron and on to Mackinac Island at the north end of Lake Michigan.

By the time you reach Lockport you'll be itching to give your vessel full-throttle and put a little break-neck speed back into your journey. More importantly, you'll be very thrilled over having shared this incredible experience – but the speed freaks among us will probably never want to do it again.

Each day is a new adventure far from the madding crowd. Each day is a lesson in history, nature, and patience. It won't be until you reach Rochester, NY that you will catch a glimpse of vehicles whizzing by at 70 miles an hour – a reminder that "life in the fast lane" is just a short distance away. And still, you won't acknowledge how enjoyable this journey has been until you realize no one aboard (even the kids) has even mentioned the words: telephone, television, or computer.

The Erie Canal is living "life in the past lane." Not only are you cruising at around five mph, you are also traveling through one of the most historic and beautiful parts of the country.

Your days on the canal will pass in timeless relaxation. Many of the canal towns have parks that provide free electrical and water connections, and when you tie up in the late afternoon, there will still be plenty of time for a bike ride, fishing, or visiting a local attraction before dinner.

Erie Canal Locks

Lockport Lock on Erie Canal

Notice the "high water" mark. This is how high your boat will be lifted in this lock, to reach the next lock level.

Keep The Dream Alive!
CaptainJohn.org

From the Hudson River (sea level), your cruise through the Erie Canal includes 57 locks that will raise your vessel 573 feet above sea level.

You will always approach the Locks dead slow – not because you are a novice, but because you are a pro. Near the lock's gate there will be an official (or unofficial) waiting or staging area. In some cases you can tie up along a wall and wait, and in other cases you let your intentions be known to the Lock Master on your VHF.

Always approach and enter the lock DEAD SLOW. If your boat approaches too fast, your wake will follow – and possibly heave you and any other boats smashing into the lock wall, or even swamping much smaller boats. On the older locks, you simply loop your dock line around the vertical guide wires or wall cleats.

Do not ever "hard tie" your vessel to anything in a lock– even the guide straps. Remember, your line and, more importantly, your boat – has to rise or fall with the changing water level in the lock. One dock line near the bow and one near the stern will do nicely.

Approach and enter the lock slow and easy. Sure... the first time, you will feel a little anxious and unsure, but by the third time – you'll be the pro!

Once all boats are loaded and secured, the lock doors close, and the water begins to rise. All the while, you simply keep a hand on the line you have looped around the guide wire, watching to make sure it (or your boat) moves up as the water level begins to fill the lock chamber. If your boat or line gets caught or snagged, it could create a major disaster. Normally the Lock Master will send the smaller boats out first. So pay attention. Don't hesitate to ask for information or help if you need it. The Lock Masters are friendly and eager to see you through the lock without incident.

NO NEED TO RUSH: If you feel the need for speed on the Erie Canal, you just need to be patient. Rushing, being in a hurry and speeding will NOT get you to your destination any sooner. Each Lock and Bridge Master is aware of your speed – they are in constant contact with each other, and know exactly how long it takes at speed limit for you to travel from one lock or lift bridge to the next. So to avoid longer waits at locks and bridges, and avoid a stiff fine for speeding, bridle your urge to speed and go with the flow of the other boats.

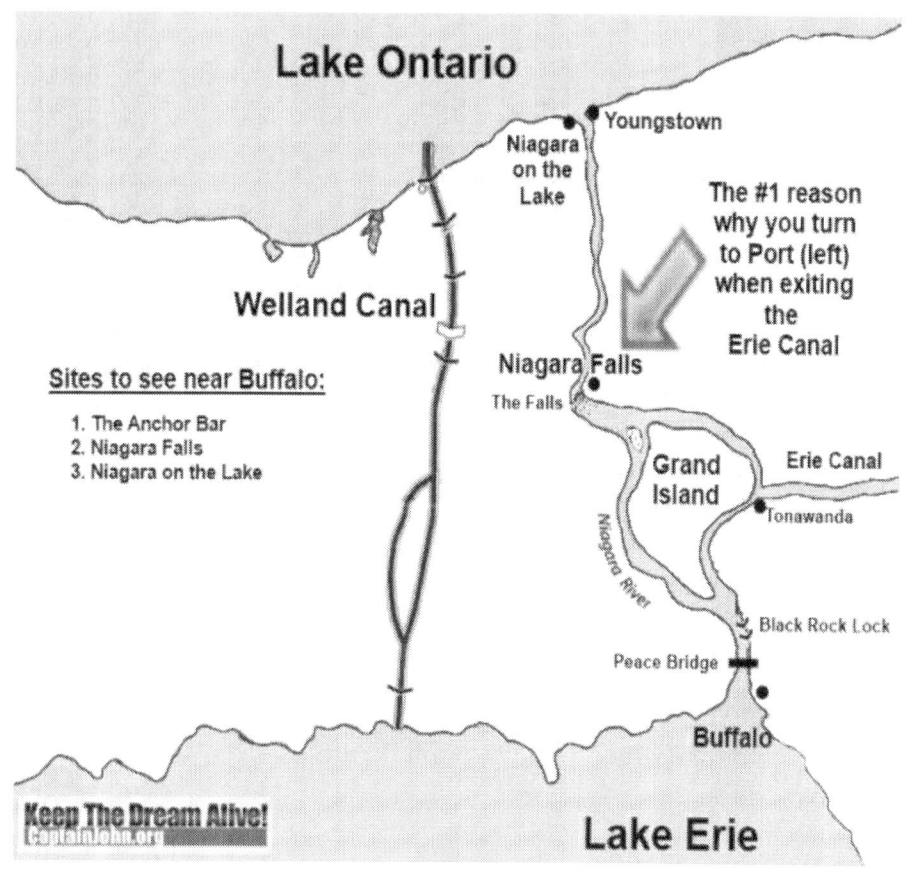

New York State's second largest city, Buffalo, will surprise you. It looms up in a cluster of skyscrapers like a miniature Manhattan on Lake Erie. The city's early twentieth-century prosperity (which collapsed while many other American cities were booming) exempted Buffalo's historic buildings from destruction and replacement, and is reflected in such architecturally significant structures as the towering 1928 City Hall (the tallest City Hall building in the USA).

Dining out in Buffalo is more than just chicken wings. In fact, there are more than 1,400 restaurants, bistros, cafes, pubs and grills in the Greater Buffalo Area. That figure doesn't include the annual food festivals where thousands come out to taste local specialties such as Beef on Wick. But if you like "Buffalo Style" chicken wings, there is no better place in the world to have them than at the Anchor Bar – where they originated.

Buffalo's downtown offers a mix of dining styles and cuisine, ranging from the frugal Towne Restaurant open 23 hours a day to E.B. Green's Steakhouse (Western New York's only five-star steakhouse) with a 24 ounce porterhouse and a three pound Maine lobster, a real treat but real expensive.

Near Buffalo, a trip to Canada's Niagara-on-the-Lake is well worth your visit. I also recommend you visit Niagara Falls from the Canadian side. (Sorry Niagara Falls, NY – but you really need to clean up your act.)

And by the way... you really don't have to worry about accidentally boating over Niagara Falls – it is eight miles (by water) from the Erie Canal junction with the Niagara River.

I have boated through and fished all around in the upper Niagara River on several occasions. In fact, believe it or not, this is the place I caught the biggest ugliest looking fish of my life (and I had a witness onboard). The fish was so ugly and so large I cut him loose at the stern of my boat only to discover later it was a large sturgeon. Fishermen in these waters fish their whole lives to catch one of these large sturgeons, which are taken from the waters of the Niagara every year. Many claim they are the best tasting fish in the world. Me? I just can't stomach the thought of eating something uglier than I am. I'll stick with the walleye, trout, and salmon, thank you very much!

The Great Lakes

If you take the most direct route, this leg of your voyage is 892 miles from the International Peace Bridge at Buffalo, NY to the Chicago River Lock at Chicago, IL.

The Great Lakes, of course, are the largest bodies of fresh surface water on earth. From the moon, astronauts can see the lakes and recognize each one.

I remember (believe it or not) in fifth grade our teacher taught us to remember the names of the Great Lakes by remembering the word "HOMES" for lakes Huron, Ontario, Michigan, Erie, and Superior. The Great Lakes cover more than 94,000 square miles. If the dam breaks on these freshwater seas, it would flood the lower 48 states ten feet deep under water.

The channels that connect the Great Lakes are an important part of the system. The St. Mary's River is the northernmost channel, a 60-mile waterway flowing from Lake Superior down to Lake Huron. Here, you will find the St. Mary's rapids; however, the Soo Locks bypass these rough waters, providing safe transport for boaters.

The St. Clair and Detroit Rivers, at Lake St. Clair form an 89-mile long channel connecting Lake Huron with Lake Erie. The 35-mile Niagara River and the Welland Canal link Lakes Erie and Ontario, and sends approximately 100,000 cubic feet of water <u>per second</u> over Niagara Falls.

On each of the Great Lakes, with the exception of Lake Ontario on a beautiful day, you can boat far enough out from shore, that you will not be able to see any land in any direction. On a clear day, however, boaters in the Youngstown-Rochester, NY area can see Toronto. But of course, if you are one that prefers to stick a little closer to shore, you can safely do that too. One could probably spend a lifetime cruising around all the Great Lakes and never see all the wonderful sites or experience all the incredible adventures this land of lakes has to offer.

The large size of the Great Lakes obviously increases the risks of water travel; storms and reefs are common threats. Historically, many commercial merchant ships have successfully crossed oceans only to meet their doom on the Great Lakes. Most of the shipwrecks are at Thunder Bay near the point where eastbound and westbound shipping lanes converge. The "Shipwreck Coast" runs from Grand Marais, MI to Whitefish Point on Lake Superior. So don't worry, you don't have to voyage that area if you don't want to.

The last major ship wreck on the Great Lakes was the SS Edmund Fitzgerald, which sank on November 10, 1975, just over 30 miles (50 km) offshore from Whitefish Point. The wreck of the Edmund Fitzgerald and the Museum are but a short detour from Mackinac Island as you enter Lake Superior. (It's worth the side trip.)

Now, having mentioned the ship wrecks... it would be OK if I scared you into being a little extra safe when cruising the Great Lakes. However, the fact is that for the exception of a couple of boiler explosions and fires in the 1800's, all the ship disasters on the Great Lakes have been a result of freak early winter storms. So, if you are voyaging the Loop by "seasons" (as suggested) it would be advisable to be well off and far south of the Great Lakes before the winter storm season threatens your vessel.

Besides, with today's technology such as GPS on boats, with accurate weather forecasting on the news, and your VHF radio you have nothing more to worry about on the Great Lakes than you do in your own marina. In fact, the Great Lakes make up what would be the "Boating Capital of the World" with more than one million US and Canadian recreational boats.

Lake Erie

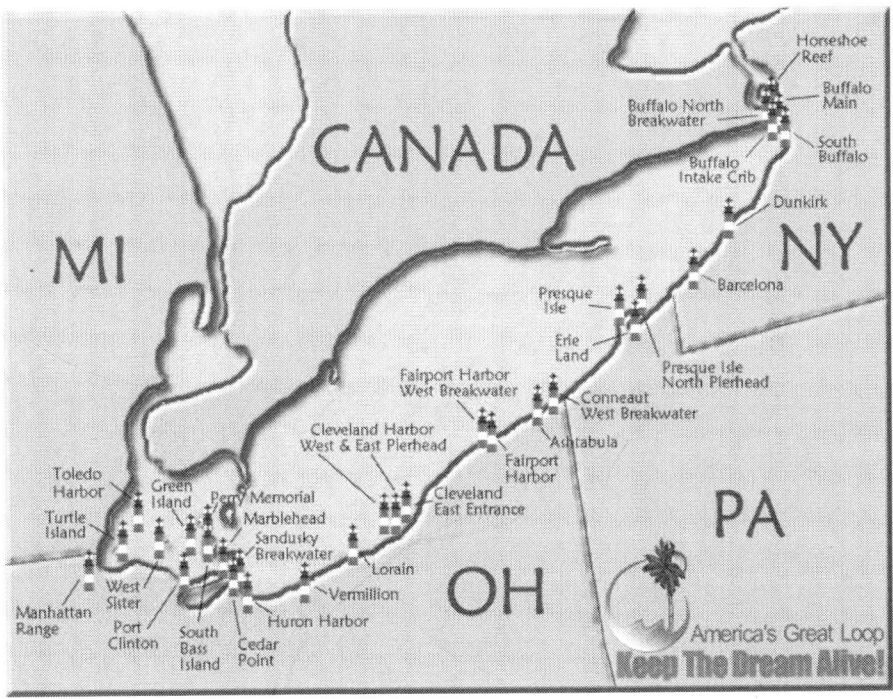

If you are cruising the Erie Canal, then Lake Erie will be the first of the Great Lakes you will cross. The average depth of Lake Erie is only 62 feet, and the western basin area averages only 24 feet. It warms quickly in summer and freezes over quickly in winter. Lake Erie is 241 miles long. If you take the US side around, your favorite stops will be Dunkirk, Erie, Conneaut, Cleveland, Sandusky, and Toledo. I enjoy Sandusky Bay and stop at Famous Dave's restaurant every time I pass by.

Once out of the Erie Canal, you will head into the Niagara River. Yes, you are now only a few short miles from Niagara Falls – so don't turn right (or to starboard) when leaving the canal. Your journey "south" on the mighty Niagara River will be against the current. Indeed, this river runs north. The current against you will be the strongest you will ever encounter. Swimming is great, but don't do it without a life line to your boat. Believe it or not – if you dive off your boat in the Niagara River, you will never, no not ever, be able to swim back – the current is that strong.

Sailboats and slow boats will need to enter the Black Rock Lock just before the Peace Bridge at Buffalo. This lock will by-pass the swiftest and strongest current where all of Lake Erie flows into an awfully narrow portion of the Niagara River.

For stronger, faster, more powerful boats, by-passing the Black Rock Lock is an option. You can (if you want) throttle up against the current and beat your way on up and under the International Peace Bridge and into Lake Erie. I've done this on many, many occasions in big engine and twin engine vessels over 30 feet. The ride is absolutely exhilarating – but it's not for the faint of heart. It's much like Whitewater rafting, only upstream. So if you have any doubt at all about you or your vessel's ability – take the Black Rock Lock.

When the wind kicks up, Lake Erie sings no lullabies. While generally Lake Erie does not create big waves (as does Lake Ontario), it can be very smooth and clear, or it can be very choppy. The chop is no hazard, of course, in a live-aboard size vessel, but you may want to have your fillings checked at the dentist when it's all over.

There are 24 islands in Lake Erie, nine of which belong to Canada. The most interesting islands are Kelley's Island, South Bass Island, Put-In-Bay, Johnson's Island, Middle Bass Island, and Canada's Pelee Island.

Buffalo is known for its "lake effect "snowstorms, the result of winter weather patterns that pick up moisture from the lake and deposit it on top of Buffalo in the form of snow. Having lived in

Buffalo for too many years, I can tell you with in-depth personal experience and knowledge – it gets cold and the snow gets deep!

Lake Erie is home to one of the largest commercial freshwater fisheries in the world which provides the largest supply of yellow perch to the United States and Canada. Major ports along Lake Erie include Buffalo, Erie, Monroe, and Toledo. Cedar Point and Sandusky, however, are Lake Erie's most favorite recreational boating stops.

Lake St. Clair

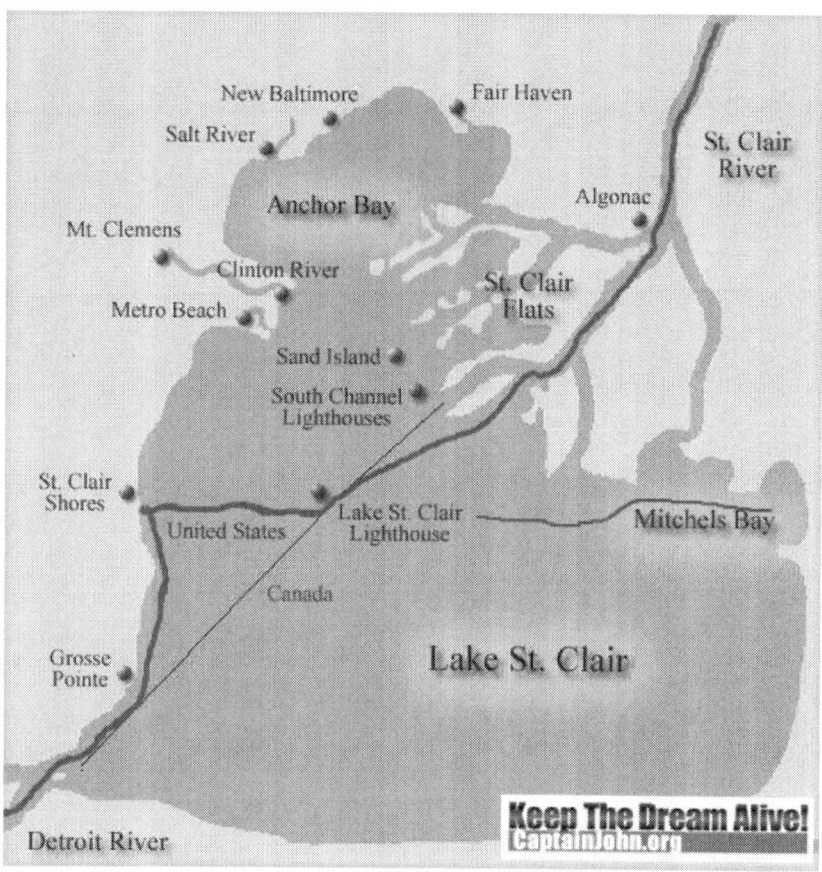

Lake St. Clair is your link from Lake Erie to Lake Huron. In comparison, it is a relatively small but it is packed with big things to do and see. I always look forward to my arrival on this lake.

My favorite stop on Lake St. Clair is the "Nautical Mile." It is the hub of Detroit's boating life and one of the largest concentrations of pleasure boats and marinas on the Great Lakes. Located along St. Clair Shores the Nautical Mile provides a number of great dining and nightlife destinations along the waterfront.

The Great Lakes Maritime Center at Vantage Point is also a great visit. Located at the junction of the Black River and St. Clair River, this place gives you a variety of opportunities to learn about the history and current events of the Great Lakes. You can also grab an ice cream and some hand-cut fries, and check out the live underwater camera feed of activities below the surface along the St. Clair River. If you are into fishing, you will love this place. Here is a good place to not only drop a line, but to learn about the hottest fishing spots along your way up Lake Huron, Georgian Bay, and Mackinac Island.

Mitchell's Bay is a small community on the east shore of Lake St. Clair. Mitchell's Bay and Mitchell's Bay Marine Park are known throughout the entire region for its great fishing. Mitchell's Bay offers some of the best walleye fishing (my favorite) to be found anywhere in North America, and it attracts fishermen from all over the world.

The Nautical Mile on Lake St. Claire

It is worth the visit.

St. Claire Shores

You will love St. Claire Shores on Lake St. Claire. You will boat right by it along your way by the Nautical mile.

Lake Huron

From Lake St. Clair, Lake Huron is your link to Lake Michigan. It is 206 miles long, and is 183 miles wide. Lake Huron has an average depth of 195 feet and a maximum depth of 750 feet.

On the north and eastern shores of Lake Huron, the granite islands (which are typical throughout Georgian Bay) surround Canada's North Channel. Lake Huron will take you to the Straits of Mackinac. Mackinac Island is at the top of our list of favorite stops.

Huron is the second largest Great Lake by surface area and the fifth largest freshwater lake in the world. It has the longest shoreline of all the Great Lakes, counting the shorelines of its 30,000 islands, which include Manitoulin Island – the largest freshwater island in the world. Georgian Bay and Saginaw Bay are the two largest bays on the Great Lakes.

If you have the time – and you should have the time – I strongly suggest a cruise to and through Huron's Georgian Bay's 30,000 Islands area. It is simply some of the most beautiful waters in the world.

Georgian Bay's 30,000 Islands offer some of the best cruising in the world. When you cruise it, the first thing you will think of is how in the world such a place has remained so untouched and original. It is much like traveling back in time before man and machines destroyed the landscape to build homes and factories. It is simply an amazing display of nature's natural beauty. Today, by far most of the islands remain untouched and unspoiled. Most of the islands are totally uninhabited and without any buildings whatsoever. The entire area is the largest group of fresh water islands in the world. If you already cruised through New York's 1,000 Islands, and gasped with amazement how beautiful it was, wait until you see this!

At the top of Lake Huron you won't be able to miss the Mackinac Bridge. It is one of the longest suspension bridges in the world. It connects the upper and lower peninsulas of Michigan and spans 5 miles over the Straits of Mackinac where Lake Huron meets Lake Michigan. You will boat directly under this bridge. FYI – at this point, you will be closer to the North Pole than you are to the Equator.

My favorite stop–One of my very most favorite stops on this leg of the voyage is Mackinac Island. The very first thing you will notice about this beautiful island is the horse-drawn carriages. There are no automobiles on the island. All transportation is either by foot, horse-drawn carriage, or bicycle.

While Mackinac Island is absolutely NOT a "frugal" destination to visit, I – the most frugal of frugal voyagers – make this stop my most expensive exception. I just can't pass it up. This is the one place I rent a hotel room, spend a few hours soaking in the tub, and then go visit the amazing shops. If you like homemade fudge and chocolates, and you're in the mood for a bit of window shopping – this is the place.

The Grand Hotel on Mackinac Island – features 386 rooms, of which, no two are alike.

Lake Michigan

From Lake Huron, after your visit to Mackinac Island and the Straits of Mackinac, you will enter Lake Michigan. Traveling south from Green Bay and Milwaukee to Chicago, the western shore is lined with big city landscapes. This area, combined with the southern shores of Indiana is home to over a whopping 120,000 US registered pleasure boats.

Many of the waterfront areas on all the Great Lakes offer some very tempting sites to visit. All of Lake Michigan has a beautiful shoreline that encompasses some of the most popular beaches on the Great Lakes. In addition, there are plenty of opportunities for adventure with sand dunes to climb; big cities to visit; pristine waters to sail, swim, and explore; as well as postcard-perfect sunsets to enjoy. Plus, don't forget about the fishing – I certainly never do.

There is an awful lot to see and do on Lake Michigan. Our very favorite stop on Lake Michigan is Leland (Fish town), MI. Leland is a picturesque little village located on a sliver of land between Lake Michigan and Lake Leelanau on the Leelanau Peninsula.

Leland (or Fish town) is certainly one of my most "highly recommended" overnight or weekend stops! So don't miss it. The people are extremely friendly and the unique shops and restaurants are surprisingly well worth a visit.

As summertime closes on Lake Michigan, you will want to be in a position to leave Chicago and begin your voyage down the Illinois

River to the Mississippi, and on to (if you take the Tenn-Tom route) the Ohio, Cumberland, Tennessee Rivers, Kentucky and Barkley Lakes and the Tenn-Tom Waterway. Your destination, of course, is the Gulf of Mexico.

You are about to enter the water-world of America's Heartland. You will be voyaging miles of tempting side trips. From Chicago through the Midwest, to the Deep South, each region will seem as distinct worlds. You will see cities melt into farmlands, and farmlands rise into hillsides. Eventually it will all fade into swamp land before you reach the beautiful beaches along the Gulf ICW.

By now, you may have already journeyed half of the 5,600 miles or so that it will take you to complete the Great Loop. Depending on your starting point, you may already be familiar with the challenges of traversing locks and dealing with bridge height restrictions, which (believe it or not) you will find again on this next portion of your journey. In addition, faster currents, silting, wing dams, fewer anchorages, and barge traffic may all be new challenges you will face on the rivers. With proper planning, however, this portion of the trip will prove to be every bit the most adventurous, easy, enjoyable, and relaxing of all.

Chicago's Navy Pier

If your boat can clear 17' . . .

You can boat right through downtown Chicago.

The Illinois River

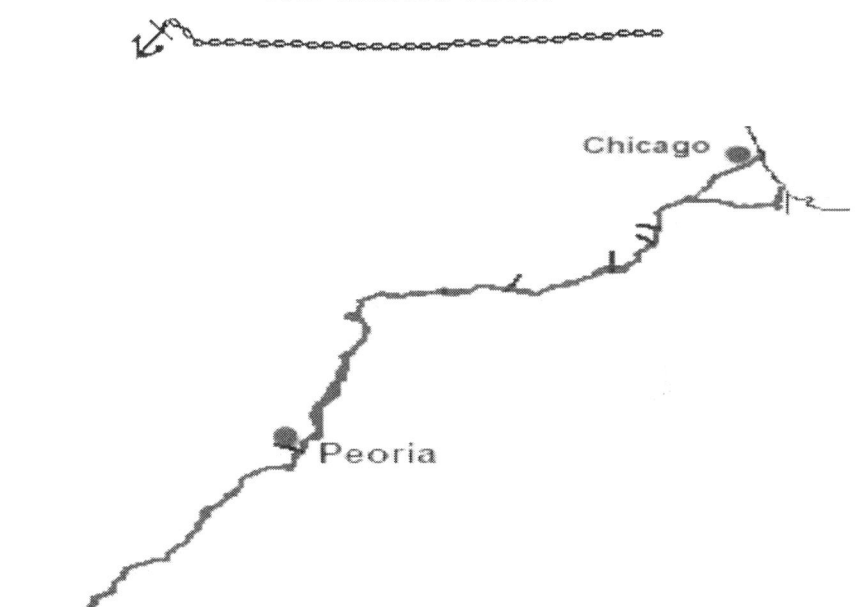

This leg of your journey is 327 miles, and extends from Chicago to Grafton, IL at the convergence of the Mississippi River. The most scenic route takes you from Lake Michigan, through the Chicago River Lock, and right through downtown Chicago.

In order to take the route through Chicago, your vessel must clear a 17' fixed overhead bridge. If you cannot clear 17', you will need to continue 11 miles south on Lake Michigan to the Cal-Sag route. Both these routes merge about three miles upriver from that 19'1" bridge you must go under.

"That 19' 1" Bridge"– Obviously, rainfall and water levels effect the height of this bridge. In 2011 (draught year) the height of this 19' 1" RR bridge was measured at 20' 7" above the water. We also heard of one Looper that flooded his bilge with enough water to pass under. But, we are not about to tell you that you can do the same. The result of failure here is most likely to result in wintering your boat in Chicago.

Just past that 19'1"bridge, you will soon approach a very intimidating **DANGER** sign. This sign indicates you are about to enter the U.S. Coast Guard's Electric Asian Carp Barrier Field at mile marker 298.

The Electric Fish Barriers are designed to prevent fish from entering the Great Lakes. The barriers are formed of electrodes that are secured to the bottom of the canal. A DC pulse is emitted through the electrodes creating an electric field in the water. Fish attempting to penetrate the electric field are exposed to electric shock, which prevents them from swimming through the electrified area.

The USCG also mandates that "everyone" on deck must wear a Coast Guard approved Type 1 PFD (life jacket) when boating through this Fish Barrier.

Asian Carp – Asian carp have become notorious for being easily frightened by boats and personal watercraft, which causes them to leap very high from the water and numerous boaters have been injured by them. Surprisingly, some of these injuries which include broken arms and noses have happened to boaters on live-aboard size vessels. On my last trip through Tennessee, the news reported Asian carp were recently spotted in the Cumberland River as well as on the Illinois, Ohio, and Mississippi Rivers.

Asian Carp on the Illinois River jumping - frightened by the boat traffic.

The Asian carp, in fact, seriously threaten the very closure of America's Great Loop. For sure, once you are south of the Electric Fish Barriers, you will encounter these fish. When you do – be aware Asian carp are known to batter boaters and even knock them into the water at the sound of a passing motor. They are voracious feeders that can grow four feet long and weigh a 150 pounds. The good news is that as soon as you make your way past the USCG Fish Barrier, you will soon find yourself on your way, voyaging at last, on your own adventure in the wake of Tom Sawyer and Huck Finn down the Mighty Mississippi. The next 297 miles of the Illinois River promises a welcome glance toward what's in front of your bow, for you are now headed into what is about to become the very best part of your adventure.

Your first great stop on this route is the Peoria Transient Marina. While some guide books mentioned it has "no services available" – the fact is that it has a machine on the dock that accepts dollar bills, and allows you to enter the amount of time you will spend. It then prints a receipt showing your departure time... the price is only a $1.00 an hour regardless of the size of your boat. (WOW! I love that!) Better still, at this very location in Peoria, you will find one of the best riverfronts on the Great Loop. Only problem is, you have to get off your boat to enjoy it.

There are a dozen or so great riverfront restaurants only a hundred feet or so away from the dock...starting with Joe's Crab Shack, Damon's Steakhouse, Hooters, Cafe' 401, and the Rhythm Kitchen. So for $12 to $24 you can get 12 to 24 hours for overnight dockage with time to eat out and do a little sightseeing. Additionally, one block from the dock, is the Peoria Riverfront Museum which is also worth a visit.

Starved Rock – on the Illinois River

Bald Eagles – While cruising the ICW along the Waccamaw River near Wacca Wachie Marina, you may have *thought* you saw a Bald Eagle. On the Illinois River, however, you won't have any doubt. Not only will you see one, you are most likely to see hundreds. So be sure to keep your camera handy for this rare American treat.

At the lower end of the Illinois River, you find **The Illinois Riverdock Restaurant** (at mile 20.9). Pay attention, or you will miss it. This is one of our top ten places to stop and eat on the entire Great Loop. In our opinion, it should be a mandatory stop for some great eats. So, don't miss it unless you absolutely have to.

Grafton Harbor Marina at mile marker 0 (zero) is the end of the road on the Illinois River. It is also mile 219 on the Upper Mississippi River. This 200 slip marina has a nice general store, gift shop, restaurant, and super shower and laundry facilities. It also has satellite TV, Wi-Fi and just about anything you could ever want or need.

America's Great Loop
THE MISSISSIPPI RIVER

The USACE (Army Corp of Engineers) has divided the Mississippi River into two halves. The Upper Mississippi River (or UMR) is one half, and The **Lower** Mississippi River (or LMR) is the other. Cairo, IL is the dividing point, and while we know the Mississippi River is only one river – when navigating it, you need to think of it as two: the Upper and the Lower Mississippi – otherwise, you are going to get terribly confused.

The Mississippi River's mouth is located 95 miles south of New Orleans at the Gulf of Mexico. From this point, distances on the Mississippi River are measured in statute miles. The mouth, or "Head of Passes" as it is referred to, is the point from which all mileage on the Lower Mississippi River is measured.

Cairo, IL, is at mile marker 954 on the Lower Mississippi. That means it is 954 miles from the Gulf of Mexico. It is also the end of the Lower Mississippi River and the beginning of the Upper Mississippi. Therefore, Cairo is also mile 0 (zero) on the Upper Mississippi River. All Mississippi River miles above Cairo give you the distance from Cairo. All miles below Cairo give you the distance to the Gulf of Mexico (95 miles below New Orleans).

For Great Loopers, the Mississippi starts at Grafton, IL where the Illinois River joins the Upper Mississippi at mile 219. Grafton, of course, is therefore mile marker 219 on the Upper Mississippi. To determine Grafton's distance from the Gulf of Mexico, simply take Grafton Mississippi mile marker 219 (the distance from Cairo) and add it to the Cairo mile marker 954, and you get the distance (219 + 954 = 1,173). Grafton is therefore 1,173 miles from the Gulf of Mexico. So your voyage to New Orleans from Grafton is 1,173 miles minus 95 miles or 1,078 statute miles.

Cairo is not only the dividing point on the Mississippi River, it is also your "decision point" on whether or not you want to cruise the full length of the Mississippi River to New Orleans or take the Tenn-Tom route to Mobile Bay. Either routes (or courses) will land you on the Gulf ICW. Your decision on which route to take should be considered seriously. In addition to the question of fuel range, your provisions and lack of facilities along the Lower Mississippi route are important considerations.

Sadly, the voyage down the Lower Mississippi is no longer the carefree romantic journey it once was. Despite what you may have heard, boating the Lower Mississippi River together with what you expect to find when you arrive in New Orleans will <u>NOT</u> be what you dreamed or thought it to be. Trust my experience on this one… when it comes to boats, boating, bugs, tugs and barges – the Lower Mississippi and the Mississippi side of New Orleans will (most likely) turn out to be something you will wish you had avoided altogether – especially if it comes as a surprise.

What matters most in making the choice of what route to take, is your vessel's fuel range. After that, it will depend on your lifestyle and comfort zone.

In order to cruise the full length of the Lower Mississippi, your boat's fuel capacity must provide you with a fuel range of 352 miles if you use diesel, or 449 miles if you use gasoline. This difference in fuel distance between gas and diesel is a result of a single optional <u>trucked-in diesel fuel delivery service</u> which is <u>not available</u> for gasoline users.

While the Tenn-Tom route offers over 60 marinas between Cairo at the junction of the Ohio River and Mobile Bay – the Lower Mississippi River offers only two marinas between Hoppies Marina at mile marker 158.5 on the Upper Mississippi and New Orleans. There are no services or fuel from Hoppies to Mud Island Marina (mile marker 737) on the Lower Mississippi River at Memphis. This is a distance of 376 miles. There are also no services or fuel from Greenville, MS until you reach the Gulf ICW. There are also no pleasure boat docks or facilities at or near New Orleans on the Mississippi River.

There are no marina services between the Greenville Yacht Club at mile 539 until you pass through the Harvey Lock south of New Orleans at mile marker 93, and then proceed three more miles east on the Gulf ICW to SeaBrook Marine. This makes your distance from Greenville Yacht Club to SeaBrook Marine a total distance of 449 miles, and makes it (by far) the farthest distance between fuel stops on the Great Loop.

Regardless of fuel, in both cases, from Hoppies Marina you have: Mud Island Marina and the Greenville Yacht Club. These two marinas are the only shore access points and marina services for nearly 400 miles in either direction. So, if you need fuel, showers, laundry, ice, beverages, or provisions of any kind, you will NOT find them until you reach Mud River Marina. The only other marina until you reach the Gulf ICW is the Greenville Yacht Club. The Lower Mississippi distance, (on average) takes me 10 to 12 days. Therefore, you will be anchoring out in places with no shore access for this length of time (provided you don't get caught in two or three days of bad weather). So plan ahead, and plan accordingly.

Now, if you have the fuel range, the Lower Mississippi can be a very exciting and enjoyable voyage – if anchoring out and spending that amount of time exclusively on your boat fits well into your lifestyle. If you can carry the provisions you want and need, and you enjoy your solitude, it will be a voyage to remember.

I know it sounds as if I am being negative about this route. I'm really not. My intention is not to encourage, or discourage – only to inform. Fact is, the recent decade of floods has (over the years) simply washed out all the riverfront restaurants, marinas, fish camps, and shore access that used to be there. Now, all of that has been replaced with high levies on one side and shallow swamp lands on the other.

Regardless of which route you take, when navigating the inland rivers you will want to practice patience. Delays, towboats, tugboats, wing dams and weir dams are simply a fact of life when boating on the rivers.

In addition, you want to make sure you reach a good anchorage before dark. You want to already be anchored, and make sure your anchor is set when dark is approaching. There are two really good reasons for this. One is you want to make sure you are in a good safe anchorage. The other is, in the late evening just before dark, you are most likely to get swarmed by bugs – mostly, mosquitoes. Believe me, you will want to be safely tucked away inside your mosquito proof cabin, long before these pesky little blood suckers attack your vessel.

You also need to make sure you have a "great" electrical system – not only on the rivers, but also for your entire Great Loop route. Why? Safety! Folks, a single anchor light, (especially atop the mast on a sailboat) is woefully inadequate (insufficient, inept, and unsuitable). If you want to be safe, and "feel" safe, you will do as I do and light up your vessel like a Christmas tree. No, I don't use colored lights, but I do have four bright shining white lights (one on each side and both ends of my vessel) that shine inward on my boat to light it up. For the most part, fishermen are the culprit. At night, they will speed around the river bends at the pace of an Indy 500 car. These guys are locals, and undoubtedly know the rivers like the back of their hand, but if you're anchored off the channel and in their path – you want to make sure they see you in time. You don't want a single (especially dim) anchor light. I have three high-capacity 12 volt batteries on my vessel and a solar panel – just to make sure my night lights (anchor lights) are ALWAYS burning bright – all night long.

Regardless of the route you take, as you cruise south for the winter, long pants and long sleeves may be your uniform of the day. In some cases, in some locations, even though it may still be hot, such clothing will greatly reduce that "field of dreams" for those truly southern American mosquitoes.

DON'T BE MISLEAD. Cruising the Lower Mississippi can certainly be a fun and exciting adventure. If you are Tom Sawyer traveling with Huck Finn, and carrying enough fuel or jerry cans to refuel your vessel and hike out a mile or more to get fuel, ice and provisions as needed. If this is you, you will be thrilled boating down the Lower Mississippi.

If, however, you are Captain Clean cruising with Ms. Manicure, and both of you are social boating butterflies, you are likely to be miserable voyaging down the Lower Mississippi. Most Loopers (even those that have the fuel range) bid farewell to the Mississippi in Cairo, and take the Tenn-Tom route – and they do so for very good reason.

The Mississippi River is the second-longest river in the United States. The longest is the Missouri River, which flows into the Mississippi. Taken together, they form the largest river system in North America. If measured from the head of the Missouri, the length of the Missouri and Mississippi combination is 3,895 miles long.

From Cairo to St. Anthony Falls in Minneapolis, the Upper Mississippi River has 27 locks that lift your vessel to a total of 725 feet above sea level. There are no locks on the Lower Mississippi River except for the New Orleans Industrial Canal Lock to Lake Pontchartrain and the Harvey Lock at the Gulf ICW.

The Upper Mississippi River

Believe it or not, for most Great Loopers the voyage down the Mississippi is only 219 miles. Yep! That's a fact.

The Upper Mississippi River (UMR) leg of your journey is only 219 miles from Grafton (end of Illinois river) to Cairo on the Mississippi river at the junction of the Ohio. Most of us take this route to Kentucky Lake, the Tennessee river, on down the Tenn-Tom to Mobile Bay and the Gulf ICW just north of the Gulf of Mexico. The fuel range required for this leg of your journey is 250 miles. You will have to make it from Hoppies Marina to either the Kentucky Dam Marina (mile 22) or Green Turtle Bay Marina (mile 25) on the Tennessee River.

Cairo is mile 954 on the Lower Mississippi River. Cairo is also mile 0 on **the Upper Mississippi River.**

Cairo is your decision point. If you haven't made up your mind to take the Tenn-Tom by the time you reach Cairo, well, the river's current may make it up for you.

Obviously, the Mississippi River had to start somewhere, for Great Loopers, it starts in Grafton, IL. While Grafton is mile 0 (zero) on the Illinois River, it is mile 219 on the Upper Mississippi River. Cairo is mile 954 on the Lower Mississippi River. Therefore Grafton is (954 plus 219) or 1,173 miles from the Gulf of Mexico, and 1,080 miles to Harvey Lock at the Gulf ICW.

From the junction of the Illinois River at Grafton, your next big city is St. Louis, and surprisingly there are limited marinas and good anchorage options in the immediate St. Louis area. This is where you will experience the fastest current of your entire voyage. In fact, you will race past the St. Louis Gateway Arch.

Just below the junction or the Missouri and Mississippi Rivers, and before you reach St Louis, you will see this sign:

Make sure you follow its directions. Don't even think about continuing straight down the Mississippi River.

This sign is directing you to enter the Chain of Rocks Canal. It is located at the Upper Mississippi River mile marker 194.1 and is the last (and most southern) Lock (#27) on the Mississippi River between here and New Orleans. This eight- mile long Chain of Rocks Canal (as the name implies) takes you safely around the Mississippi's chain of rocks reach and rapids.

The canal ends at mile marker 184 just upstream of St Louis.

Cruising south on the Mississippi River, the St. Louis Gateway Arch will be on your starboard side at Upper Mississippi River mile marker 180 just before the Poplar Street Bridge.

Your next stop will be Hoppies Marina in Kimmswick, MO, at mile marker 158 (22 miles away) and this is a <u>must</u> fuel stop. It is 238 miles from Hoppies to Kentucky Dam Marina or 250 miles to Green Turtle Bay Marina (your nearest fuel stops) on the Tenn-Tom route. Hoppies Marina is not only a must fuel stop, it has also become somewhat of a "rite of passage" for Great Loopers. No matter which route you take from Hoppies – you <u>must</u> stop and get fuel. If you don't, you may run out of fuel before your next available fuel stop.

Not one single Great Loop voyage is complete without a stop at Hoppies Marina. Just do it. You will be glad you did, and you will need the fuel anyway.

From Hoppies, and for the next 158 miles or so you will discover wing dams. Wing dams extend and direct the river's flow toward the center of the river. The USACE has built over 1,000 wing dams on the Upper Mississippi River. If the river is a little high, you may not see them. If you know what to look for, wing dams can be recognized by the ripples on the surface of the water.

Wing Dams: locations are marked on your charts and GPS system. Going down the rivers, it is important to know what these are, where they are, and how to identify them.

At Cairo, you can take the Ohio River route straight to the Tennessee River at the Kentucky Lock and Dam, or you can continue another 12 miles up the Ohio, and take the Cumberland River route. Both these routes will end up at the same place near the Green Turtle Marina and you can get to Green Turtle Marina from either route. If you are concerned over fuel range, the Tennessee River route to Kentucky Dam Marina is about 12 miles shorter, but the wait time in the Kentucky Lock is often considerably longer.

Or of course, you can head on down the Lower Mississippi River to New Orleans and the Gulf of Mexico.

The Lower Mississippi River

If you take it, the Lower Mississippi leg of your voyage is 859 miles to New Orleans – it begins at the convergence of the Ohio River at Cairo and goes another 95 miles south past New Orleans and the Gulf ICW into the Gulf of Mexico. So your voyage to New Orleans is 859 miles from Cairo and 1,078 miles from Grafton.

Your "fuel range" is the major veto factor for taking this route. So too is the lack of Marinas and convenient stops. This route offers you

only two fuel stops between Hoppies on the Upper Mississippi and SeaBrook Marine on the Gulf ICW - compared to more than 30 marinas on the very most direct Tenn-Tom route which also cuts 400 miles off your total distance.

Your main problem on this route is fuel range and fuel stops. If your vessel requires diesel fuel, you will fuel up at Cape Girardeau, MO, (115 miles below St. Louis). On this route, your boat's fuel capacity must provide you with a fuel range of 352 miles if you use diesel, or 449 miles if you use gasoline. The difference in fuel distance between gas and diesel is a result of a diesel fuel delivery service which is not available for gasoline users.

You will not get a chance to fuel up again until you reach Mud River Marina in Memphis, a distance of 436 miles.

The other big problem on the Lower Mississippi River is anchorage – or I should say, lack of them. Below St. Louis, you can spend the first night at the Kaskaskia Lock and Dam, just off the Upper Mississippi River on the LDB (Left Descending Bank) at about mile 117. With the Lockmaster's permission, you can tie-up to the floating guide for free.

Mile zero of the UMR is at the junction of the Ohio and Mississippi Rivers, at Cairo, which is also mile 954 on the LMR (Lower Mississippi River). The Mississippi River runs under 20 feet deep until the Ohio; then it runs over 30 feet deep. After that, there is a safe anchorage at mile 857.

After Mud River Marina, your next fuel stop is the Greenville Yacht Club in Greenville, MS. Your timing is also critical here as you don't want to get caught boating in the dark. Many tugs and towboats (with or without barges) on the Mississippi, in fact, run after dark.

Memphis, TN is at the Lower Mississippi River mile marker 736. There is an "optional" safe overnight stop at the Merrisach Lake anchorage at the Arkansas Post Canal, which is 151 miles south of

Mud Island at Memphis. There is also a safe place to get off the river at Tunica.

Safe, quite comfortable anchorages on the Lower Mississippi are simply few and far between – and difficult to find. With all the recent floods and flood damage, guide books simply can't come close to keeping up with all the changes going on, on the Lower Mississippi.

Entrances to many marked anchorages are silted over and not navigable.

Below Memphis in Helena, AR is your next anchorage. Almost everywhere else you will find marginal depth, sand bars, and heavy silting until you reach Vicksburg, almost 300 miles below Memphis.

No marina or "gasoline" exists at Vicksburg, but you can tie-up to a barge next to Harrah's Casino. Vicksburg, however, is a must stop for diesel fuel users, because a fuel truck will bring fuel to the boat. After that, there is no fuel for 450 miles until you pass New Orleans, the Harvey Lock, and are on the Gulf ICW.

If you do take this route, when you reach New Orleans, you will undoubtedly recognize places you've either visited or seen, like the hotels on Canal Street, the Riverwalk, the Aquarium, and the French Quarter.

Inviting as the city looks from the river, and as inviting as all this seems, there simply is nowhere for a pleasure boat to stop on the Mississippi River anywhere near New Orleans (not even between Baton Rouge and the Gulf ICW). Instead, you must pass through the Industrial Canal Lock to reach Lake Pontchatrain and visit New Orleans from the east side.

If you have been researching the Great Loop routes, I'm positive you will have either heard or read many plenty of negative things about both the Lower Mississippi and the Industrial Canal.

The fact is this is not a "bad" or "terrible" experience at all. Those "bad reviews" you read or heard from those that have cruised it, are coming from boaters that simply did not know what to expect. Therefore it was not that it was so terrible, just "terribly disappointing" for them. Most of them, however, were expecting New Orleans to welcome them in all its Riverboat and Mardi Gras glory. That's not going to happen not even during Mardi Gras.

When, for example, you pass New Orleans and exit the Canal into Lake Pontchatrain, you can cruise along the street lights of Lake Shore Drive all the way to the harbor. There, when you get close enough, you will see a flashing red light at the harbor entrance, which is dimmed by the bright lights from *Joe's Crab Shack. If you* turn into the harbor entrance at *Joe's,* you will see Schubert's Marine – and that's where your fun in New Orleans begins.

The Lower Mississippi – if you have the fuel range, it's not a bad journey. It's best loved, however, by those on a "Huck Finn-Tom Sawyer" adventure.

America's Great Loop
The Ohio River

The Ohio River...it's a long one. It begins at the confluence of the Allegheny and Monongahela Rivers at "The Point" in Pittsburgh, PA, and flows 981 miles to join the Mississippi at Cairo, IL.

Cairo, of course, will be your entry to the Ohio River. There are 53 locks on the Ohio River, and you will not be the only one on it. Sometimes there are long lines of pleasure boats waiting for locks. Over 30,000 recreational boats locked through the Pittsburgh District's locks last year.

Numerous excursion boats also use our locks as they cruise the rivers entertaining and educating area residents and tourists. Many people use the navigation pools as a lake for pleasure boating without ever using a lock and some do not realize that the miles of clear channel are created by the dams. In many areas, fishing is at an all-time high, as the quality of the water and the fish have dramatically improved over the past 20 years.

It is a long up-stream ride from Cairo to Pittsburgh, and another long ride back down, but honestly, I can't think of a better use of the time spent on a boat.

Pittsburgh is a very popular long-distance boating destination. Furthermore, your voyage doesn't need to stop in Pittsburgh. The Allegheny River has eight locks and dams that provide 72 miles of navigation from The Point north to above East Brady. In addition, nine locks and dams on the Monongahela River will get you 128 more miles upriver to just above Fairmont, WV. So total miles for your voyage up the Ohio and into West Virginia will be almost 1,200 miles one-way.

I have voyaged the entire length of this river, and I must confess, it can get very crowded in areas, especially in the early fall if the weather remains warm. Everyone is friendly and no one has as much fun as boaters on the Ohio River. From tubers, to canoes, to cabin cruisers, trawlers, sailboats, deck boats, houseboats, even old paddle wheel steamboats, towboats and barges, they all seem to be wearing smiles, and all having the time of their lives.

There is no need to feel threatened in any way over the size of this river, nor of its commercial traffic or its locks and dams. The Ohio River seems a mile wide in some places and the winds can create some uncomfortable chop. While the towboats and barges can be intimidating, all in all, it is (like all the rest of the Great Loop) a simple matter of paying attention, using good common sense, and being a safe boater.

There is probably more neat stuff (and free stuff) to see and do on this river than any other. From boat shows to riverside summer concerts and fall festivals, the activities on the Ohio don't stop until the winter season closes for winter.

If you can't make the entire journey on the Ohio to Pittsburgh, you should at least give serious thought to a much shorter cruise to Louisville and visit Churchill Downs – the home of the Kentucky Derby.

Louisville is a wonderful waterfront city that is just incredibly beautiful, and extremely hospitable to visiting boaters. Famous for the Kentucky Derby, the area is surrounded by beautiful horse farms and landscapes. Much to your surprise, you will discover Louisville has much more to offer than just the Derby.

However, if you are taking the Great Loop "short" route, your cruise on this river is only from Cairo to Paducah. At Paducah you will either take the Tennessee River to Kentucky Lake, or 12 miles farther you will take the Cumberland River to Lake Barkley. Both these routes will lead to the same "land-cut canal" just below the Kentucky Lake Lock Dam or Lake Barley Lock and Dam.

While the Tennessee River route is shorter, often because of heavy commercial traffic, the Cumberland River route is quicker.

The Tennessee River

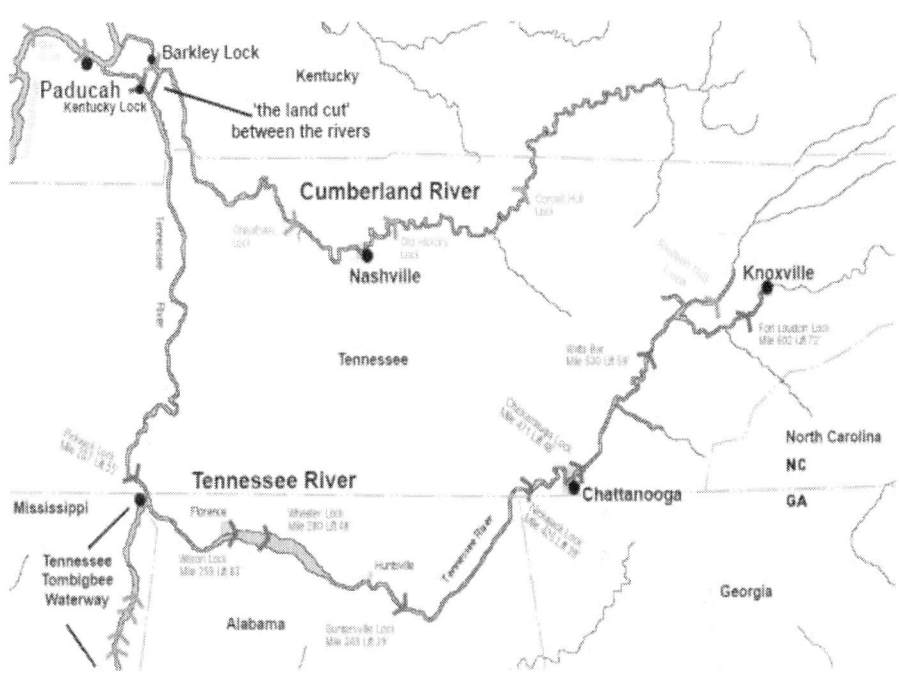

This Tennessee River leg of your voyage is a beautiful 215 miles from Paducah, KY to the junction of the Tennessee-Tombigbee Waterway. Your side trip options include taking the Cumberland River to Nashville, and taking the Tennessee River to Chattanooga and Knoxville.

Pioneers (including Daniel Boone) referred to this river as the Cherokee River. Now, the Tennessee River is one of the most popular vacation spots in America. Its rich fascinating history includes Cherokee Indians, early colonial pioneers, Revolutionary war heroes, and Civil War battles. Today, the Tennessee River provides a magnificent variety of boat-accessible concerts, festivals, museums, historic sites, landmarks, resorts, and activities.

The Tennessee River begins near its eastern border with Georgia and then flows westward, before flowing northward back into Tennessee. The largest lakes it traverses are Guntersville, Wheeler, Wilson and Pickwick.
As a Looper, if you are also an angler, sightseer, or lover of history, you will want to take a side trip along the full navigable length of the Tennessee River, from Paducah to Chattanooga and on to Knoxville. It is the Cumberland River that takes you to Nashville.

Yes, I know, it is a shame that it only takes four hours to drive your car from Nashville to Knoxville, but the good news is, you can boat from Nashville to Knoxville in about 10 days via the Tennessee River and
Cumberland Rivers. The Tennessee is one cool, clean, massive river that forms Kentucky Lake. It is not only great boating, it is great fishing and widely known for its huge small mouth bass and big blue catfish.

From Paducah on the Ohio River, once you pass through the lock to enter either the Tennessee River at Kentucky Dam or the Cumberland River Lock at Lake Barkley, there is a land cut (short canal) that allows boat traffic to cross over between the two rivers (and lakes) without having to go back through the locks to the Ohio River.

So on this portion of the Great Loop route, (if you take no detours) you will be heading south on the Tennessee River, but you will be going upstream, as this portion of the Tennessee flows north. Confusing, huh! Especially when you realize at this point you are heading south, parallel to the Mississippi River (just a few miles west of you) which is flowing south. As a footnote here, there are only two sections on the Great Loop where this phenomena takes place – the other is the Niagara River above Niagara Falls.

Birdsong Marina

Located on the south side of Birdsong Creek, 1.5 miles in the deep buoyed channel, from the scenic Tennessee River. This neat little place is right on your Great Loop route about halfway between Kentucky dam and Pickwick dam. (Tennessee River Mile marker 103.7).

The interesting thing about this marina is that it operates North America's only natural fresh water pearl farm and museum. It's a nice stop, and it is a very interesting place to visit.

For fishermen, the Tennessee River is, of late, the only place I have seen "catfish jumpin'" since I was a kid. Watching them one morning while still anchored, I had the notion to toss out some bait. Since I had none, I tossed some pieces of raw bacon – sure enough, the water began to swish and open-mouthed catfish were catching my bacon in midair.

From Nickajack Marina, Chattanooga is just 33 miles away and very well worth the voyage. If you can't go all the way to Knoxville, be sure to make it to Chattanooga. It's a great time with great things to do. Not only will you find a pretty neat aquarium, you'll get a chance to see the Chattanooga Choo Choo and discover some really great restaurants.

The Tennessee-Tombigbee Waterway

Once on the Tennessee-Tombigbee Waterway, often referred to as the Tenn-Tom, it is absolutely beautiful despite the early morning fog and possibly some questionable weather. If you are cruising the Loop by the seasons, it is after all – winter!

I have spent a lot time on the Tenn-Tom, and also a lot of time thinking about it in relationship to taking this route vs. the Lower Mississippi River route. The Tenn-Tom route cuts about 400 miles off your Great Loop journey vs. taking the Lower Mississippi River to New Orleans and across the Gulf ICW to Mobile Bay where the Mobile Bay Ship Channel intersects the Gulf Intracoastal Waterway.

Many (in fact most) Loopers rush through this leg of adventure and regrettably miss so much. Agreed, there is not a lot to do if you are one of the Loopers that thrives on Tiki Bars and nightlife. The Tenn-Tom route to Mobile is one of the most remote sections on the Great Loop. However, not only is it beautiful, it is far from boring.

The Tenn-Tom is an extensive inland man-made waterway system unlike any of its kind. It was a bigger project than the Panama Canal. This 234 mile-long waterway ends at Demopolis where it connects with the Tombigbee River. The Tombigbee River takes you another 213 miles to Mobile. So this leg of your journey from the Tennessee River is a total of 447 statute miles.

While it is the preferred alternative route to the Lower Mississippi, it too is not without its hang-ups and hazards. You will still have currents, shoaling, debris, and barges to contend with, but on a much more manageable level than the Mississippi. You also have 13 marinas counting Pebble Isle and Birdsong Marinas, on this 447 mile journey to Mobile vs. only two marinas on the 1,116 mile Lower Mississippi route from Hoppies Marina to New Orleans.

The very best way to avoid all the problems everyone else has on the inland rivers is to simply go slow and stay inside the channel markers. This might seem like common sense, but the temptation to cut corners and speed can often be stronger than the current. When you go around a bend, you have to know where the deep side will be because the shallow side will be silted. As I have mentioned before, when Loopers cut corners, they take the chance of running aground, running into barges, picking up debris, or damaging their props... then they blame someone else for their problems. Despite the hazards, if you follow the rules and use good common sense, you will absolutely love this part of your voyage. The food is good, the local natives are friendly, and this entire leg of your journey is one long stream of Kodak moments.

There are a number of locks on the Tenn-Tom route between the Ohio and Mobile Bay. Also, the great expanses of farmland and rural landscapes often surprise Loopers who are more accustomed to life and boating around major populated areas. It is narrower and most of the waters are muddy, but that seems to just make the catfish taste all that much better.

On the Tenn-Tom route you find fuel, supplies, southern cooking, and small-town hospitality so intriguing and wonderful, you'll want to eat your way all the way to the Gulf.

Bobby's Fish Camp in Silas, AL is every bit a must stop as much for their fried catfish platters as for fuel, and you will begin to smell the salt sea air. Of all the other legs of the Loop, this one ends in a great American city. Mobile is a gem of the South, and after many a day on the rivers, you will find it to be a welcome site – and a pleasure to enjoy full-service, big-city amenities before you make your way into the biggest body of water you have seen since leaving the Great Lakes – the Gulf of Mexico.

Yes, cruising America's Great Loop is a wonderful, exhilarating, and undoubtedly fun adventure and the Tenn-Tom is no exception. Your voyage all the way down river through America's Heartland will indeed be a highlight of your journey.

If you haven't already, it is here on the Tenn-Tom you will encounter other Loopers in their boats of all shapes, sizes, and all types of vessels from sailboats, houseboats, cabin cruisers, catamarans, trawlers, tugs, and anything that floats. Most of them are continuing on to Florida and will be looking to make some "cruising buddies" in preparation of crossing the Gulf of Mexico.

The Great Loop is, after all, a truly American adventure. Voyaging down the rivers of America's Heartland, it matters not what size, type, kind, or cost of your vessel. Your vessel does not have to shine, but it does have to have all the bells and whistles. At day's end you will find yourself sharing this experience with both bums and billionaires. Some Loopers will own yachts; others will own something equivalent to a floating cargo crate with an outboard engine. Most of us own vessels that fall somewhere in-between. But the fact remains – no one cares how new or old, big or small your boat is, or how much it cost. As you will discover yourself when anchored in the same harbors - gathered at the same barbecues on the same beaches, over the same steamed claims, crabs, fish fry, or potluck dinner– you will soon realize it is not the boat that unites Loopers, it is the boater.

America's Great Loop
THE GULF ICW

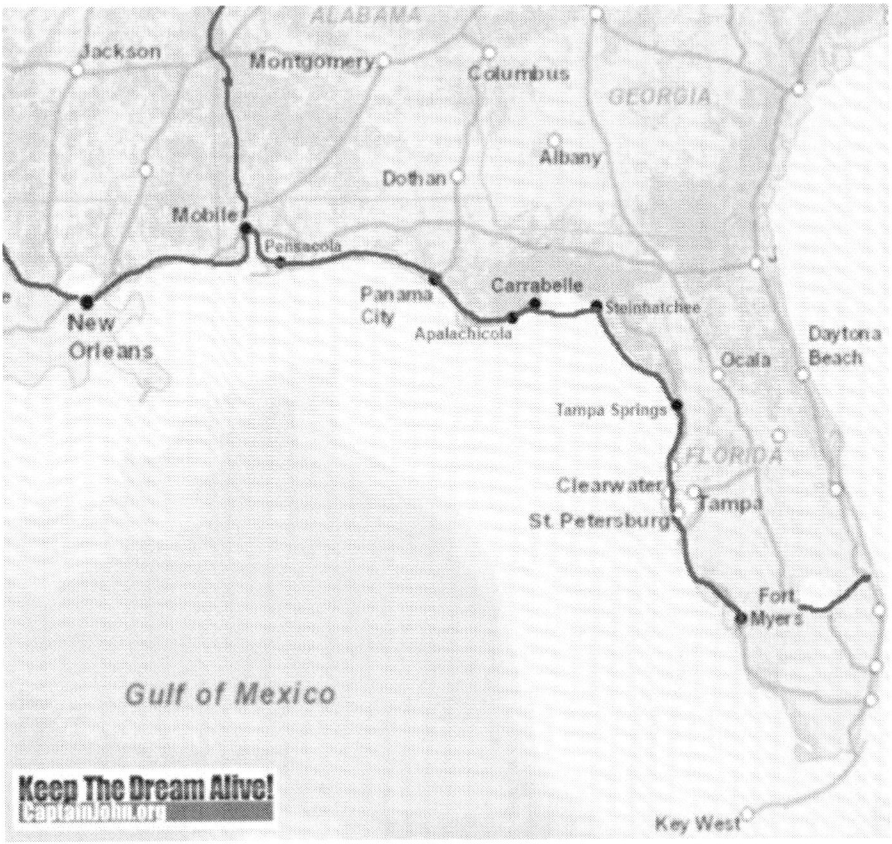

This leg of your journey is 218 miles from Mobile Bay to Carrabelle. It is 350 miles from New Orleans to Carrabelle, and 700 miles from Galveston to Carrabelle (just thought I would throw that in as Galveston is my Home Port).Aside from the brief trip down Mobile Bay's eastern shore, the entire Gulf ICW is a well-protected inside route all the way to Carrabelle.

The area has been described as the "Forgotten Coast" and "the road less traveled." That translates into fewer tourists where you would think more tourists would be. Fact is, you are about to cruise through some shockingly beautiful beaches with astonishingly aqua-tinted, gin-clear waters, and white pristine sandy beaches this side of the Caribbean.

Among the world's great waterways, America's Great Loop is indeed the greatest. It not only includes the mighty Mississippi, Illinois, Ohio, but also includes the Atlantic ICW, the Erie Canal, the Great Lakes, the Tennessee and Tombigbee Rivers, as well as the rambling 1,116 statute mile Gulf ICW that reaches from Brownsville, TX to Carrabelle, FL.

As far as the Great Loop is concerned and for all intended navigational purposes, the Gulf ICW or "The Ditch" starts in at the Harvey Locks (New Orleans) on the Gulf Intracoastal Waterway.

Here, the miles are also defined in terms of statute miles (as opposed to nautical miles) east and west of Harvey Lock, in the New Orleans area. The Hathaway Bridge in Panama City, FL, for example, is at mile 284.6 EHL (East of Harvey Lock). The Queen Isabella Causeway Bridge at South Padre Island is at mile 665.1 WHL (West of Harvey Lock).

The Harvey Lock is mile 0 (zero) as is Norfolk, VA mile 0 (zero) on the Atlantic ICW. While very heavy barges, tugs, and commercial traffic can be very stressful near the New Orleans, LA, and the East Texas portions of the Gulf ICW, you can boat the full length with little fear of getting lost. There are signs, rules, and guidelines to follow. Still it is common sense and safety (not secrets) that will make your journey successful. As a Great Looper, the GICW provides an inland protected passage for all of us voyaging from the Mississippi or Mobile Bay to Carrabelle, FL.

Starting way back at the Erie Canal and from Chicago – to the end of the Tenn-Tom –you will have gone through so many locks you can't possibly remember them all. Here is your last one until you reach the Okeechobee Waterway.

The route from Mobile to Carrabelle takes you (surprisingly to most) into and across some of the most beautiful beaches in America. In season, this area becomes the boater's playground. Heading south along Mobile Bay's Eastern shore, there are several marinas to choose from, including the Marriott's Grand Hotel Marina, Fly Creek Marina, and Fairhope Marina, all three of which are located near Fairhope.

From Fairhope, it is a short distance to the Gulf ICW (or GIWW as it is most often referred to) and your first stop on the Gulf ICW is most likely to be LuLu's in Gulf Shores, AL.

Cruising the Gulf ICW (especially in a sailboat or deep draft vessel) can be very stressful. (I am not holding back any punches here.) The commercial traffic, narrow channel, and shallow banks around New Orleans simply do not give a pleasure boater much time for carefree boating in this area. Since the commercial traffic does NOT move out of your way... you must move out of theirs. At times, this may seem difficult if not impossible to do – but it is. As long as you plan your voyage and always plan ahead for your escape from oncoming or passing traffic, you'll be ok.

Sometimes the GICW runs right along the Gulf, other times it will take you a surprisingly to a far distant inland.

Your route along the Gulf Intracoastal Waterway will take you from Mobile –mile 134 EHL (East of Harvey Lock) to the Gulf ICW where your first stop will most likely be Lulu's which is mile 155 EHL. From Lulu's and Homeport Marina, it is 12 miles to Orange Beach Marina.

If you want to visit the beach at Orange Beach, between mile 167 and mile 168 there is a marked channel off the GIWW through Bayou St. John to Perdido Pass. On the way you will cruise past a gauntlet of marinas and waterfront restaurants. The area is a great place to visit and, of course, (as you will see) the beaches are pristine, sandy, and beautiful.

Blalock Seafood & Specialty Market offers local seafood, oysters, shrimp and crayfish. They have three locations: Orange Beach and Gulf Shores, AL, and Destin, FL.

Ft. Walton Beach (mile 224) is another beautiful area with a lot of charm. Sandy beaches and crystal-clear waters are a delight. All the water and the beaches of Pensacola, Orange Beach, Panama City, Ft. Walton, and Destin are simply great.

If you are in the mood for some great off shore fishing, all the area from Pensacola to Panama City offers simply fantastic charter fishing. So, while you might not be as excited as all those "landlubbers" over the boat ride, the fishing makes for a fantastic day. Just remember to give away the fish you can't eat or can't safely store until you can eat it.

Apalachicola is a small Florida town, known in modern times for its oyster industry. It used to be one of Florida's largest ports in the 1800's due to cotton shipping. It's along the western bank of the Apalachicola River.

Apalachicola Bay is wide and runs approximately east-west. It is very shallow in parts, so pay special attention to your chart. Getting into and out of Apalachicola from the bay almost invariably requires motoring. There's a good half hours' worth of dredged channel you have to motor down, with depths of only a few feet on either side. Watch your depths and your markers. Very few sailors who home in Apalachicola haven't run aground from time to time.

There's a much protected anchorage spot just north of the US 98 bridge, east of the Intracoastal Waterway, dinghy distance from the Apalachicola riverfront.

You can anchor really just about anywhere in Apalachicola Bay, but very little of it is well protected, especially from a northeasterly or southwesterly blow. Your best bet for anchoring in the bay is to pay attention to the weather and anchor leeward of a barrier island. Also, the whole bay is tidal, so dropping a second hook is a good idea, and pay attention to dragging. Bottoms are pretty uniformly mud, with some oysters. The Cove offers some of the best anchorage in the area, with 20 foot depths, swimming distance from shore, and a view of the gulf over very low dunes.

Boss Oyster is one of the essential places to eat across the entire Forgotten Coast. Quite possibly the best oyster bar in the entire country. There are some private slips for fishing boats in front of it, but nowhere for transients to tie up. You must take your dinghy. **The Tin Shed** is another must visit, with its large collection of maritime artifacts.

The Gulf Intracoastal Waterway serves ports from Brownsville, TX, to Carrabelle, FL. At its eastern end, Carrabelle, FL, the Gulf ICW stops – it is not directly connected with its Atlantic counterpart (Florida Gulf ICW). To make this connection, you will need to either hop-scotch your way around, or cross a small portion of the Gulf of Mexico. Then you will make your way south down to and through the Okeechobee Waterway in southern Florida.

The heaviest commercial activity on the Gulf ICW is centered at New Orleans and extends to the Tenn-Tom River System at Mobile Bay, and west to Galveston. The Harvey Lock at New Orleans furnishes a direct entrance to and from the Mississippi River. Over all, while some may envision the Gulf and Atlantic Intracoastal Waterways as a superhighway on the water for boats, speed-wise it is not quite that. For the most part your speed will be limited, but it is easy to navigate your way along its miles of wide channels and narrow canals. Most of it, by far, offers lots of very interesting things to do and see along the way.

Remember, the **red** and **green day** (or channel) markers are <u>**channel markers.**</u> Just like the markers on the Atlantic ICW – only the ones with the little yellow square or triangle stickers mark the ICW channel.

These are **red** triangle (even numbered) channel day markers:

This is NOT an ICW marker   This is an ICW marker

These are **green** square (odd numbered) channel day markers:

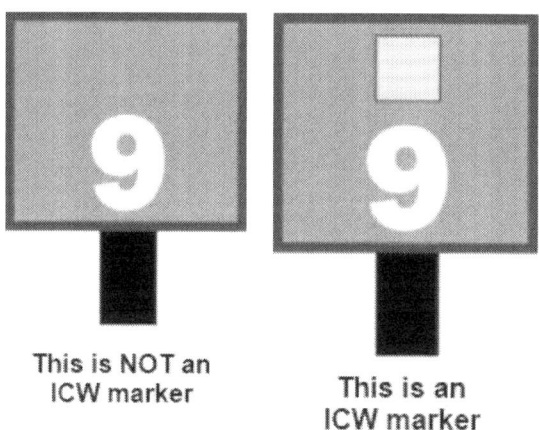

This is NOT an ICW marker   This is an ICW marker

Only those red and green markers with the small yellow stickers mark the ICW – this applies to both the Atlantic and Gulf ICW. Heading north, the RED markers with yellow triangles indicate these navigational aids should be passed by keeping them on your port (left) side.

Just remember, when cruising the Great Loop, on both the Atlantic and Gulf ICW **"Red, Right, Return" means Return to Texas – NOT return from the sea.** On both the Atlantic and Gulf "ICW" for Great Loop navigational purposes – the ICW markers assume you are always returning
SOUTH from New Jersey to Brownsville, TX. (Red, Right, Return to Texas)

In addition to the most common ICW day markers, there are places along the ICW that use "Range Markers." Range markers are typically white signs with red stripes or red signs with black stripes. They look like this:

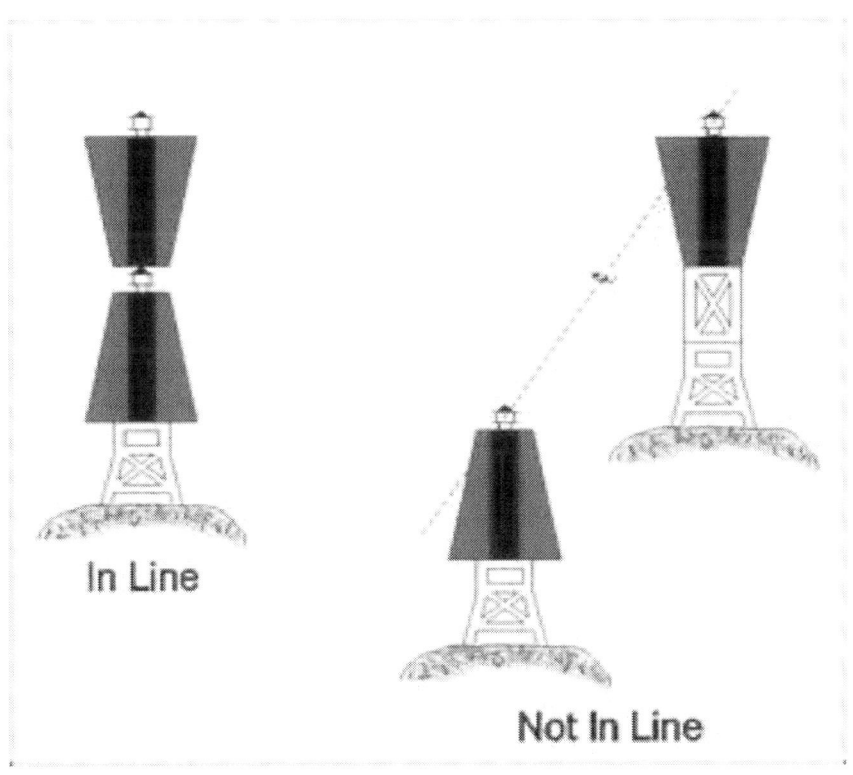

The purpose of the range marker is to keep you in the middle of the channel. Range markers are often difficult to find. They can be in the water, or hundreds of yards beyond the shore line. Sometimes they can be far up on land. Most often you will find them in bays or sounds, and sometimes where the ICW widens or makes a large wide turn. Heading north, in some places, after you make a turn these "range markers" show up behind you. So, if you don't look back you will never know they were there, until it is possibly too late.

Like the red and green ICW markers, these "range markers" mark the channel. When cruising, you follow the channel by keeping the range finders "in line" as pictured above. In the "Not in Line" picture above, the skipper would steer to his left until the ranger finder looks like the "In Line" view above. On the Atlantic ICW – Kings Bay (near the submarine base) utilizes a series of range markers for your navigation pleasure. (Lol).   Generally, where there are "range markers" it is critical to stay "in line" as usually the channel is narrow and straight, but your GPS will tell you where to look for them.

America's Great Loop

Crossing the GULF OF MEXICO

This leg of your voyage has three options. You can "hop-scotch" your way around, or you can take the short 73-mile run across the Gulf from Carrabelle to Steinhatchee, or you can take the 160-mile direct route from Carrabelle to Tarpon Springs. At first, I took the route to Tarpon Springs. After discovering Steinhatchee, it has become one of my favorite stops on the Great Loop.

Carrabelle is, of course, the perfect place to wait for good weather before making your run across the Gulf of Mexico. Your options are to shoot 160 miles directly across to Anclote Key near Tarpon Springs where the Florida west coast's Intracoastal Waterway enters St. Joseph Sound, or you can cut your miles across the Gulf to 73 by heading straight to Steinhatchee. Those with a more shallow draft can even hop-scotch their way around.

The 73 mile crossing from Carrabelle to Steinhatchee:

More accurately (or maybe I should say "less precisely") your voyage across the Gulf from Carrabelle to Steinhatchee will be between 73 to about 85 miles, depending on the weather, your course, and how well you stay on it. Regardless of how close you cut it, this is the shortest and easiest route across the Gulf. The 160 mile stretch across the Gulf to Anciote River near Tarpon Springs is the most popular. Hop-scotching your way around it is, of course, the longest route – and if you are not in a very shallow-draft boat, potentially the most dangerous.

With updated GPS, the right kind of boat, and some good weather you'll be in great shape. Regardless of your route, it is easy to find other "Loopers" in Carrabelle that are making the trip, and you can all do it all together if you wish (and most do).

If you head from Carrabelle to Tarpon Springs you will need to depart around midnight in order to make it across for a daylight arrival in Tarpon Springs. In my opinion, I believe the only reason this route is the most popular is that most guide books tell you it is – and since most Loopers like to travel in groups across the Gulf – the Looper wanting to visit Steinhatchee has to leave the crowd. Steinhatchee, however, is not only the quickest and safest route – it is also the most "charming" of places to visit on Florida's Gulf Coast.

I have taken all three routes. Truthfully, all routes can be very enjoyable or very miserable depending on the weather; but your choice of route should depend on your vessel, the weather, and your mood.

For many, the coastal route will be best, but it requires a very shallow draft. Although this route will take you three or probably four days, there is some great scenery and places to visit along the way.

Steinhatchee - Whether you shoot straight across to Steinhatchee (as I now always do), or hopscotch your way around, Steinhatchee and your next stop cruising south – Crystal River – are both places you don't want to miss. Here you have good access and protection from wind and waves when anchoring out, as well as access to shore and marinas, several good restaurants, and the local natives are quite friendly people.

The locals here are eager to help, and the marina offers a free courtesy car. In season, this is where the locals will gladly show you where and how to gather a few fresh scallops for dinner. With some real butter, a little garlic, and some pasta… WOW! Are you in for a treat.

If you love a good treasure hunt, you definitely need to try scalloping when you reach Steinhatchee. You can harvest scallops by hand or with a landing or dip net. You will need to grab your mask and snorkel and anchor out in areas where the water is between four and eight feet deep, near the grass beds. This is where you will find scallops by the thousands.

For those of you that have already crossed Albemarle Sound and the Chesapeake Bay on the Atlantic ICW, believe it or not, crossing the Gulf of Mexico may seem like a piece of cake. Given the choice, I would rather cross the Gulf of Mexico than the Albemarle Sound, any day of the week.

Most Loopers fear crossing the Gulf more than any other portion of America's Great Loop. Fact is, however, (if you take the short route and pay attention to the weather forecast) this 73 mile crossing can end up being very pleasant, peaceful, relaxing, and even enjoyable.

Obviously to "the sailors" among us, the open ocean is not at all like the protected waters of the inland lakes and rivers. Furthermore, both the GICW and AICW offer protection from the surf and seas. In the right boat, however, there is nothing to fear over crossing the Gulf. Believe me – we've had more difficulty and more bouts with seasickness crossing Albemarle Sound than on the open seas.

Crossing the Gulf is a great example of "the fear of the wolf" – making the wolf much bigger than he really is. If you are a safe boater in an appropriate, safe, and seaworthy vessel, crossing this 73 mile section of the Gulf is simply NBD –NO BIG DEAL!

The secret to crossing the Gulf, of course, is waiting for calm seas and the right weather forecast to start your crossing. Many Loopers in powerboats such as trawlers and cruisers may wait ten days or more for the most favorable conditions. Sailboats, however, seldom need to wait that long. I've never waited more than three days, and two of them were because I spent too much time trying to eat my way through all the restaurants in Apalachicola and Carrabelle. Plan on this voyage being 73 to 85 miles (ten or more hours) so you need to start your crossing at night to make sure you arrive safely in daylight.

Possibly the worst part of crossing the Gulf may be that you need to position yourself so that your midnight to 3 a.m. departure is simple and uneventful. Your cruise across will most likely take you ten or more hours. And you will want to make sure you arrive during daylight, with plenty of time to shower, shave, and go out to dinner to celebrate your crossing (everyone does).

I prefer the Gulf crossing from Carrabelle to Steinhatchee because I love Steinhatchee. I also like to visit Crystal River before cruising on down to Tarpon Springs.

I suppose one of the reasons many Loopers don't enjoy this part of the coast as much as the rest is because they have never seen Steinhatchee, and because the navigation is not as straight and easy as the Carrabelle to Tarpon Springs route. Obviously, running close to shore one has to go slowly and be aware of the shoals and reefs. It is also 104 miles from Steinhatchee to Tarpon Springs and the water never gets over twenty feet.

The west coast of Florida from Apalachicola to Anclote Key near Port Richly on the Gulf of Mexico is known as the "Nature's Coast" or the "Forgotten Coast" and is centered around Apalachicola, Carrabelle, and Steinhatchee.

The coastal area from Apalachicola to Port Richey is the "Big Bend" area of Florida. The coastline is nearly 300 miles long and is a sizable part of Florida's entire coastline.

West of Apalachicola, the coast is a well-protected part of the Intracoastal Waterway. East of Apalachicola, you have an area of the Gulf to cross. While the ICW continues south to Ft. Myers, it is not nearly as calm and protected as the rest of the Intracoastal Waterways on either the Atlantic or Gulf.

At the "other side" of the Big Bend from Carrabelle, the Florida coast south of Anclote Key the ICW extends south to Ft. Myers, which is mile 0 (zero) on Florida's Gulf ICW, and where you will turn east for Lake Okeechobee where you will eventually connect to the Atlantic ICW.

Loopers heading across to Tarpon Springs or Tampa Bay need to leave no later than midnight in order to arrive at their destinations during daylight. Many often take 16 hours or more for this crossing. For sure, you need to be "accurately" aware of the speed capability and fuel range of your vessel to make the crossing to Tarpon Springs. Remember, your mpg (miles per gallon) will be woefully inaccurate when calculating your fuel range – you need to know your vessels gph (gallons per hour) fuel burn rate. Thinking you can cruise 160 miles at 20 mph is one thing – taking 16 hours to do it – instead of 8 is another.

Soon enough (if you don't run out of fuel) the dolphins will be escorting you all the way to the channel markers into the Steinhatchee River. I follow the markers into the Sea Hag Marina, and usually stay a night or two before making my way to Crystal River.

From Crystal River you want to head to the Anclote River, which takes you to Tarpon Springs. On your way you will see the shrimp and sponge boat docks, where you will find an amazing array of sponge shops. From Tarpon Springs it is 150 miles to Ft. Myers on the GICW, which is a greatly protected waterway that runs through a gauntlet very popular boating areas.

Finally, depending on where you start your Great Loop voyage, you will have already made your way across the Atlantic bays and sounds, and across the Great Lakes. So yes! Compared to some of that, your voyage across the Gulf will be a piece of cake. You can do this!

THE OKEECHOBEE WATERWAY

Here it is…a series of five locks helping boats through the 154 mile long waterway across the lower peninsula of Florida. The "canal" depth of the waterway is approximately eight feet and the width of the canal varies from 80 to 100 feet.

Most cruisers access the waterway from the Florida's Gulf ICW through Ft. Myers, shortening their trip to the east coast of Florida and bypassing the Florida Keys.

Okeechobee (at times) can be very shallow and is always full of alligators – for sure Captain Hook would not like it here.

America's Great Loop

Once you've made your way down Florida's Gulf Coast to Ft. Myers (to cross Florida from west to east), you will take the Okeechobee Waterway. This leg of your journey is 154 miles and extends from the Gulf of Mexico at Ft. Myers to the Atlantic ICW at the St. Lucie Inlet.

Surprisingly, Lake Okeechobee is the second largest freshwater lake <u>entirely</u> in the US. That's right – it is second only to Lake Michigan. Of course, this is because the other Great Lakes share borders with Canada.

There are two routes across Lake Okeechobee. The most direct is the "Open Water Route" and the other being the "Rim" or southern route. There is only 11 miles difference between the two routes.

If you're not in a hurry (and you shouldn't be), the Rim Route offers more protection from winds and choppy waters. It only takes about an hour longer, and the sightseeing opportunities are much better.

On either route you take, Clewiston (mile 75.7) is a very worthwhile stop. It offers Anglers Marina and Roland Martin's Marina with groceries, marine store, and restaurants. In addition, the Clewiston Inn provides free transportation to and from the marina for diners.

Lake Okeechobee covers over 730 square miles and is connected to both of Florida's coasts via the man-made Okeechobee Waterway. The Lake is 33 miles long from north to south, and 30 miles wide from east to west.

For Loopers, access to the Okeechobee Waterway is at Ft Myers, and takes you to the Atlantic ICW at St. Lucie Inlet at Stuart. This is not only a protected inside route, it shortens your journey to the east coast of Florida bypassing the Florida Keys.

Fishing is among the most popular activities on this Lake. Largemouth bass, blue gill, catfish, and crappie are some of the species of fish that can be found in the Lake. Birds, beautiful scenery, and the water all combine to make this a nature-lover's paradise, as well as a Mecca for boaters.

However, the Lake is very shallow, and since we can't control the rain, the lake levels vary seasonally to levels as low as five feet (or less) in the main navigational routes. If you have more than a 3' draft boat, you don't want to cross this waterway in rough weather – if you do, your boat will be bouncing off the muddy bottom of the lake (and that's personal experience talking).

A series of five locks operate from 6 a.m. to 9:30 p.m. daily, unless otherwise noted in Coast Guard published "Notice to Mariners." Hail locks on Channel 13. Pursuant to operating procedures, once Lake Okeechobee reaches 12.5 feet the Corps will begin implementing lock restrictions on the Okeechobee Waterway at the W.P. Franklin Lock (west) and the St. Lucie Lock (east). This means the locks will be closed to all traffic.

As beautiful as it may be on a nice day, this little lake is no cake walk to cross for anyone sailing or with a draft of 4' or more in anything other than near perfect weather. We've sailed it when winds kicked up a two-foot chop and our keel came down and hit the sandy bottom on many more occasions than I could count. Very much a Pogo Stick ride, we bounced our way across the bottom. Visions of my boat ripped to pieces with my crew and I wearing USCG approved PFD's in a pool of hungry alligators flashed through my mind the entire time across.

Therefore, while we don't want to scare anybody off this waterway (seriously), for anyone planning their Great Loop route using the Okeechobee Waterway, it is simply advisable to stay in touch with the

Army Corps of Engineers for lock status, lake levels, wind and weather.

If your vessel's draft is 4' or more feet, it is certainly best to wait for lake levels to be up and the day's weather to be nice. Do this, and your journey will be a carefree and beautiful one.

All along your route on the West Coast of Florida to the Atlantic ICW, and especially on the Okeechobee Waterway, you will want to keep a good look astern – not so much for traffic but for keeping in line with the channel markers.

From Tarpon Springs to St. Lucie, it is not wise to travel at a fast pace. You need to a keep a concentrated effort to stay in the middle of the channel. In many areas just a few feet either way to the side of the channel and you will run aground. While I have never run aground on this leg of the journey, I have seen a few that have.

All along this route, including Lake Okeechobee, the bottom is mostly soft mud or sand, running aground at a rising tide and at a slow speed is much safer than getting stuck on a falling tide. Even with a 3' draft, you will find yourself holding your breath across the shoals.

For sailors, the lowest fixed bridge from the Gulf to the Atlantic is 49 feet. For the exception of crossing Lake Okeechobee _in bad weather_, navigation is simple, piloting is easy, and all your navigational aids are better than in many areas with bays and sounds. So have no concern for getting lost, just stay in the channel.

Mile 0 (zero) of the Okeechobee intersects the Atlantic ICW at mile 987.8. If you plan on boating the Florida Keys, or crossing the Gulf Steam to Bimini (our favorite) we suggest you take the more protected Okeechobee route to St. Lucie, then head south to the Keys, or across the Gulf stream to Bimini (only 50 miles away).

BEYOND THE LOOP
Great Loop Side Trips & Detours

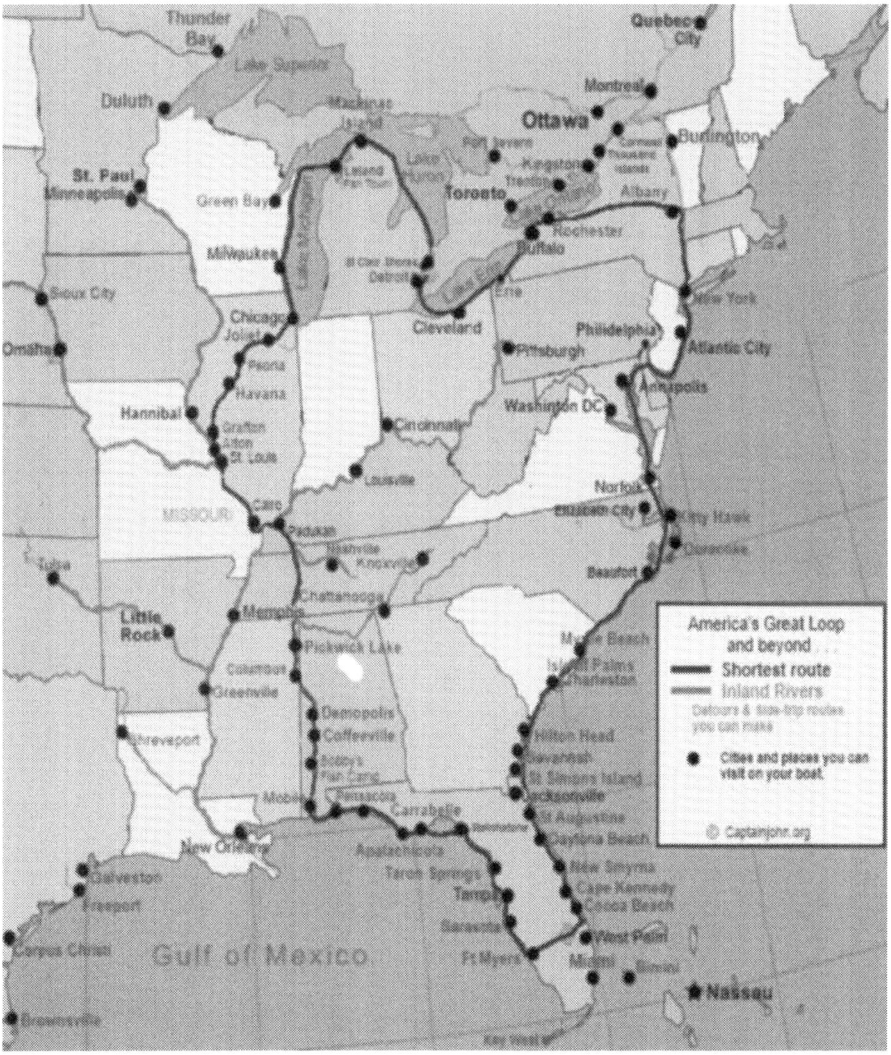

America's Great Loop is simply an amazing adventure. Likewise, what lies within your reach "beyond the Loop" is the land of quaint villages, surprising big cities, remote uninhabited islands, and a boat load of travel treasures so numerous you couldn't possibly fit them all into your boat, much less in a book or even in one single voyage around the Great Loop. However, many wonderful highlights of your journey will be the result of a detour or side trip off the main Great Loop route.

Take Lake Superior for example: From Mackinac Bridge dividing Lake Michigan and Lake Huron in the north, one can take a side trip from Mackinac Island to the Soo Locks – your gateway entrance into Lake Superior. From the Soo Locks, you are just 273 statute miles away from Thunder Bay, Ontario which is 195 miles (by water of course) from Duluth, Wisconsin.

Lake Superior

Home of the Great Lakes Shipwreck Historical Society which features the wreck of the famous Edmund Fitzgerald. The Society was founded by a group of teachers, and educators to commence exploration of historic shipwrecks in eastern Lake Superior, near Whitefish Point in Michigan's scenic Upper Peninsula. The Great Lakes Shipwreck Museum, located just inside the entrance to Lake Superior at Whitefish Point Light Station, and the U.S. Weather Bureau Building, at the Soo Locks Park, Sault Sainte Marie, Michigan are all worth the trip. The Whitefish lighthouse is the oldest operating lighthouse on Lake Superior, and the wreck of the Edmund Fitzgerald is just 17 miles northwest of Whitefish point.

Lake Superior of course, is the largest of the Great Lake. In fact, (bet you didn't know this) it is so large that it could hold the water from all of the other Great Lakess. WOW!

The waterway (boating) distance from the Atlantic Ocean via the St. Lawrence Seaway to Thunder Bay is 2,342 statute miles. From the Soo Locks however, you are only 273 miles away. From Mackinac Island to the Soo Locks, you are less than a day's sail away and as close to Lake Superior as most boaters will ever be.

The lake is bounded by Ontario to the north and Minnesota to the west, and Wisconsin and Michigan to the south. It is generally considered the largest freshwater lake by surface area in the world. It is the world's third-largest freshwater lake by volume and the largest by volume in North America.

The Soo Locks (your entrance to Lake Superior} are a sight to behold. Often referred to as one of the great wonders of the world and it is still the largest waterway traffic system on earth. Your boat will travel along the international shoreline of the lower harbor letting you experience all the sights, sounds, and excitement of Michigan's oldest city, Sault Ste Marie.

Here, you can watch 1,000 foot freighters being raised and lowered 21 feet between the levels of the St. Mary's river - right along with your very own boat in a Lock System constructed in 1850. If you like to fish, Lake Superior is known for Lake Trout to 43 lbs, Whitefish up to 3 lbs, and King Salmon over 30 lbs.

One of the most fascinating aspects of boating Lake Superior is the large number or large commercial vessels. Folks, we are talking 50 – 60,000 ton vessels here, a 1,000 feet long. Needless to say, they deserve all the room you can give them.

Additionally, local boaters will tell you right up front, that when the weather turns for the worse, Lake Superior can become extremely dangerous for vessels of any type and size. So you will want to make sure you keep a good watch and listen to your marine weather forecasts if you plan to venture out across Lake Superior.

Having said that however, whether you plan a short visit into Lake Superior (just so you can say you've been there) or if you want to visit the Shipwreck museum at – or voyage all across the lake to Thunder Bay. . . It is a voyage through some of the coldest and most beautiful fresh water you will find anywhere in the world.

Cold water is also a yearlong danger. Except in shallow bays and beach areas, the water in Lake Superior seldom reaches as high as 55 degrees. As a result, Shock & Hypothermia is an ever present danger, even in the summer. So you might want to avoid the temptation of diving off your boat into deep water.

Paradise, Michigan just 11 miles north of Paradise, Michigan just past the entrance of the Soo Locks makes for a very interesting and worth the effort stopover. In addition to the Shipwreck Museum and lighthouse, they have everything from beaches to bear. Besides, your Great Loop voyage takes you to Mackinac Island anyway – so why not take the detour (Cheboygan, MI is just 17 miles away) and visit Lake Superior? You may never be this close again. After all, you are now only 324 miles from Chicago, and you have until mid-September to get off the Great Lakes.

All things considered, this is a prime boating vacation area, and you will have plenty of time to cruise it, if you are cruising the Loop on a seasonal schedule. Between the Grand Hotel on Mackinac Island, the Mackinac Bridge, taking a detour up the St. Mary's river through the Soo Locks to visit Tahquamenon Falls State Park, Pictured Rocks National Lakeshore, Paradise, Michigan, Whitefish point, and the Shipwreck Museum and wreck of the Edmund Fitzgerald, you can take a week or two, or three, and experience some wonderful sites to see and places to go. You are an easy (rubber necking) day away from Whitefish Point when you reach the Soo Locks.

The Soo Locks

Huge ships pass between Lake Superior to the lower Great Lakes through the Soo Locks. These Locks pass 10,000 ships a year despite being closed for 3 (or more) months a year, depending on the winter weather. The Locks bypass the St. Mary's river rapids between Lake Superior and Lake Huron.

The St. John's River – Atlantic on the ICW

The St. John's river: Heading north on the Atlantic Intracoastal Waterway, near ICW Mile marker 740 – just about 35 miles north of St. Augustine at Mayport - you can enter the St. John's river, it offers a 145 mile detour inland. Along the way you will boat to Green Cove Springs, into Lake George and on to Blue Springs State Park, Lake Beresford and Lake Monroe near Sanford.

The Carolina Loop

The Carolina Loop: If you are having difficulty deciding which route to take from Albemarle Sound to Norfolk, the "Carolina Loop" might be just the route. It allows you to make a circle so that you can experience both Coinjock on the Virginia Cut and Elizabeth City at the Dismal Swamp.

Chesapeake Bay

I know that Chesapeake Bay is part of your necessary, straight-shot, short route on the Great Loop to the C&D Canal and Delaware River, but this is also part of your route that should not be overlooked. So I am adding it again to that part of your adventure that is "Beyond the Loop." I could go on and on and back and forth across Chesapeake Bay. It is that fantastic. You should not miss this opportunity to explore it, and the choices of where to go, what to do and see are virtually endless.

From Deltaville, VA., Broad Creek, and Rappahannock, you will discover plenty of marinas, wonderful restaurants and beautiful boats all along the way. If you happen to be looking for boat parts here's the place. You will find it all in and around Deltaville, from Coffee shops to grocery stores, specialty shops, seafood market, and several new and used marine stores selling all sorts of boat parts, along with boat and boating supplies, and a maritime museum. This area of the Great Loop is about as nautical and nice as one can get.

From Deltaville a short run up the Rappahannock will take you to Irvington and along some large protected fishing bays, waterfront towns such as Milford Haven, Gwynn's Island, Mathews, Cape Charles and Onancock – all of which are great places to see and visit, and you don't have to spend a lot of money to have a great time.

In the Chesapeake Bay, Deltaville, Irvington, Kilmarnock, and Reedville are all well worth a stop and go, and mostly you will discover, they are easy to stop at, and very difficult to go. So don't be surprised if you end up spending more time around here than you thought you would. That's what's so wonderful about anchoring out. You can stay an extra day or two or three, and it costs you little of nothing more than what you eat and drink. When you get to Charlie's Tiki Bar, tell them Capt. John sent you.

Chesapeake Bay from the Eastern Shore to the "mainland" is simply a wonderful storage of eye candy. From spending time anchored out (or gunk holing) among the many, many anchorages and harbors to spending nights in some of the better (more strategically located) marinas – it's just filled with things to do and see.

On the east side of Tilghman Island is Dun Cove, a wonderfully protected anchorage where you can spend a peaceful night watching the stars. Then you can take a cruise through Knapps Narrows, one of several man-made passages that create shortcuts from the extensive backwaters of the Eastern Shore. Several marinas and small towns on either side of the draw bridge will sure look inviting. This is one place your dinghy can get an awful lot of use.

From Annapolis, and the Naval Academy, and from the biggest of yachts to the most humble of boats – you will find t-shirt shops, bars, and an amazing selection of ice cream stands.

At Rock Hall you can even enjoy the hospitality of the free public dock, and this is a neat and inviting little town with a long maritime heritage.

Obviously, of course, the Chesapeake is also your connection to the **Potomac River.**

The Potomac River

The Potomac River to Washington DC: Possibly the very best way to see Washington DC is on your boat, although many are simply unaware of this fact.

Once you enter the Chesapeake Bay, you may want to plan a week or two to cruise up the historic Potomac River and spend some time in Washington, DC. This detour is a 270 mile round trip journey, and well worth the time.

The Potomac River is about four miles wide at the Chesapeake and gradually narrows as you get closer to Washington. About 15 miles before Washington DC, you will pass by Mount Vernon sitting high on a bluff overlooking the Potomac. Within the hour, the Washington waterfront will present you with the famous and familiar Washington, Jefferson, and Lincoln Memorials in plain view.

Baltimore and Baltimore's Inner Harbor is one of the most photographed and visited areas on the Great Loop. It is easy to get to and it has been one of the major seaports in the United States since the 1700's.

Baltimore's Inner Harbor offers a wide range of great food and fun– fine dining, cultural experiences, and a busy nightlife.

From your boat, you have the best seat in the house for some breathtaking views of the harbor and skyline. There are daily street performances (weather permitting) right on the waterfront. Baltimore's Inner Harbor offers more to see and do than you might imagine.

Located in the heart of the Inner Harbor on Pratt Street, you will find lots of unique shopping, diverse dining, and a variety of entertainment right on the beautiful waterfront.

When you cruise the Inner Harbor on your own boat, you can't resist the temptation to stop and walk the waterfront.

Upper Mississippi River

On the Mississippi River you can boat 2,320 miles through ten US States; i.e.: Minnesota, Wisconsin, Iowa, Illinois, Missouri, Kentucky, Tennessee, Arkansas, Mississippi, and Louisiana. Major cities you can boat to include New Orleans, Baton Rouge, Vicksburg, Memphis, St. Louis, St. Paul and Minneapolis. It is true that the entire Mississippi River features fabulous boating!

On your Great Loop voyage if you turn north at Grafton, the Upper Mississippi River will simply astonish you on a voyage that will take you past Hannibal, MO and as far north as Minneapolis and St. Paul. You can also boat through Lake Pepin to Winona, MN near the Iowa border. A cruise on the scenic St. Croix River will take you to Hudson, WI and the clear St. Croix River is a breath taking beautiful National Scenic Waterway.

Some tugboat captains I've met along the way moving large barges of grain refer to the Mississippi River as the "Breadbasket of the Nation." Even today, it remains the method for the majority of this country's grain getting to market.

The US Army Corps of Engineers struggles in their effort to keep this waterway open for navigation. Dredges work around the clock to dig and maintain a minimal 9' channel deep enough for the barges and tows.

The Corps has built an impressive series of locks and dams to control water levels and allow river traffic to move as the Mississippi descends in elevation on its way south to the Gulf of Mexico. It is the tugboats, tows, and barges that pay for maintaining the waterways and all of us "pleasure boaters" get to use the waterways for free.

When you pass through the locks, whether ascending or descending, while holding onto your lines in the locks, you can't help but notice that permanent wet mark on the lock wall that shows just how far your vessel will be raised to or was lowered from, one level to another.

The Ohio River

On the Ohio River you can boat along the Ohio for 980 miles to or through the states of Pennsylvania, Ohio, West Virginia, Kentucky, Indiana, and Illinois. Major cities you can boat to, in addition to Cairo and Paducah, include Henderson, Evansville, Owensboro, New Albany, Jeffersonville, Louisville, Cincinnati, Portsmouth, Ashland, Huntington, Wheeling, and Pittsburgh.

The Tennessee River

"Pardon me boy, is that the Chattanooga Choo-Choo?"

The Tennessee River is actually a tributary of the Ohio River. You can take your boat 652 miles along this river through Tennessee (of course) as well as Alabama, Mississippi, and Kentucky. Major cities you can boat to on the Tennessee River include Bridgeport, Chattanooga, Cherokee, Clifton, Decatur, Florence, Grand Rivers, Guntersville, Huntsville, Kingston, Knoxville, Lenoir, Savannah, and Waterloo.

The river was once popularly known as the Cherokee River. The Tennessee River will take you to Knoxville and Chattanooga. From Knoxville, it flows southwest through Chattanooga before crossing into Alabama. It loops through northern Alabama and forms a small part of the state's border with Mississippi before returning to Tennessee.

It is the U.S. Corp of Engineers' project that provides navigation on the Tombigbee and the Tennessee Rivers and the Tombigbee Canal that links to the Gulf of Mexico Port of Mobile, AL. The Tenn-Tom waterway reduces the navigation distance from Cairo to the Gulf ICW at Mobile Bay by 400 miles.

The placement of Kentucky Dam on the Tennessee River and Barkley Dam on the Cumberland River led to the creation of the "Land between the Lakes." As a result, a navigational canal located at Grand Rivers, KY links Kentucky Lake and Lake Barkley. The canal also allows for a 20 mile shorter trip for river traffic going from Paducah on the Ohio River to the Cumberland River.

The Cumberland River

The Cumberland River is navigable year round and winds 192 miles from Nashville to Smithland at the Ohio River. It flows through ridges and valleys and is an absolutely beautiful cruise. All told, the Cumberland River is 688 miles long, and starts in Harlan County in far southeastern Kentucky between the Pine and Cumberland Mountains. It flows through southern Kentucky, and crosses into northern Tennessee.

The bulk of the traffic is to and from Nashville to the mouth. There are but two barge terminals above Nashville, a DuPont Chemical dock just above Old Hickory and a TVA coal-fired steam power plant at Gallatin, 54 miles above Nashville.

While the Cumberland is technically navigable up to mile 381, (190 miles above Nashville) there is no commercial navigation above mile 244.

Celina, TN is the beginning and ending of navigation for commercial vessels. If you have an extra two weeks or so, you can cruise the beautiful and historic Cumberland River. I usually make my connection by heading south just past Paducah and start my Cumberland River adventure from Green Turtle Marina.

From `Green Turtle Marina` you will head south through Lake Barkley on the Cumberland. Lake Barkley State Park Marina is at mile marker 59.1.

Clarksville is at mile 126.1. From Clarksville it is an easy 32 miles and one lock to Ashland City and then another 32 miles to Nashville.

Nashville is a great river city to visit. They have a nice riverfront with courtesy docks for those visiting the city by boat. There are plenty of restaurants near the landing that is located right downtown.

The river is quite narrow through Nashville so when towboats are present it is wise to give them plenty of room. Along your voyage on the Cumberland, you can head out to the Cherokee Steak House, and cruise by Reba McEntire's home (what a site to see from the river) that is located just North of Lebanon, 30 miles east of Nashville.

On your way there, you can cruise past the homes of Tanya Tucker, Barbara Mandrell, and the late Johnny Cash. From the Cumberland River at mile 33 you will enter the Barkley Canal. This is a one-mile-long canal that leads to Kentucky Lake on the Tennessee River. All things considered, this is a safe wonderful Great Loop side trip.

Obviously, I don't need to tell you all about the gentle hills and farmlands of central Tennessee, or that Nashville attracts millions of visitors each year to its mainstream showcases like the Country Music Hall of Fame and the Grand Ole Opry. So, I won't. However, I will tell you that Nashville, especially if you have never seen it, is well worth a short cruise down the beautiful Cumberland River.

The Tennessee-Tombigbee

The Tennessee-Tombigbee (Tenn-Tom) is something not to be over looked. While your Great Loop distance on this waterway from the Tennessee to the Gulf is only 234 miles and not really a detour, the Tenn-Tom Waterway is one of the most incredible components of America's Great Loop – and should not be over looked. Many Loopers rush through this portion of the Loop in their hurry to reach the Gulf. This world class transportation waterway (a canal project larger than that of the Panama Canal) is not only part of the Great Loop, but also it can link you to the Sunbelt states and 14 different river systems that could add another 4,000 miles (or so) to your existing 5,600 mile Great Loop journey.

The Missouri River

The Missouri River is a marvelous Great Loop side trip. This is the river of Lewis and Clark, and makes for a fantastic and adventurous side trip. It flows more than 2,300 miles from Three Forks, MT to St. Louis, MO where it joins the Mississippi River. You can cruise the Missouri River 811 miles all the way to Yankton, SD which is located downstream of the Gavin's Point Dam and the Lewis and Clark Lake which is just upstream of the confluence with the James River. The United State National Park Service's headquarters for the Missouri River is also located in Yankton. While Sioux City is considered the commercial navigational head of the Missouri River, the actual limit to your navigational ability on the Missouri is the Gavin's Point Dam which is another 58 miles upstream from Sioux City at Yankton SD. From Sioux City, however, the US Army Corps of Engineers maintains a minimum river depth of 9' for 753 miles to the Mississippi River. Since no locks were constructed, commercial navigation on the Missouri cannot proceed above the Gavin's Point Dam, four miles beyond Yankton, SD. The Gavin's Point Dam is located on the Missouri River at mile marker 811. Kansas City is at mile marker 363. St. Joseph is at mile marker 448, and what a wonderful worthwhile trip this is.

Of course, the Missouri waters continue on to the Gulf of Mexico, making the Missouri/Mississippi River complex the fourth longest river and the third largest in the entire world.

The Alabama River

The Alabama River is another Great Loop side trip you can take. Thanks to the Army Corps of Engineers dam projects constructed in the 60's and 70's to facilitate navigation. The Alabama's 315 mainstream navigable river miles flow through or borders nine Alabama counties. At the southernmost tip of Clarke County the river joins the Tombigbee to form the Mobile River. The Alabama River is navigable to Montgomery and its main tributary, the Coosa River, is navigable to Rome, GA.

The Arkansas River

The Arkansas River is called the "Waterway to the World," and if you live in this part of the country, you would know why. The Arkansas River Navigation System is a 445 mile waterway that links Little Rock, AK and Tulsa, OK and the surrounding five-state area with the Great Loop and ports all around this great nation's 24,000 mile Inland Waterway System.

The Arkansas River is a super-surprising Great Loop side trip. This southern waterway is operational year-round regardless of weather conditions. You can make this boating connection from the Lower Mississippi River at Montgomery Point between Rosedale, MS and Arkansas City. What surprises almost everyone is that the Arkansas River is navigable from the Mississippi River to Tulsa, OK.

Cruising Canada

Cruising Canada: Folks... it is true, I love cruising America's Great Loop but I have to admit, cruising Canada is world-class cruising. It is truly the icing on the cake when it comes to cruising the Great Loop. Both the Rideau Waterway and the Trent-Severn Waterway have to be two of the three best-kept cruising secrets in North America. Georgian Bay and Canada's "Thirty Thousand Islands" area has to be the third.

The Rideau Waterway is located in eastern Ontario. The waterway links Ottawa on the historic Ottawa River, at one end, and Kingston on Lake Ontario at the other. Along the Rideau you will find a magical mix of city life and country life (both with their own kind of wildlife).

You'll cruise through incredible scenery and past the finest of fine dining restaurants in the world. There is great fishing, quaint hotels, magnificent museums, historic sites, and scenic, peaceful backwaters. This is the ultimate place where past and present, nature and culture, meld in a setting of tranquility and charm.

All along the way, you learn little by little about the rich heritage of this part of Canada. There are 24 lock stations and almost as many museums. Many of the locks are virtually as they were well over 150 years ago – peaceful and secluded. They will take you back to the 19th century.

This is the region that is the most popular tourist, recreation, and boating areas in all of Canada. Every year 90,000 boats pass through these locks. Millions of people visit the parks, beaches, and historical sites along the canal. The waterway (as was the Erie Canal in the US) was an amazing achievement in 1826. Today, this series of rivers, lakes, wetlands, man-made canals, and locks come together in the most beautiful, scenic, and historic waterways in the world… it is truly a cruiser's dream.

The Rideau Canal

On the Rideau Canal, you will cruise 125 wonderful, safe, scenic miles from Kingston, at Lake Ontario, to Ottawa - Canada's Capitol City.

It is a Great Loop detour that is well worth your time & effort.

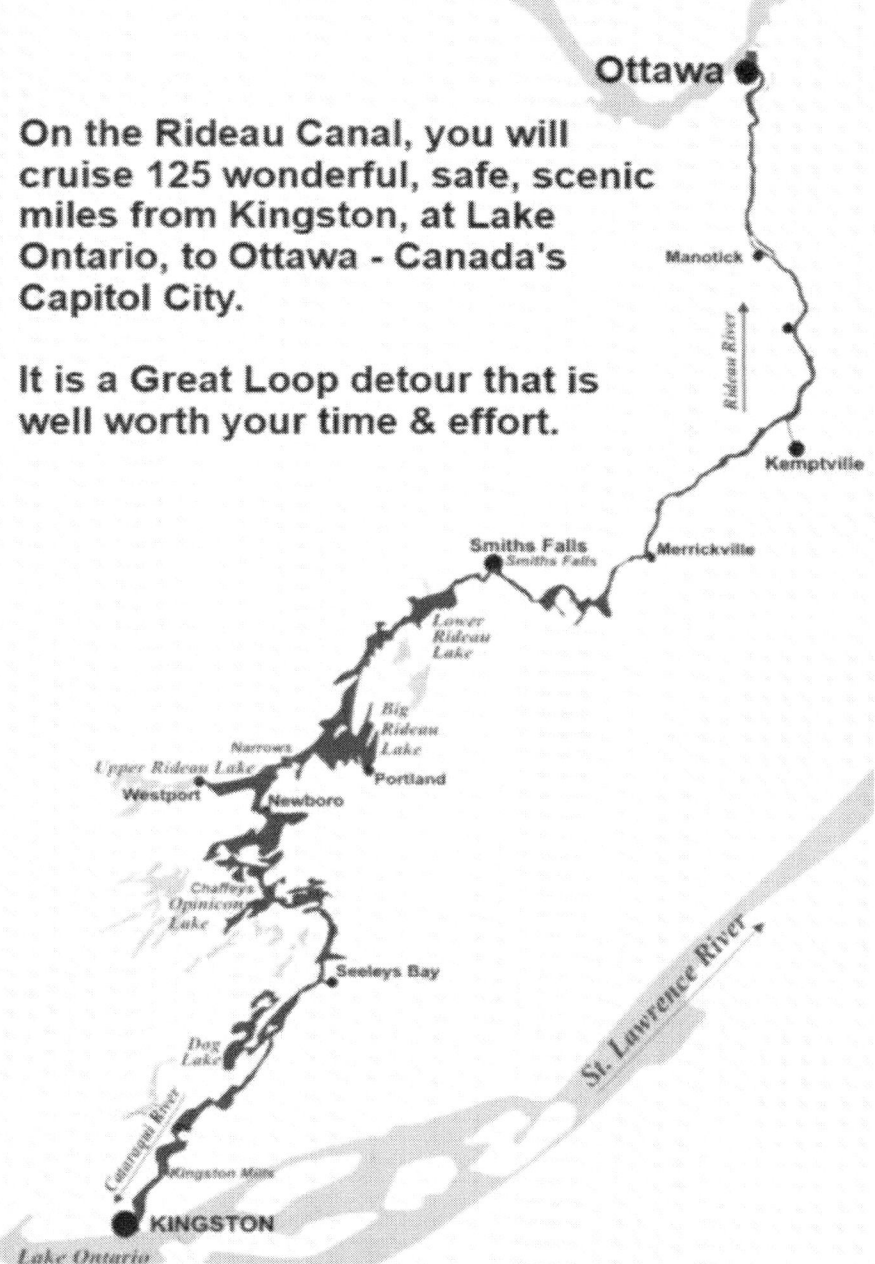

The Rideau Canal is like a trip back in time. It is the oldest continuously operated canal in North America and the locks are operated today much as they were when first opened in 1832.

Most locks provide washrooms, overnight mooring, and picnic facilities including tables, benches, and barbecue grills. I love it!

On the Rideau Canal you will cruise 125 miles and right into the shadow of Canada's Parliament Buildings. It stretches from Kingston at the foot of Lake Ontario to Ottawa, Canada's capital. Maintained by Parks Canada, it is the most scenic and historic waterway in North America.

The Rideau Canal is like a trip back in time. It is the oldest continuously operated canal in North America and the locks are operated today much as they were when first opened in 1832. Each lock is unique and the lock staff is always ready to offer boaters assistance. Most locks provide washrooms, overnight mooring, and picnic facilities including tables, benches, and barbecue grills. I love it!

This is where a giant flight of locks will raise your boat 77 feet from the Ottawa River to the canal that winds through the city.

The canal merges with the Rideau River at Hogs Back Lock station. Heading south from Ottawa the first town is Manotick. On the river in the center of town is one of the most splendid historic mills in Canada, Watson's Mill, built in 1860. South of Manotick is the Long Reach – the longest section of the waterway without a lock and a very popular place for canoes and kayaks.

At the next lock station, Burritts Rapids, a canal lined by massive cut limestone blocks and cedar forests bypasses the rapids. A few miles farther is the historic town of Merrickville. The town is one of the most picturesque in Ontario, with its historic buildings, ruins of a wooden mill, a blockhouse museum, and the headquarters of the

Canadian Canoeing Association is located just south of the locks in Merrickville.

Continuing, the Rideau cuts through a series of marshes and shallow lakes on the way to Smiths Falls. In the center of Smiths Falls is one of the three lock stations on the system operated by hydraulics. A pleasant saunter from the Combined Lock is the Rideau Canal Museum. You certainly will want to take a trip to the Hershey's Chocolate Factory that is just a short walk from Old Sly's Lock. A narrow channel lined with limestone blocks winding through cedar forests and wetlands links Smiths Falls to Lower Rideau Lake.

An interesting side trip leads from Lower Rideau Lake up the Tay River to the historic town of Perth. For many, the most scenic section of the Rideau Waterway stretches from The Narrows, between Big Rideau Lake and Upper Rideau Lake to Jones Falls. The keystone arch dam at Jones Falls was the highest in North America when it was built in 1830. You can still hear the sound of a hammer striking hot iron in the 1840's blacksmith shop. The hilltop lockmaster's house has been restored to give you a glimpse of the life of a lockmaster in the 19th century.

The Trent Severn Waterway

The **Trent Severn Waterway** is a sight to behold. Its overall length is 240 miles. It features 44 locks including the first and second highest lift locks in the world, two flight locks, and one marine railway. It took 87 years to complete. The Waterway Locks take you up 596' to the summit at Balsam Lake and then you descend to 262' down to Georgian Bay. Initially, the first elements of the waterway were dams and locks; built primarily to accommodate water-powered mills and the move timbers. Boaters are abundant, as the Trent Severn is shared by locals with boaters renting cottages, houseboat rentals, fishermen, as well as us fortunate Great Loop and other long-distance cruisers. The Trent Severn is an integral and very enjoyable part of the Great Loop. When you are through it, you will be hardly able to stay at your helm - for wanting to tell all your friends and family about it. And you will be biting at the bit for the first chance to swap stories with all those other fortunate souls making the trip.

No matter how long your journey lasts, boating along the Trent Severn, the Rideau Canal, and all of Canada will be an adventure you will forever wish holds a return trip.

The fees on the Trent Severn are the same as those on the Rideau. As of 2012, you could purchase a One Way Pass for $4.65 per foot, a Six Day Pass for $5.05 per foot, and a Seasonal Pass for $8.80 per foot.

There are, of course, rules and regulations for Canadian Boating, and for Canadian Customs. You will need to know what they are. The Canadian Coast Guard Office of Boating Safety lists requirements for Foreign Recreational Vessels in Canadian Waters. Visiting boaters staying in Canadian waters less than 45 days are exempt from most regulations for safety equipment if their boat is legally fitted and licensed in their home (U.S.) state. However, visitors must follow all other Canadian boating regulations with speed limits, toilet and discharge regulations, age and power restrictions, drinking and boating laws.

TAKE NOTE: As of 2009, if you plan to be in Canadian waters, all boat operators are now required to show proof of competency to operate a boat in Canada - this includes all visitors and all non-residents. So, even if your home state does not require it, you will need to take (and pass) your home state's "NASBLA approved" Boat Safety course.

If you plan to set foot on Canadian soil, you must report to a Canadian Border Services Agency (formerly Canada Customs) immediately upon arrival. It is illegal to stop or anchor anywhere in Canadian waters before checking in. What you want to obtain (and they will give it over the phone) is a Customs Report number. When you get it – for heaven's sake – get the number correct and don't lose it.

Kingston Mills (the most southern Rideau Canal lock) is an official Canada Customs Report Site. American boaters can call directly to Canadian Border Services Agency and receive their Customs Report number when entering the Rideau Canal as their first Canadian stop arriving from the United States. You will need your state's "NASBLA approved" Boat Safety Card, boat insurance and registration, as well as a list of full names, citizenship, birth dates, and addresses of all persons on board your vessel. You will also be required to show vaccination papers for pets on board. You should be prepared to keep all passengers on board until you have cleared entry procedures.

If the above sounds like too much trouble – it's not really! Furthermore, any effort it requires, I promise, is well worth the effort to cruise through the beautiful Canadian waters and waterways. If you do it, I guarantee that you will be glad you did.

How big a boat do I need? The maximum size of boat is 90' length, 26' width, 19' height.

How deep is the channel? The navigation channel that is clearly marked by buoys and maintains a 5' of water under normal circumstances.

Is the Rideau and/or Trent Severn Canals difficult to boat? No – it's very easy. The Rideau was built as a "slack water" system, meaning there is no excessive current in the rivers. Waves with some chop can develop on the bigger lakes but boaters can easily seek shelter near shore. Each lock has 3 or 4 canal staff that are used to dealing with novice boaters and will help out in any way they can.

Do I need a navigation chart? Yes – there are two sets of navigation charts that cover the Rideau.

When are the Canals open for boating? The locks operate from mid-May to mid-October.

Do the locks operate 24 hours a day? No, like the Erie Canal the hours vary and the locks and lift bridges close at night. During most of the season the locks open at 9:00 a.m. In the summer they stay open until 6:00 p.m. On the Rideau there is a 5 p.m. "last lock" time. So you need to be in the staging area no later than 4:30 p.m.

How long does it take to boat the Rideau Canal? A one-way trip normally takes six days each way. It can be done in five if you plan it right and get lucky. A general rule of thumb is to assume 30 minutes for each lock and an average speed of 10 mph.

How much does it cost to go through the locks? The 2012 fees were $0.90 (US) per foot for one lock. If you want to travel through locks for the whole season, you can buy a season lock pass for $8.80 a foot. There are also options for six-day, one-way transit, and 12-day both ways transits.

What about docking, anchoring overnight? You can always anchor your boat in one of the many sheltered bays. You can moor at most of the lock stations for a fee. For those wishing more services such as shore power and showers, there are plenty of marinas with services to transient boaters.

Do I have to stock up on gas and supplies? No – there are many services available along the Canadian Heritage Canals. Both the Rideau and TrentSevern have lots of marinas so it's easy to get fuel. There are several communities along the canals that have grocery stores within easy walking distance of a docking area so you can stock up on food, ice, drinks, etc. Have fun, you'll enjoy!

Inland Islands and More

And you don't want to confuse the two.

Canada's Georgian Bay "Thirty Thousands Islands" are NOT to be confused with the New York State's "1,000 Islands" on the St. Lawrence Seaway. While they are both absolutely beautiful, they are totally different and in totally different regions of North America – and the great news, of course, is you can cruise through both.

Canada's Thirty Thousand Islands are also known as the "Discovery Islands," and the area is filled with innumerable humps of granite rock and barely submerged shoals that lie between Severn Sound and the French River. This area is the world's largest freshwater archipelago, an intensely beautiful island landscape of battered bedrock and windswept pines. It is also the largest concentrated area of freshwater islands in the world.

If you are coming from the Trent-Severn, on your approach to the Thirty Thousand Islands from the big open waters of Georgian Bay, and you'll find it difficult to differentiate one island from another. The large islands near Penetanguishene are easier to distinguish. Hope, Beckwith, and Christian Islands are also easy to approach because they're surrounded by deep water with open anchorages and long sandy beaches. Large boats often anchor here. If you do want to explore the channels woven through the island chain, you're safer to stay between the channel markers. The route from Port Severn to Killarney is about 175 miles long.

Pene tan What? Penetanguishene (however you pronounce it) has a rich heritage of cultures and people. Recognized as having one of the most beautiful and protected harbors, it is a haven for boating enthusiasts. Being within Simcoe County it offers many attractions and events. Many of those large attractions are native to Penetanguishene and it is your gateway to exploring the 30,000 Islands.

Georgian Bay Islands National Park encompasses 59 islands in the southeastern part of this region, and dozens of provincial parks and conservation reserves are scattered along its shore. The "Discovery Islands," though a nightmare for boaters, are a paradise for fishermen and photographers!

OOPS, did I just say the area was a nightmare for boaters? Well, it can be, for sure. The good news is, however, the channels to the big islands are well marked and you can boat into a marina, and you can safely explore the islands in your dinghy – if you wish.

Canada's Georgian Bay is much like America's Chesapeake Bay in that I could spend a whole day talking about it or write a book about it. If I ever did, I would have to include the time a Black Bear jumped off a 20 foot high granite rock and landed in the cockpit of my boat. Obviously, his intent was to jump in the water, and he did so as I just happened to come cruising by. With the sudden and violent "bounce" of my boat, my friend Terry and I were startled – thinking at first we hit an underwater boulder. Looking aft, there in the cockpit was a bear looking at us – with a look on his face that said he was just as shocked and startled as we were. At that, he quickly jumped into the water and made his escape.

Tucked into Ontario's Lake Huron, Georgian Bay is almost as big as Lake Ontario, earning it the nickname "The Sixth Great Lake." With more than 1,240 miles of black-grayish-pink granite shoreline, it is a summer freshwater playground for boaters and anglers.

The Bay has 32 historic lighthouses and 30,000 (plus) islands which form the world's largest freshwater archipelago and Georgian Bay Islands National Park – which you definitely need to navigate. They are accessible by water only and you can cruise between the island in your cruiser or dinghy.

If you are boating the Loop by seasons (as I suggest) you will be in Georgian Bay at just the right time. June through August is the time to be here and in mid-July each year there is a the three-week long "Festival of the Sound" with music celebrations staged on the waterfront at the Charles W. Stockey Center for the Performing Arts in Parry Sound. For beach-going, try seven-mile Sauble Beach in the town of South Bruce Peninsula; of the crescent-shaped Providence Bay beach and boardwalk on Manitoulin Island; or Wasaga Beach at the southern end of Georgian Bay, a nine-mile stretch of white sand that bills itself as the world's longest freshwater beach. For camping in the archipelago, a late mid to late August visit is just right.

Where to Eat: All of the ingredients used to prepare wood-fired, thin-crust pizza, the local fresh menu items at Haisai, are grown or raised on nearby farms, including Eigensinn Farm which is part of the Canadian Culinary Apprenticeship Program. Along with the restaurant being run by award winning chefs, the Singhampton Haisai restaurant and bakery follows a strict farm-to-table philosophy, and the fish is as fresh as it gets – right from Georgian Bay. Haisai is open for lunch and dinner Friday through Sunday. It's a treat worth planning for.

At **Grandma's Beach Treats** in Wasaga Beach you can taste homemade, hand-scooped ice cream with flavors like Black Raspberry Thunder and Blueberry Ripple, using local berries. My favorite, however, is the homemade butter tarts – flaky crust with pecans and gooey pecan filling – they are what set this place apart from other lakeside ice cream stands.

On a final note about cruising Georgian Bay – experience talking here – you want to make absolutely sure you keep your eyes on your depth sounder and the boulders. Pay special note to the fact, you CAN NOT do this while looking at the shore line through your binoculars… especially when you cruise by Canada's largest (and most popular) nudist colony.

Montreal on the St. Lawrence Seaway

Montreal is Quebec's largest city and like the St. Lawrence's Thousand Islands area is simply a must see, if you can possibly make the time. When do you want to go? In June! June is Montreal's Jazz Festival time – the city is in full stride with musicians from Mile End and chefs from Old Montreal at the top of their game. Take it all in, then use the mountain that the city was named after – Mount Royal – as a *trou normand* (palate cleanser).

Where to Stay: If you are ready to splurge a bit, and spend a night or two off your boat, you can sleep in at Pierre Du Calvet (built in 1725), or at the Fairmont Queen Elizabeth where John Lennon and Yoko Ono recorded "Give Peace a Chance" in room #1742 and staged their "bed-ins" for peace in 1969.

What to Do: Visit Wilensky's Light Lunch for a trip back in time and experience authentic Montreal smoked meat–the cured, smoked, and gently steamed beef brisket cousin of New York pastrami –not Texas BBQ. Compare the bagels at the Fairmount and St. Viateur. Then make sure you visit Comptoir which serves up a top-notch (real British version) fish and chips on a shiny wooden counter.

New York State's 1,000 Islands

Bolt Castle in the Thousand Islands

The *Thousand Islands* are in the St. Lawrence River, running along between the USA and Canadian borders from Kinston to Brockville Ontario, a distance of about 50 miles. The St. Lawrence National Park is on the Canadian side of the Canada/US border in the middle of the river. This area is one of the best and most beautiful cruising areas anywhere in the world with protected anchorages, beaches, fishing, riverside towns, campgrounds, and parks on both sides. Remember to check in with government officials before you dock, moor, or anchor in Canada, or whichever "other side" of your country you hail from.

While the actual number of islands in this area is officially 1,793, but in my opinion, I believe the number would vary dramatically depending on when the islands were counted. In a "dry season" for example, low water levels would cause more islands to appear, and of course causing others to come in contact with more boat props. Updated charts are quite important here! I ALWAYS follow behind the bigger (deeper draft) tour boats (there are always a lot of them running) and I've yet to damage a prop in the Thousand Islands.

The **St. Lawrence Islands National Park** has 21 islands and numerous islets. Most of the Park islands have docks, picnic tables, and walking paths and can only be reached by boat. It's a great place to stay overnight. There are many places to anchor for the day, and my favorite overnight anchorages include Leek (Thwartway) Island. There are a lot of "novice" boaters in this area, so you want to make sure you set an anchor light (or lights) that are brightly visible in all directions.

Anchoring in the islands near Gananoque usually means weeds and mud. So I go farther east toward Rockport. There you may anchor in deeper water. Brakey Bay in the "Forty Acres" south of Howe Island is also a favorite of mine and many sailors.

Caribbean Island Hopping

Cruising the Bahamas & Caribbean

While many may not consider the Bahamas & Caribbean as an optional detour or side trip to cruising the Great Loop – fact is, if you have the right boat, at least a portion of the Bahamas are a very realistic (and pleasant) detour off the Great Loop route.

For those having completed the Great Loop, fact is, the Great Loop is actually a fantastic "training ground" for cruising the Caribbean. For example: Did you know you can "Island Hop" your way south from Bimini to Trinidad and Venezuela without ever having to cruise through the night? That's right! Just as with the Great Loop, you can island hop your way all the way to Venezuela and be safely anchored out in some Paradise Island, Cay or Cove every single evening in time to watch a beautiful sunset.

If interested, Bimini Island is your nearest and shortest open sea gateway to the Bahamas and Caribbean. It is just a 50-mile day run from Ft. Lauderdale, FL. If you start in the early morning, you'll be having lunch or dinner on one of the most beautiful islands in the Caribbean – Bimini!!!

Caribbean Island Hopping
Keep The Dream Alive!

Obviously, cruising the full length of the Caribbean takes some serious planning. It is the type of voyage that requires plenty of fuel, and fresh water. While the Caribbean has more than 7,000 islands, most of them are uninhabited and not only do they not have a Starbucks or McDonalds, most Islands and Marinas do not have fuel.

In addition, fresh water in the Caribbean is a precious commodity. Lack of fresh water turns back as many sailboats as lack of fuel turns back power boaters. Between Nassau and Aruba there are fewer than 45 marinas and most of them are located in the more popular tourist areas north of the US and British Virgin Islands. In 2013, fuel averaged over $6.50 a gallon. In some locations fuel is over $7.00 a gallon. Water at most marina docks (that have it) is metered at $0.50 a gallon. Therefore an unsuspecting couple wishing to fill a 200 gallon fresh water tank and take a couple of showers on the boat at the dock, could easily cost you $150.00. Furthermore, you don't want to be too quick to pick up a few bags of ice - many marinas charge $10.00 a bag. That is the bad news!

The good news is that in the right boat, planned right and equipped correctly one can cruise from the US mainland to Trinidad, Tobago off the coast of South America while never having to spend an entire night cruising through the night on the open sea. If you follow my "Caribbean Island Hopping" route, your voyage is all on the "leeward" side of the islands – which are much more comfortable cruising grounds than the windward side on the Atlantic.

So when planning your voyage around the Great Loop, if you are also in need of a boat, and think you might enjoy a voyage into the near Bahamas, a sailboat or very economical, long-distance capable cruiser should be at the top of your list for consideration. A short voyage to Bimini and Nassau is very safe and attainable in most any vessel you make the Great Loop journey in. On the other hand, an extended voyage into the Caribbean can be extremely safe and economical in a sailboat equipped with a water maker.

Finally

Cruising America's Great Loop, is in itself, a most fantastic safe boating adventure. It is best if planned and cruised on a seasonal basis, boating each area according to the best weather. Boating north in the summer, south in the winter, and cruising up the Atlantic ICS in the spring, and down the inland rivers in the fall.

If you cruise the Loop on a seasonal basis, you will have plenty of time to take several side trips and detours, many of which will be like icing on the cake to your Great Loop voyage.

The Great Loop Boat

Think Goldilocks! You don't need one that's too big, and you don't want one that is too small.

While most of us dream of a "big or bigger" boat, fact is, long distance pleasure boats are simply not as big as we think. According to USCG 2012 statistics, of all the more than 13 million pleasure boats registered in the United States (and the 9.5 million unregistered), 86% of them are under 26 feet. Less than 1% are 40 feet long or longer – and of that 1% only 1 in 10,000 over 40 feet is larger than 48 feet. So keep this in mind when you think you need a "big" boat. Most pleasure boats are simply not as big as we think, and furthermore, when it pertains to boats, "bigger" is actually seldom "better."

I get the question about boat size all the time. Mostly from dreamers wanting to know whether or not a 60 foot boat is big enough. After that, we get the boaters that want to know about a perfect size "Great Loop" boat. Most are thinking much larger than they need. While we have all heard the phrase "bigger is better" when it comes to living aboard and cruising… the "bigger is better" theory is a big myth. Big pleasure boats for a cruising couple or a lone sailor has its very safe limits – and those "safe" limits are much smaller than most people think.

Unlike driving a car with brakes, even a stopped boat is in constant motion, pushed one way by currents, another way by wind. That isn't a big deal in a small boat. You can always fend off from some obstacle with your hand or even a boat hook. But when it comes to a 34 foot (plus) live-aboard size pleasure boat – it weighs tons and isn't so easy to move or fend off the dock or another boat even when at the marina. Especially when winds are strong, currents are swift, and waves or someone's wake comes crashing in on you.

You need to think safety first, then think comfort and economy. Don't buy a boat one foot bigger than you need. Keep in mind long after your boat is paid for, most cost you encounter will be related (one way or another) to the length of your boat.

Like shoes, there simply is not a "one size fits all" when it comes to cruising America's Great Loop, (or anywhere else as far as that goes). Long-distance, long-term, living aboard and cruising is much more about comfort. For this reason, I never recommend "a specific boat" or even a particular "type" of boat; but I can give you points to consider for what you need – and you can decide what kind, type, and size is best for you.

If you're on a budget (and who is not?) you need to be very careful in your boat selection. Boat price and any loan payments set aside, the very moment you choose your boat you have predetermined your long-term cruising expenses. Here are a few "boat related" items you need to consider for cruising America's Great Loop:

"Go or No Go"
Great Loop boat restrictions

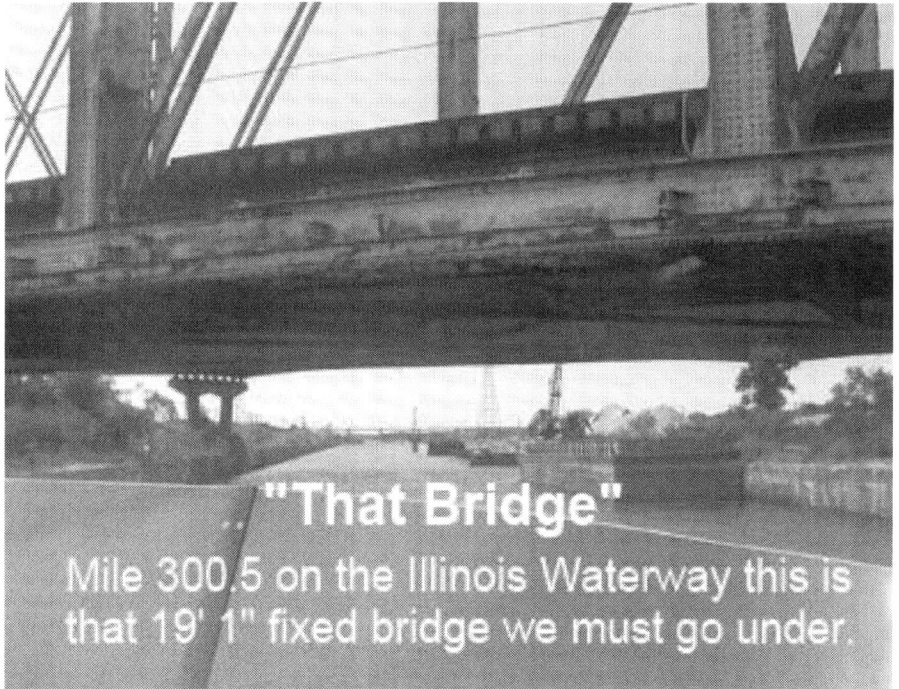

Your boat <u>must be able to clear a 19' 1" fixed bridge.</u> This means, after taking off or taking down, any removable objects on your boat such as Bimini, masts, antennas, etc., your boat's super-structure must be able to pass under a fixed bridge between Chicago and the Illinois River with a height above the water of 19' 1". <u>There is no alternative waterway route around this bridge</u>. If you cannot clear this fixed bridge, your Great Loop will become a Great U-turn.

Your boat <u>should</u> **have a draft of less than 5'**. In other words, all that part of your boat that extends below the waterline should not be deeper than 5'. In fact, I cannot stress enough, **the shallower your draft, the better.**

Note: Some cruising guides and older books, blogs or websites will tell you a "6 foot" draft is OK. I'm sure it is, but I wouldn't do it myself and I don't recommend it. Based on my most recent trips, I would not even consider a 5' draft boat for cruising the Loop. I ran aground twice in the last two years with a 4' draft. If your plans include cruising the (optional) Canadian Heritage Canals, your full load draft <u>must</u> be less than 5 feet. We've all heard of "white knuckle" flyers... if you don't want to be a "white knuckle" Captain at the helm – you'll want a shallow draft.

Fuel –your boat must <u>have a minimum fuel range of at least 250 miles</u>. This is currently the farthest distance between fuel stops if you take the Tenn-Tom route. It is located between Hoppies Marina on the Upper Mississippi River and Green Turtle Marina or Kentucky Dam Marina. Green Turtle Marina is located on the Cumberland River (Lake Barkley) at river mile marker 31.5. Kentucky Dam Marina is located at mile marker 23 on the Tennessee River (Kentucky Lake) just south of the Kentucky Dam Locks, 25 miles from Paducah. The City of Paducah, however, has plans to build a marina in its new waterfront development, so hopefully (by the time you get there) this will cut your minimum fuel range to 225 miles on this route.

So, as of now, unless you plan on carrying additional fuel in jerry cans, your boat's fuel tank(s) capacity must allow you a cruising range of **at least 250 statute miles.**

NOTE *(optional route)*: If you plan to cruise the entire **<u>Lower Mississippi River route</u>** from Cairo to New Orleans, your "**diesel powered**" **boat will need a cruising range of <u>376</u> miles. Your** "**gasoline powered**" **vessel must have a cruising range of at least <u>449</u> miles.** (Those are exact miles leaving no fuel in reserve.)

Your comfort both inside and outside is critical.

Length– between 26' to 36' is really as good as it gets. This is big enough for comfort, but not too big to be unsafe or excessively expensive. I'm not saying you can't do the Loop in a something smaller, larger or longer, you can. Single or "back packer" types can cruise the Loop in smaller boats, and those who have the bigger budgets can do it in bigger boats. Just remember, when you choose your boat, you are predetermining your long-term cruising expenses.

Height (above the waterline) – you vessel's super-structure (with mast, Bimini, antennas down) <u>must</u> be able to clear a 19' 1" fixed RR bridge in order to avoid turning the Great Loop into a Great U-turn. If you can clear 17 feet you can cruise right through downtown Chicago. If you can clear 15' 6" you can cruise the full length of the Erie Canal and will have totally unrestricted cruising on the Great Loop, both in the USA and Canada's Champlain Route and Heritage Canals. Sailboats obviously must take their masts down.

Depth (below the waterline) – Some Cruising Guides will tell you - that you can do the Loop with a 6' draft. I'm sure you can, but I (personally) wouldn't want to in anything over a 5' draft. Less draft is better – much better, and will be an awful lot less stressful. My last two trips around, I ran aground on the AICW for the first time with a 4' draft. This is why I always cruise on a rising tide.

Your draft must be less than 5' to cruise the Canada's Heritage Canals. Other than that, the less draft you have, the more worry free and relaxed your entire journey will be.

Note on draft: Since 2008 the Government has continually cut back on many programs. As a result, the Army Corp of Engineers has had a serious lack of funding for dredging the waterways and canals. As a result, the waterways are not as well maintained as they were in the past. As a full-time Looper I can tell you the depth changes and increased amount of problem shoaling areas are very obvious. So, where years ago a 6' draft would have been no problem... it is "white knuckles" cruising today, but I'm sure you can do it if you are careful.

Beam– For *pleasure* boats in the USA, this is never a problem. You must have a beam of 23' and under to cruise the Canadian Heritage Canals.

Fresh Water capacity– It depends on how often you want to stop and get water. Usually, five days' worth will be about perfect – you will probably go ashore more often than that anyway. If your plans include boating the Lower Mississippi, you'll have to stretch your water to last ten days (maybe more depending on weather). If your side trips or after the Loop voyage includes the Caribbean, you will want or need a fresh water maker.

Holding Tank capacity–Guys need 9 gallons, girls need 900 gallons (Lol). Both fresh water capacity and holding tank capacity will depend much on your lifestyle, type of boat, and number of individuals aboard. If your boat has a shower, couples will want a minimum 100 gallon water tank. More of course will be better. Your holding tank should be at least 30 gallons.

Electrical "Shore" Power– It depends on your amenities aboard. I recommend two 30-amp vs. one 50-amp. In addition, in a few locations you will need a 30-amp female to 15-amp male reducer. On shore power, I run my air-conditioner, TV, microwave oven, toaster oven, coffee pot, etc.

Top-side and Deck– We highly suggest vessels with unobstructed walk-a-round decks with flat, clear, easy access from bow to stern. For working docks and locks, the flatter and wider the walkways, the better. You will most likely pass through over 120 locks on your journey around the Great Loop.

Anchors– A two bow anchor system with both a Danforth and a Plow /Bruce anchor is ideal for the varying bottom types and/or for a twin 60 degree anchor placement. At least one anchor rod should have very heavy chain the length of your boat. Normally, I only use one anchor. I have only used two when anchored out in heavy storms.

Fresh water filter – If you drink the water from your fresh water tank, you will want a filter. It's not required, but it sure will make your coffee and water taste better.

TV– If TV is important, you will need a unidirectional digital air TV antenna. On the Great Loop route you will be able to receive all the major (free) networks. I can't recall the last time around when I could not watch the news and football games.

Bimini top– You will need a BIG one. The stronger and bigger the more shade it provides, the better and more comfortable you will be. Keep in mind by mid-morning and late afternoons, the sun will be low in the sky and very hot. More times than not, you will want to be under the shade.

Your boat's engine(s) – Remember… it will NOT matter much at all how fast your boat is capable of going. On America's Great Loop your speed is very limited over most of your entire voyage. If you truly need or want to make this voyage on a frugal budget, it will be imperative to select a boat or an engine based on a <u>minimum hourly fuel burn rate</u>, and it will also be vitally important you know exactly what it is.

Battery "Underway" Power – This is difficult to answer. It greatly depends on the boat and your electrical needs and amenities. It also depends on your pocketbook, and whether you want or need only 12 volt or also need 110 volts.

My sailboat is equipped with four 12 volt batteries. I also have a solar panel that keeps them in good shape.

Starting with the very basics of electrical needs, I strongly suggest you plan to light up the outside of your vessel like a Christmas tree. No, I don't mean you need a string of colorful blinking lights, but I do mean you will want more than a woefully inadequate anchor light – especially if you're on a sailboat and the light is 40 or more feet up in the air at the top of your mast. Remember, you may be anchoring out 4 or more nights a week. When you do, you will want your boat to be easily seen for a safe distance. A single dim anchor light atop a mast can be easily mistaken for distant star.

Many boaters buy those (cheap) solar powered yard lights that are made to stick in the ground and light the path of your driveway or landscape around the house – and put them on all four sides of their vessel.

I have four small (very bright) LED 12 volt spots that shine down on my pearl white vessel from the mast spreaders. They illuminate my vessel like a glow stick in the night.

Obviously, this would not be necessary if all boaters were experienced and alert – but they are not. Your most frequent midnight speedboat visitor will be fishermen checking lines and crab pots. These guys know the local waters and their "boating" is work. They run on a schedule and want to get home. If you are anchored in what you feel is a safe anchorage that happens to be in their off channel path – you want them to see you well in advance. Believe me, long before this voyage is over, you wish you had brighter anchorage lights.

I have four marine deep cell batteries and solar panels to keep my batteries charged. It works very well for me and it keeps my navigation lights, anchor lights, and 12-volt electronics running good and bright.

Underway and anchored out, I use my outside propane grill for cooking, my propane stove top for heating water for coffee, and my refrigerator/freezer is also propane and requires very little electricity for the thermostat. I also have a laptop computer that I use a lot when anchored out. I often turn on the TV (with a 12v to 110v inverter) to watch the news, and sometimes long enough to watch a movie. On really hot evenings anchored out, I will close the hatches and turn on my air conditioner long enough to cool down the cabin before going to sleep.

Your comfort is the key to how small your boat can possibly be. For sure, living aboard and cruising long distance over an extended period of time demands a boat that you and your mate or crew can live on comfortably and safely.

How large should your boat be? It should be absolutely no larger than one person can safely handle alone. Now, if your first thought was "the bigger the better" – shame on you. Frugal or not, this is an important safety feature when it comes to cruising. Accidents happen. We all get sick. Some of us have been known to bruise, bust or break a toe or finger. When it comes to on-board accidents almost anything can happen. Certainly if someone falls over-board, it will not be the first time.

Boat size: In our experience with both power and sail, and with sailboats, cruisers and trawlers, we have found that a vessel in the 26' to 36' range is about as good as it gets. After 36' it gets much more expensive and difficult to handle. Smaller is not only more economical, it is safer and easier to handle.

Trawlers: Are very popular vessels for living aboard and for cruising. The main reason for this is they provide the most living space and comfort of any boat of comparable size. If you are cruising on a budget, a small (full displacement hull) trawler with a small single engine offers the very best in comfort and amenities, as well as economy when compared to all other powerboats. On the economy scale, a small 25'-30'"pocket"trawler or tugboat with a small single engine will average about 3 gallons an hour. That is a fuel cost of about

$7,000 (compared to $21,000 or more for a larger trawler) for 110 cruising days on one trip around America's Great Loop.

The "Trawler" for its length, offers more interior live-aboard space than any other on the market. Beware, however, that some "trawlers" are not really trawlers at all – they just look like one.

The "true" pleasure boat trawler has a full-displacement hull with a long keel, a single engine, and a top cruising speed of about 10 knots. Remember, a full-displacement hull is the trademark of an ocean capable vessel. These hulls can carry more payloads and are more stable than any other vessel on the water, due to their design. The hulls do not plane and all the power, power train, and hulls are all designed and engineered to simply push the hull through the water – not on top of it.

The other type of pleasure boat "trawler" is not a "true" trawler at all. It just looks like one (above the water). It sports a semi-displacement hull. The semi-displacement hull is designed to provide <u>lift</u> and therefore partially raise the vessel out of the water for the sole purpose of speed. These vessels most often have twin engines and offer much greater speed (typically 24 knots), but they do so at a tremendous sacrifice of fuel economy.

Now, don't get me wrong. I love a true trawler. I would have one if I could afford the fuel to take it 10,000 or more miles every year, and allow me to cruise the Caribbean. Many trawlers have a large fuel and water capacity to enable extended cruising and they offer interior live-aboard space and creature comforts that are simply unmatched by any other type pleasure vessel afloat. If you future plans include cruising deep into the Caribbean however, you will want a sailboat. Most powerboats from the U.S. mainland cannot go farther south in the Caribbean than the Turks or Virgin Islands. I know – it looks like one could make it all the way to Trinidad or Venezuela, but many of the islands south of the Dominica Republic don't have fuel. Saba Island (for example) has it, but the only way to get it is using your own Jerry cans and carrying fuel out to your vessel in your dinghy. (Not a happy thought when you need 800 or more gallons to reach your next fuel stop.)

What the difference means to you:

The <u>full-displacement</u> **trawler** is designed to direct all of its power to pushing your vessel forward through the water. The full-displacement trawler is built for about 9 knots (10 mph) sustained cruising speed. It will burn much less fuel at its designed cruising speed, than a semi-displacement trawler will burn at a near idle speed.

The <u>semi-displacement</u> **trawler** is designed to lift as well as push your vessel through the water. Therefore, much of vessels fuel economy is lost (even at very low speed) in the energy it requires to lift the front of the vessel out of the water, rather than move it smoothly and slowly forward.

The semi-displacement trawler, along with cabin cruisers were designed for higher cruising speeds in the 17-24 knot sustained cruising range, and have a very poor (make that terrible) fuel economy.

A true trawler (or tugboat) in the 25' – 32' range make excellent live-aboard vessels. They have a head and shower (smart) and make for a great long-term and long-distance cruising vessel. For a boat they offer much comfort and have both cabin and deck space.

Trawlers in the 32' – 36' range - are easy for a couple to handle and very comfortable for long-distance cruising. They often have two heads and showers (dumb – who needs two bathrooms less than six feet apart?) but they are comfortable, and can accommodate guests for longer stays. By the time most "Looping couples" are halfway into their voyage, they have already converted the second head and shower into closet and storage space. So you will be wise to do that before you ever cast off.

Both full and semi-displacement trawlers can be found with both single and twin engine configurations. Most true full-displacement trawlers, however, will only have one relatively small diesel engine.

The primary advantage to twins is NOT (as most people think) for having a back-up if you lose one engine. That just happens so seldom, the chances of it ever happening to you are slim to null. The real advantage of a twin engine vessel is maneuvering in close quarters (I love a twin screw or twin engine boat for that reason). The disadvantage in twin engines is twice the cost to maintain: two of everything, and twice the fuel consumption (I hate both of those).

That's right! Don't let any boat salesperson try to convince you that two engines won't burn twice the fuel as one. It simply is not true – they will! Small single engines offer much lower fuel consumption even though they are more difficult to handle in close quarters. Another advantage of a single engine, in addition to fuel efficiency, is easier access and engine maintenance due to more room in the engine compartment.

Trawlers & Trawlering (the magazine) not long ago featured an article on "The Great Loop's Ideal Boat" wherein they outlined all the wonderful features of a twin-engine planing trawler – and indeed, they are wonderful features.

What they fail to mention, however, is that this cruise (at today's fuel prices) will cost you $35,000 (or more) in fuel alone.

Here for example is one Looper's actual final stats for cruising America's Great Loop in a twin-engine semi-displacement hull trawler: Average number of miles traveled on cruising days = 41 miles. Total fuel consumed gallons (gas) = 8,724 gallons. Average cost of fuel = $4.17 per gallon. Total cost of fuel = $36,370.00

I enjoy reading magazines such as *Trawlers& Trawlering* magazine, and this should be no reflection on them. They certainly can't be expected to offend their primary advertisers who want to sell you a trawler… but I don't have a problem offending their advertisers. So, if you think spending $35,000 (or more) for fuel is NBD (No Big Deal) go right ahead and buy that trawler. I know you will love it – I used to own one. They make wonderful live-aboards. In fact, (my opinion) you won't find one better.

It is magazine articles that promote the large semi-displacement hull, twin engine Trawler as "the perfect Great Loop boat". This, along with many "Looper blogs," fuel the fire and feed the myth that cruising America's Great Loop requires a big expensive boat and even bigger budget.

Sadly, some Loopers and some Great Loop cruising blogs and websites would have you believe it takes $350,000 or more to purchase a Great Loop boat, another $20,000 to outfit her, and $35,000 in fuel.

On top of that, many talk of spending every night in expensive marinas for an additional $20,000 in marina fees – when the fact is, you don't have to do any of that. I don't mean to be negative about the boat. They are wonderful boats. My only point is that such a boat is a matter of choice – not a requirement – as some would have us believe.

Just a year ago I cruised into a marina, docked, and on my way to the marina office stumbled into a small group of about 30 people seated auditorium style by the pool listening to a man speaking from a podium about "CRUISING THE GREAT LOOP" (this, of all things for me to stumble upon –Lol). So of course, I had to pause and listen.

Within minutes, the speaker was either consciously or unconsciously bragging or complaining (I'm not sure which) about how much money he spent cruising America's Great Loop – making it sound like what he spent was not only a surprise to him, but a requirement for others. Never once did he mention his boat choice, or his choice to spend every night in a marina – was "his choice." All I could do was think about how many potential Loopers walked away from his "seminar" with a shattered dream.

Cabin Cruisers: Live-aboard size powerboats such as cabin cruisers and semi-displacement hull Trawlers (and any other vessels capable of planing) will be your very most expensive vessel to take around the Great Loop. These vessels simply were not designed for fuel economy, nor were they designed for slow speed. For an example, years ago, a cruise down the Erie Canal (at 10 mph and less) in my twin-engine 32' Chris Craft cruiser, cost me $200 a day in fuel, and that was long before gas reached $3.00 a gallon. If you're planning on cruising the Loop in a cabin cruiser, a planing hull (powered) live-aboard size vessel, or an over 32' twin engine semi-displacement trawler, you can expect your fuel cost to exceed $25,000 for one very slow trip around America's Great Loop.

Few of us have money to burn. And burning money (in the form of fuel) is exactly what a 30' plus (whatever brand) cabin cruiser or planing hull live aboard size vessel will do. In today's economy, as we sit here facing $4.00 a gallon (and higher) fuel prices at the marina, it simply is not a good time to even think about cruising the Loop in a fuel-inhaling, fire-breathing dragon fast boat.

It is great for those that have no concern over a budget. For most of us, however, we have to operate within a budget.

For that reason, and due to the fact that our experience has taught us that cruising the Loop can be done safely and comfortably on a very frugal budget, we simply do not recommend cruising the Loop in a live-aboard size, planing hull vessel – especially one with twin engines.

If, however, you have a small planing vessel with a single engine or outboard and a Bimini top, you can certainly cruise the Loop in good fashion.

Sailboats: For the voyager on a <u>very frugal</u> budget, or someone that wants to extend their Great Loop voyage into the Caribbean, a sailboat (even if you never sail and only power your way around the Loop) is for sure the <u>cheapest</u> way to go. No other affordable vessel will give you the economy of a sailboat under power. Of course, being able to actually sail it offers an even greater advantage. Powering the entire way around the Great Loop in a live-aboard size sailboat is possible to do with a fuel burn rate below 1/2 gallon per hour. Last year, I averaged slightly less than .4 gph in my 30 foot sailboat. That came to a total fuel cost (for one year and one trip around the Loop) of only $1,300.00 in fuel cost at an average price of $3.41 a gallon. In any other vessel you would spend at least five times that.

For the frugal voyager, a sailboat is a great option. Even if you don't know how to sail and never learn – even if you take the mast off and sell it – an "auxiliary powered" (live-aboard size) sailboat offers the very most economical long-distance voyaging of any vessel available.

Now that I have said that, there are of course, three possible exceptions: The small non-live-aboard vessel, human powered vessels, and totally electric vessels (if you can afford one). Notwithstanding the exceptions, the full displacement hulls of both the mono-hull and multi-hull sailing vessels offer the most efficient slow speed fuel economy of any gas or diesel powered vessel on the water.

It seems that many "sailors" visiting our website are totally unaware that one can cruise America's Great Loop in a sailboat, but you can and many, many do. If your mast is less than 65' above the water (and most are), and your draft is less than 6' the trip around is very possible. Sure, there are both long and short stretches where you have to take your mast down, but there are places strategically located along the way to have this done. While we strongly suggest a draft less than 5' (mine is 4'), motoring your sailboat around the Loop opens a wide range of very frugal cruising options.

Of course, sailboats must have their mast removed before entering the Erie Canal, and before entering Chicago or the Cal-Sag. There are facilities to raise and lower your mast at each end of these locations. It is also impossible to actually "sail" in many areas of the Great Loop.

What you may not know is that the design of the sailboat's displacement hull makes it the very most economical vessel on the water. Think about it! Sailboats are designed to move easily through the water in the slightest breeze. As a result, it requires a very minimum amount of horsepower to move these vessels through the water.

For example:

A 32' to 36' (live-aboard size) sailboat might be rated for a 15 to 25hp engine and have a fuel burn rate of 0.4 to 0.6 gallons per hour, at a speed of about 8 mph.

A 32' to 36' single engine trawler might be rated for a 175 to 250hp and have a 10 mph fuel burn rate of 4 to 5 gallons an hour. Twin engines might have a fuel burn rate of 8 to 10 gallons (or more).

Fuel burn rates:

By the way, there is always an on-going debate about hourly fuel burn rates. I don't wish to get involved with all those disputes. However, as a former Trawler owner (and I'm sure I will own one again when I stop cruising so far) I can tell you for fact, the problem is not so much the fuel burn rate you "can" get, as the fuel burn rate you will "actually" get. Here's why:

All boats have a "sweet spot" or comfort speed. Some in fact, have several. So when a Trawler salesman or a Trawler owner tells you that you can get 1.5 gallon an hour fuel burn rate at 2,500 rpms (for example) you probably can. . . Problem is, the ride you get at 2,500 rpms may in fact be the roughest most uncomfortable boat ride of your life. Your vessel's low speed "sweet spot" may in fact be at 3,100 rpms, and therefore, you just jumped your fuel burn to 2.5 gallons per hour.

The other problem with faster boats – is the fact they go faster. It is never hard to go 8 mph (for example) in a boat that will only go 8 mph. If you have a boat that will go 25 mph however – guess what? You will never be comfortable or willing (for long) to simply go 8 mph. I know, I've been there and done that. It's human nature. The faster your boat will go, the faster you will be going in it. This is the entire reason, when someone tells you the fuel burn rate of running a "fast boat slow" simply never works out to be what you thought it was going to be.

For these reasons, you cannot obtain a more economical live-aboard vessel than a sailboat to cruise the Great Loop - even if you take off the mast or never raise the sails.

We met two such Loopers on our last voyage that had removed their mast and left it at home. We met another couple that had inherited an old 50-foot ketch. They didn't know how to sail and simply cut the old wooden masts off at a height about eight feet above their deck. From that, they mounted their antennas, and rigged a great Bimini top.

Learning to sail, of course, is easy and fun. Surprisingly it comes natural once one realizes there isn't anything hard or difficult about it. With a few lessons a sailboat will open your "side trip" options to include a greater range of boating capabilities – such as the Caribbean and the rest of the world.

Regardless of your boat choice–With the "KISS" boating philosophy of "Keep It Simple Sailor" the kind of boat you have, or choose, for making this voyage must be no smaller than one you can live comfortably on for an extended period of time. It should also be no larger than one can safely handle alone.

Additionally, you need to pay as much attention to the cockpit and helm station area on your boat being as comfortable (if not more so) than your cabin. If you voyage the Great Loop by each area's boating season, you will be cruising through 95% of good to great weather. As a result, 95% of your time will be spent in the cockpit. Not in the cabin.

Don't overlook the cockpit. It is easy to be caught up in the dream when looking on the "inside" of a boat: good headroom, nice galley, great salon and berths, etc., and while all that is important, it is also important to remember you will be spending the vast majority of your "awake" time in the cockpit –not in the cabin.

Therefore, it needs to be comfortable and as roomy as possible. It also needs to provide plenty of shade. Good comfortable seating, a large Bimini for shade, and room for a few amenities such as food and beverage trays or table, etc. will make your day at the helm a much more enjoyable and comfortable one.

If there are two things most Loopers start out without, or not enough of. . . It is not enough shade, and not enough light. The longer you cruise, the more shade you will want in the day, and the more lights (to light up your boat) at night – will be two things you will be scrambling for before your journey is over.

The most experienced long-term, long-distance boaters are justifiably bored being told that "size matters"– possibly because the phrase is rarely used to say anything clever or accurate by anyone that knows anything about what they are talking about. Size does matter, but in ways that are not ever obvious to new boaters. Many boaters have spent a lifetime on the water just to learn a simple truth: They had the most fun on the smallest and most humble boat they ever owned.

There was a time (40 years ago) that I too dreamed of a 50 footer. Slowly, as my experience grew, my dream boat shrunk. I no longer think of my boat as my "home on the water." It is instead my "suit case" – that just happens to have a galley, a bed, and a head.

Should your boat be NEW or USED?

The answer of course has to do with your lifestyle, philosophy, and pocketbook. For sure, the frugal voyager will buy used. I do, my son does, and most all of the more experienced and most accomplished boaters buy used. It is a simple matter: "Do you want to give your money to the boat dealer, or do you want to keep it in your cruising kitty?"

Our experience over the years with both new and used boats is that you get what you pay for. Truthfully, buying NEW does NOT guarantee you any less trouble than buying used.

Boats– all boats – and especially sailboats are so unlike cars, it is unbelievable. Unlike used cars, used boats over 10 years old can most often be found with fewer than 200 hours on its engine. Folks, this is the equivalent of driving your brand new car with a 30 minute commute to work and back for less than one year. As far as the "structure" goes, there is far less wear and tear on a boat than a car. So don't make the serious financial mistake of comparing a used 20 year old boat to a 20 year old car. There is a world of difference. If you do, you will miss some of the most fantastic boat buys on the market. It may also help you to know that the "average age" of all registered powerboats in the US is 23 years old. The average age for sailboats is 27.5 years – and the average age of cars registered in the US is 11.

Additionally, while most of us can easily still tell the difference in a newly painted or refurbished 1980 automobile vs. a brand new one – few, even experienced boaters – can tell the difference in a 1980 newly painted or refurbished boat vs. a new one. So if you keep your vessel in "ship shape" – no one is going to know how old it is anyway.

When you are 1,000 miles from home and it comes to a Coast Guard, BoatUS® or Sea Tow rescue or emergency – a new boat warranty won't do you much good. In most cases, a BoatUS® or Sea Tow "tow" to the nearest marina will cost you $600. An actual boat "rescue" will cost you upwards of $2,000. A new boat warranty will not cover the cost of either. Both BoatUS® and Sea Tow offer insurance for these services for less the $200 a year.

Out here the bottom line with a new or used boat is safety – not shine. It is important to remember, that the primary purpose of your vessel is to get you safely and comfortably where you want to go – not to show the world how far you've come.

For sure when it comes to cruising and living aboard, it really doesn't matter to anyone else if your vessel is new or used, small, medium or large, or even shiny and bright.

If you are new to boats and boating, we suggest that before you buy at a <u>very minimum</u>, you should never buy a boat without first taking it out for a good long test run. Don't be embarrassed about putting the vessel through its paces. Furthermore, if you have any doubts about what to look for, or what to check, then you should seek the help and assistance of a professional Certified Boat Surveyor. I've shaken hands on many deals based on a $100 down payment, with the cash paid in full upon receipt of a satisfactory (to me) certified boat survey.

Of course: Your vessel should be safe, seaworthy, comfortable, and (we suggest) fully paid for. You DON'T want to go cruising with "Capt. Boat payment" at your helm, especially if you have any intentions of cruising on a frugal budget.

What type of boat is best for you?

At $4.75 - $5.00 (or more) per gallon for marine fuel... it may be time to rethink "the perfect Looper Boat."

It may also be time to reconsider the perfect boat for you. As mentioned in the prior chapter, a sailboat is the most economical way to cruise the Great Loop. In addition, they can take you through the Caribbean and even on around the world.

If "power" is your thing – it may be time to think "Slow Boat" rather than a fuel burning twin engine dragon. It's all a matter of whatever fits your philosophy, lifestyle, and pocketbook.

Learning to sail is easy and fun. Surprisingly to many beginners, it comes naturally once they realize there really isn't anything hard or difficult about it. With a few lessons, a sailboat will also open your "side trip" options to include a greater range of boating capabilities – such as the Caribbean and the rest of the world.

Many trawlers and tugs (like sailboats) have full displacement hulls – which also makes them a perfect economical choice for cruising the Loop. Some of them, with true full displacement hulls, a single small engine, are ideal long-distance cruisers. While not nearly as fuel efficient as motoring a sailboat, for sure they are the next best thing. In fact, they can be the "very best thing" if you can fit all the fuel in with all the fun, and still have some money left over in your pocketbook.

In addition, a trawler or recreational tug under 36 feet both offer an exciting amount of live-aboard comfort inside, as well as plenty of useful, comfortable, safe deck space outside. Their uncluttered walk-around decks are very safe for handling your vessel in the 120 or so locks you will pass through. The properly equipped long distance tug or trawler can also take you into the Bahamas.

When choosing a boat that is right for you, careful thought needs to go into your "long range" plans. Cruising the Loop is one thing – what you plan to do, or how you intend to use your boat, after the Loop is another.

Currently, in today's economy, the used boat market for any type live-aboard size vessel is at absolute all-time low. It is a "buyers' market." It's GREAT if you are buying, and rock bottom terrible if you are selling. So, if you are thinking of buying a boat, cruising the Loop, and then selling it – for sure you need to buy used, and buy smart.

If you are looking for a used boat – forget the advertisements for used boats advertised in all the boating magazines. While these are great to look at and dream on – they are by far the very most expensive and over-priced vessels on the market. Avoid getting serious over any of these boats. I'm not just talking saving a thousand, or two, or three… I'm talking spending tens of thousands more for a great, safe, seaworthy boat then you have to.

If my own experience of driving in my car from the Gulf to the Great Lakes and from up the Mississippi to down the Atlantic seaboard in search of a boat didn't tell you something, then I will tell you now: There are absolutely many steals of a deal on live-aboard size vessels all over the place – wherever you can find big water and navigable waterways to reach it, you will find great deals on used boats.

Since 2008 to date, I have seen dozens upon dozens of great boats sold for rock-bottom prices. From a perfectly great live-aboard size 32 foot sailboat that sold on "Boat Angels" for $52.00 to a 1989 34 foot trawler that sold for $5,000 – both of which I actually climbed on and inspected. Both of which would have sold for $20,000 more if the job market and economy wasn't in the dumpster.

To find these deals, however, requires both patience and work. And if you don't think you have the "time" for an extensive boat search, you might want to think again. It took my son and me seven weeks to find the Albin Vega used for our most frugal voyage around the Loop. We traveled, left business cards, built a network, and ended up with a vessel perfectly suited for our needs for only $3,000. At the time, there were three such vessels on the market. One on Craig's list – that when we saw it, was junk listed for $11,000; one in a boating magazine for $19,000; and one floating in a slip in New Jersey for $15,000. We saved over $12,000 in our seven week search. That savings equals a net income of $1,700 a week for our effort. Not too many people make that kind of money these days.

If you are looking for a bit bigger and more expensive boat – a good boat search can of course, result in a much greater savings.

A good boat search can save you thousands. And the best place to look is north of Cocoa Beach, FL to New Jersey. The Cape Kennedy/Canaveral area in Florida north to and including St. Augustine (due to the NASA layoffs) is an especially good place to look. The deals are either floating in slips or on land in the marina yards. The owners either have abandoned these vessels or simply don't have the money to spend advertising their vessels – so the "for sale" posters are plastered on the marina bulletin boards.

Now… I'm not going to try to sell you on my boat, or one like it. Fact is, I've had dozens. From fast cruisers (in my younger days) to trawlers, catamarans, and mono-hulls – I loved them all – and they all suited the purpose for which they were intended. And that is the point. Make sure your vessel fits well within your intend use.

So my very best advice for finding a vessel that best suits your needs is to consider the Great Loop boat restrictions, your pocketbook, your lifestyle, and comfort zone, as well as your "after the Loop" plans. Then go climb on a hundred or so live-aboard size boats. Until you do this, you will never have a good idea of what you really want and need.

Provisioning your Boat

Provisioning your boat for cruising America's Great Loop is not nearly as challenging as provisioning a boat for the Caribbean or for crossing an ocean. Reason? You are seldom far from shore or places to re-stock your supplies. Whether it is fresh water or fresh vegetables – you will pass plenty of places to purchase supplies on a daily basis. The only exceptions to this is if you elect to cruise across the center of the Great Lakes in one continuous journey, and/or take the Lower Mississippi River route to New Orleans. In addition there are a few places on the ICW where your distance will require you to anchor out in the absolute middle of nowhere. These places are easily recognized on your navigational charts, and your Skipper Bob's Anchorages Along the Intracoastal Waterway Guide will also indicate where you can, or cannot, anchor and reach nearby facilities.

When it comes to food on your boat, one sure thing holds true – if you don't eat it at home, you won't eat it on your boat. So don't go thinking "boat food" is going to change your likes or dislikes or your eating habits.

For some reason (which to me surpasses all understanding) I have met Great Loop boaters that initially left shore with all kinds of "survival" food (which they will probably never eat), and all other kinds of "food stuff" packed away in every nook and cranny on their boat.

The reality, however, is that you are cruising America's Great Loop – not sailing around the world non-stop. You don't need to pack or even attempt to stock up with more than a week's worth of food – and that's for convenience, not because you have to. Your shopping opportunities cruising the Loop will not be much different than your shopping opportunities at home.

The biggest difference is actually a money-saving difference, as well as a healthier one. On your boat, you don't have all those "Convenience Stores" at every corner to tempt you with chips, snacks, candy, or big gulps. You can't (for example) be cooking dinner and realize you forgot something, and just run out of your boat, hop in your dinghy, and go conveniently to the corner store. So you do have to plan ahead; you just don't have to plan "that much" ahead.

Things you need to think about before running off to the store, include the amount of "space" on your boat. This includes pantry space, as well as refrigerated space – both of which will be very limited compared to what you have at home.

In addition, nothing you buy will last nearly as long on your boat as it does in your home. The reason for this is heat and humidity. Other than that, you will want to have a good supply of Ziploc freezer bags or small Tupperware™ containers for re-packaging most everything you need to fit in your tiny refrigerator, and also for many thing that don't need refrigeration, but you want to keep fresh. I am continually amazed at how long and fresh my used Folgers plastic coffee containers keep my left over cookies, crackers and such fresh.

Cooking is also another big consideration. In the small confined space of a boat, when you cook, the inside of your boat heats up like a charcoal briquette. So normally, food you can serve cold or food that cooks fast is best. This is why you will see so many outside propane BBQ grill units on the stern of cruising vessels. If you buy one (and we suggest you do), you will want to "bite the bullet" and get the best. Marine grade is a must; otherwise, it will be completely rusted out and totally unusable before you are halfway around the Loop. Remember, not only are you on the water for half your voyage, but also you will be in salt or brackish water where everything rusts at an astronomical super-fast speed. This will also include your cooking utensils and canned goods.

What foods should you take? Take only what you love to eat. I personally love seafood, and when cruising the Great Loop, I catch all the fish, shrimp, lobsters, clams, scallops, etc. I want to eat. So I stock up on basic staples... rice, beans, pasta, potatoes with all the spices and seasonings that go well with seafood and can make a meal even without seafood. I very seldom have red meat on my boat. I like to reserve that for eating out. I also always have the makings for a good salad on the boat with fresh tomatoes. And I always have a few cans of soup, stew, and a few things that are quick and easy to fix for days that weather might prevent me from wanting to go ashore.

The fact is cruising America's Great Loop is totally different than crossing an ocean. Food provisions on your boat are not nearly as critical when it comes to planning ahead. The best thing you can do is simply make sure that you have some bad weather back-up food handy. Other than that, on most days you will have many opportunities to go ashore and get supplies.

Equipping your Great Loop Boat

You will need navigational charts. All navigational charts are the responsibility of NOAA. Yes, they get lots of help from both the USCG (Coast Guard) and the Army Corp of Engineers, but NOAA is the single source responsible for the publication of all navigational charts, both digital and paper. Furthermore, NOAA has already announce it is discontinuing the production of paper charts. That means, if they continue to be on the market, they will come from third party printers.

Paper charts: It is my opinion paper charts are as outdated as the hard-wired telephone. I have not used them in years, and obviously I am not the only one as NOAA is discontinuing them. However, if you think you need them, by all means buy them (as long as they are available).

Electronic or digital charts: Since NOAA is the original source of all nautical charts, I have chosen to back up my GPS and battery power (in case of equipment or electrical failure) instead of buying paper charts (which become outdated very quickly).

On Cruising Guides and Paper Charts: Believe it or not, current, updated, official navigational maps and cruising guides are things that few cruisers will think about until they are underway. On the Great Loop your electronic GPS with automatic NOAA updates will be tremendously safer and more valuable than paper charts. The bad news is that paper charts produced by third party printers will be terribly outdated almost as soon as they hit the stores.

Street Maps: For many reasons, you will find an Atlas of US street maps very handy. NOAA weather reports (for example) will reference weather by counties. Do you have any idea for example where Kaufman County is? It's not on your chart.

This is where an area "road atlas" will provide this and more great useful information for the area where you are cruising. In fact, I love using my AAA trip packs for seeing what nearby interesting sites and places are along the route I am cruising. Also, most State tourism offices will send you information packages that will include tourist type maps and a lot of information on places you may want to visit.

The more you know about exactly where you are, the more you will enjoy your Great Loop trip. Many museums in the US are free and some small town museums and galleries are surprisingly great.

All Cruising Guides are indispensable but NOT infallible. In my humble opinion, the most current Skipper Bob's Great Loop and ICW guides are the only ones worth buying. They provide a tremendous amount of information, plus you can get on-line updates.

Not only are the Skipper Bob's guides "cheap" (they are black and white print on copied paper and spiral bound) they are also easy to read and free of advertising clutter. While the more expensive cruising guides are full color and have great photos, they are mostly full of glossy advertising. In some sections one has to page through a dozen or more quarter, half-page, or full-page ads to get to the meat of the matter. Skipper Bob's, however, is free of advertising and reads like an AAA TripTik. You just follow line by line along your route and the information you need is at your finger tip.

You might also be surprised to know that most independent, for-profit Cruising guides rely on boaters (like you) to report navigational hazards such as shoaling, silting, route changes, etc. When you "study" these cruising guides, most of them offer little more than glossy advertising for overpriced marinas – and if you actually look at their marina "rating" system in the guide book, and compare it to the advertising, you will discover that the bigger the advertisement, the better the rating.

Even if you never intend to stay in a marina, I highly recommend you purchase **Skipper Bob's** "anchorages" and "marina "guides as you will need information contained in both. Skipper Bob's also relies heavily on cruisers to keep up to date with information. The difference, however, is that his information is subjective. When Skipper Bob's says a marina or anchorage is a good one, it generally is (he's not getting paid to say it). When he says it's a bad one – don't waste your time and effort there unless you absolutely have to.

There are bigger, full-color cruising guidebooks. I buy used ones now and then when I find one newer then my old ones. They make good reading (if you can get past the advertising) and they have lots of great "general" information on the areas in which you are cruising. For navigation, however, they won't keep you out of trouble, but they will point you to the most expensive marinas, and if you're looking to "anchor out" (as I do five or more days a week) you can forget them altogether. Free anchorages don't pay for advertising space.

You need a GPS navigational system: I use a mid-priced Lowrance GPS system for navigation. It works very similar to the GPS in most cars. I turn it on, and as soon as it gets a fix on my position, it displays the channel boundaries and markers, and gives a magenta line path to follow. It also shows water depths, hazards, mile markers, and marinas along the way. It also has an optional off/on switch that allows us to find the nearest Walmart, Starbucks, restaurants, hospital, pharmacy, rental car, airport, shopping, site-seeing and interesting sites along the way. (Columbus would have loved this!)

You need a depth sounder: I have a depth finder on my vessel even though my GPS gives me the depth. I feel more comfortable with having both. In fact, I suggest you have both. That way if one goes on the blink for any reason, you should still have (or might have) the use of the other. Knowing the waters depth on the Great Loop at all times is critically important.

You need a VHF radio: Not only is your VHF important for safety, such as contacting the USCG and getting USCG hazard reports, it also gives updated weather. You can also contact BoatUS®, and/or Sea Tow. You will also need it for daily contact with Lock Masters and Bridge Tenders along the way. Additionally, it is great for getting local information from other boaters as well as approach and docking instructions from the marina.

You need a dinghy: While a good <u>used</u> (hard-bottom) dinghy might cost you upwards of $600 and a new one might cost $1,600 (or more), a good dinghy will save you more than it cost over the length of your adventure. Most areas you will be boating in offer free "dinghy docks" whereas, without a dinghy, you will pay to dock your vessel. **Your dinghy will be the single biggest "money saving" device you can buy for your boat!**

You need some Cruising Guide Books: As mentioned above, at the top of my list of cruising guides is Skipper Bob's. I also have a few used (outdated) Waterway Guides. That's because the Waterway Guides don't change that much from year to year. They are mostly into advertising dollars. My Skipper Bob's, however, is my constant companion at the helm. I refer to them every day, several times a day. In fact, I would not leave the docks without them.

Caution and consideration <u>should be used when reading any books and blogs, or any dated material</u>. Don't blindly expect fuel stops, docks, piers, marinas, safe anchorages, or even water depths to be there when you are. If there is one thing you can expect cruising the Great Loop, it is the unexpected.

In fact, as I write this book, Hoppies Marina is in danger of closing. Paducah is in the process of building a new city marina. In addition, even the Great Loop is in danger as a result of the Asian Carp invasion. A "hard lock" closure will result in the passage between the Great Lakes and the Illinois/Mississippi and inland rivers being closed. Let's pray that doesn't happen! If it does, I guess my next book will be on the "Great U-Turn".

So, I suggest you not spend your cruising cash on paper charts. (Yes, I get a lot of heat over this suggestion.) However, <u>if you insist</u> on using them, don't buy the expensive most current ones <u>until</u> you are ready to pull up anchor and go. Paper charts are <u>dated material</u>. If you buy them six months before you start your voyage, chances are they will be more than a year old by the time you start your journey and two years old by the time you are half way finished.

Note: your GPS will be much more accurate, because you can download updates as soon as NOAA enters the change. Since NOAA is the original source of, and is responsible for, the production of <u>all</u> nautical charts, you get them as soon as the paper chart publishers get them. This is why we have chosen to back up our GPS and our battery power (in case of equipment or electrical failure) instead of buying all those expensive paper charts.

Ground tackle:

Unless you plan on staying at a marina every night (which is impossible to do, by the way) your vessel's ground tackle will be an extremely important part of your incident-free voyage around the Great Loop. When it comes to the proper anchoring of your vessel, I strongly suggest you pay attention.

If you have never done it before, anchoring out in the tidal currents can be a real shocker – especially along the Atlantic ICW. If you are new to anchoring in tidal waters, believe me… your anchor is going to drag somewhere at some time, and most likely it will be in the middle of the night in a crowded anchorage. Once you let that happen, you will never sleep that soundly or ever let it happen again. You will undoubtedly learn this lesson the hard way – most of us did! After you hear that "bump" in the middle of the night (that usually comes after the tide change) you will then remember the seriousness of what I'm telling you now.

If you just bought a new production vessel, chances are about 100% certain that the anchor and anchoring system that came with it is woefully inadequate for use around the Great Loop. When you get "out here" with the anchoring system that came on your vessel, you will immediately realize how silly it looks when compared to that of the more experienced and accomplished cruisers.

You have probably heard and read it before, but let me reinforce the fact that the safety value of a good anchoring system and knowing how to use it is vital. NEVER just drop an anchor. Make sure it is holding by using your engine to back off until you know your anchor is set.

In addition, you should always cruise prepared to drop your anchor at a moment notice, if need be. An engine failure at the wrong place and wrong time, could get you in real trouble if your boat drifts out of a channel into shallow waters.

Remember, tides cause the current to reverse directions which will make your boat swing around in the opposite direction. If you have a 100 feet of anchor ridden out, your boat will swing in a circle with a radius of 100 feet plus the added length of your boat.

Heavy chain the length of your boat helps your anchor reset. A good anchoring system is one that resets itself when the tides change. A good anchoring system, in fact, is better for a good night's sleep than a Sleep Number® bed. So, consider yourself warned.

Cruising on a frugal budget

Yes, America's Great Loop can be cruised on a frugal budget.

Having said that, don't be misled. When I speak of cruising on a frugal budget, I am speaking strictly as a matter of choice, NOT as a result of financial hardship or an impoverished situation.

In order to be a happy boater, (and who doesn't want to be a happy boater?) cruising on a frugal budget must be a matter of choice, not a matter of adverse or unfavorable financial circumstances. "Frugal Voyaging" is making a smart, conscious financial decision to spend the majority of your money on yourself – rather than on your boat. It is a decision for more fun vs. more fuel – between paying $70 a week in a smaller boat to dock overnight for two nights at a marina vs. paying $420 a week for docking seven nights in a larger boat.

Anchoring out is free, and spending the money you save anchoring out will pay for an awful lot of great meals at some wonderful restaurants and entertainment along your way. Cruising on a frugal budget successfully is the decision to be a happy long-term, long-distance cruiser vs. a short-term, short distance consumer.

Let me also make it clear being a "Frugal Voyager" does NOT mean skimping or neglecting your boat – it simply means owning an economical boat. One that is economical to purchase, own, easy to maintain and operate.

Frugal Voyaging - What does it really cost?

The first and most important aspect to cruising on a frugal budget is to realize your cost of cruising will be directly related to your own comfort zone, lifestyle, philosophy, and pocketbook.

I wish I could tell you that cruising the Great Loop will cost you a set amount of dollars, but I can't. Maybe this will help you understand why:

When cruising, your money is like your water...
No, I'm not getting off the subject here, as it takes both (money and fresh potable water) to keep you happy when cruising.

According to the US Dept. of Environmental Conservation, inside the home the average American couple uses 160 gallons of water every day. Flushing the toilet = 30 gallons, showers = 25 gallons, brushing teeth = 4 gallons... etc. etc. That's over 300 gallons a day, and 2,100 gallons a week.

Problem is, most affordable live-aboard pleasure boats have 90 gallons (or less) of fresh water storage – so without an onboard water maker that 90 gallons (or less) might, in some cases, have to last a cruising couple for a week.

So the question is: "How much fresh water do you really need?" Do you shower twice a day? Once a day? Every other day? Once a week? Do you let the water run while showering or turn it off while soaping up? Do you brush your teeth with the water running? On your boat, will you wash the dishes in lake or salt water and rinse with fresh? Or wash them entirely with fresh water? How do you rinse the dishes? Do you fill the sink with water? Or let the tap run? Do you have an electric water pump or a foot pump?

I could go on but I'm sure you get the point. When cruising, your money is much like your potable water. How you use it, how much you conserve it, all depends on your lifestyle and comfort zone.

The point is that there are simply too many variables to tell you how much fresh water you are going to need on your boat.

For example: if I told you that I used 200 gallons of water last week, and you didn't think that you could do that…what would you do? Would you give up the idea of cruising? Or would you buckle down and get creative with conserving and/or storing more water? Possibly even purchase a water maker?

Now, substitute the word money for water. What if I told you that it cost me $8,062.00 in 2011 to cruise around America's Great Loop? Now what if I told you that included the purchase price of my boat, and $1,300 of that was spent on fuel? Would that information be relevant to you?

My oldest son and I did in fact spend $8,062.00 cruising the Loop in 2011. That included the boat, and all my boat related and marina expenses. IT DID NOT however, include food, clothing, sight-seeing, entertainment, souvenirs or dining out expenses.

However, some live-aboard cruisers I meet along the way spend much more. Some spend much less. So, if you thought my analogy on water use had variables… just imagine what it would be over money. I know cruising couples that spend $10,000 a year eating out. I know others that spend $30,000 (and more) just in fuel. So the question of "How much will you spend?" Of course, I have no idea. But I can tell you this: The very day you select your boat, you predetermine your long term (boat related) cruising expenses. Aside from that, the rest depends on your lifestyle and in what it takes to keep you happy and in your comfort zone.

Whether cruising America's Great Loop, or sailing off to paradise, boaters with less – will spend less. Those with more – will spend more. Just as those who have less water, will use less water.

I know, and truthfully understand, that all of us would love to be able to "buy a ticket" that included all our fuel, food, and fun for a voyage around the Great Loop – but that just isn't going to happen, at least not when cruising on your own boat.

So, when I say that it's <u>not possible</u> for anyone (including me) to give you a safe, dependable minimum amount of money you need to cruise America's Great Loop – that's as true a statement as there ever was one. I can, however, let you know what it cost me in hopes of giving you an idea of what it <u>might</u> cost you.

When it comes to cruising on a frugal budget, your lifestyle and comfort zone is of primary importance. Whether you are cruising America's Great Loop or sailing the seven seas, the type and size of boat, the distance traveled, the time it takes, the amenities on board, and the final cost demands you to remain in your comfort zone. The major expense of which always boils down to your own individual lifestyle, philosophy, and pocket book. I spend an awful lot just eating out. This is why it cost me much more to spend a year on the Loop, than a year in the Caribbean. The wonderful opportunities to eat out at great local restaurants are simply much greater cruising the Loop.

We are all creatures of habit. There are simply some comforts we all have that we are not willing to give up. These are the things that keep and make us happy. They don't change! On land or sea we all have our "comfort zone." Our individual needs and wants don't change, no, even when cruising in paradise.

For most, the question is: More fuel? Or more fun? My boating philosophy has always been, "Go small, go now, and stay out longer." And if you are one of those that dreams of a big yacht that holds 10,000 gallons of fuel (or more) and you "think" you want to go long-distance cruising... think again. What you probably don't know is that those vessels have a fuel range that is limited to where all the beautiful people are. It is a "look at me and see how far I've come boat." It is NOT a get me where I want to go boat (unless of course) you don't want to go very far. A good example of this is Tiger Wood's yacht "Privacy" Bet you didn't know he couldn't cross the Atlantic it in, unless he took the very shortest distance between landfall – and slowed it down to a speed slower than my sailboat. It's true. Why? Not enough fuel and not enough fuel range.

For the frugal voyager, "going small, going now, and staying out longer" makes for a great plan. This allows you to spend more of your money on yourself, (eating out, entertainment, stopping to see the sites, etc.) instead of on your boat for fuel and boat related expenses.

It is a philosophy that understands your boat should be one that gets you where you want to go, NOT to show the world how far you've come. As a result, going small is what allows a frugal voyager to be a happy voyager.

While some will tell you a good live-aboard boat for cruising will cost you upwards of $200,000, I say, give me a frugal voyager, and I'll show you someone who can not only buy the boat, but also have enough change left over to go cruising for several years. Again, it is a matter of lifestyle, philosophy, and pocketbook.

So, is your dream one of a dreamboat? Or is your dream one of long distance cruising? There is a huge financial difference in the two. Long distance cruising does not require a "dream boat." In fact, if your dream is of the cruise and adventure, "the dream boat" may in fact be the single biggest obstacle preventing you from living your dream.

Fact is, "out here" on either the Loop or on the Seven Seas, most experienced cruisers have purchased used boats under 36 feet, costing $36,000 or less – and they are living the dream. While those dreaming of cruising in a "dream boat" are still working every day to (hopefully someday) be able to afford the boat, and then afford to go cruising in it – and this is a sad fact.

FACT: Out of almost 130 million recreational boats registered in the USA in 2012, 85% are under 26 feet, less than 1% are 40 feet or over, and of those, less than 5,400 are 60 feet or larger. And to give you some more "boat ownership" facts that will surprise you: The "average" new boat buyer is a "first time" buyer. (That's why they love you at the boat shows.) In addition, the average age of US registered boats in the US is 27.5 years for sailboats and 23 years for powerboats (not counting PWCs). So fact is, if you've been thinking of buying a brand new, big shinny boat – you are going to stand out in the crowd as a rookie.

Anchoring Out is another huge money-saver. I anchor out an average of five nights a week. I only stay overnight at marina in places I really want to visit. At those locations I also plan for doing laundry and buying provisions. You can plan your stays at a marina around the things you want and need to do. I have never paid for a "mooring" as there are almost always good anchoring locations near mooring fields and even near most marinas. Mooring fields cost you money, anchoring out costs you nothing.

Marinas: Docking your boat for a half day usually cost you $10.00 or more. Overnight most marinas charge $1.50 (or more) per foot for the length of your boat. Many charge extra for electric, water, cable TV, Internet hook-ups, and pump-outs. Information on marinas such as fees and amenities can be found in Skipper Bob Publications as well as in most waterway and cruising guidebooks. This information, however, (remember?) is dated material, so it is a good idea to call ahead for two reasons: 1) to verify they are still in business, and (2) to verify their fees. We have discovered (especially of late) that this is a great time to negotiate your dockage fee. Most (if not all) are eager for your business, and will quickly drop the price and/or offer you some extras.

Shopping: Along your route in many areas, it will appear that you are as far away from civilization as Easter Island is from Hawaii, but never fear – there is almost always a Starbucks and/or a Walmart nearby. Plan your shopping. Avoid having to buy your provisions at a marina or convenient store.

Food – Provisions & Eating Out: You can manage your food budget, and eat better and healthier if you plan your meals and plan ahead to obtain your provisions at area supermarkets. Trust me, prices for ice, food, and beverages as well as for all the things you need and want at most marinas, will be even higher than the highway-robbery prices of expensive roadside convenience stores. Here again is one of the reasons a good dinghy will save you money. In many cases you can dinghy within a few hundred yards of a supermarket or Walmart, where otherwise, you may be miles away if you have to walk from the nearest marina.

If you love seafood and like to fish, you're in luck, and you're in for a real money-saving treat. It is very seldom that I don't have fresh seafood on my vessel's "catch of the day" menu. In fact, I can't remember ever having steaks or red meat on my boat, as I reserve that for when I'm eating out. Likewise, I seldom eat seafood out, unless it is at a place known for its scrumptious seafood specialties (i.e.: places like Hurricane Patty's, Bobby's Fish Camp, and the Fisherman's Wife, etc.). There are a lot of these wonderful places on the Loop.

Along any route you take, you will discover lots of tempting places to stop and visit. From small town areas to the big city lights, you will cruise by state and national parks, museums, historical sites, famous landmarks, and many more really great waterfront restaurants. The good news is that a lot of places to stop along the way are free. Almost all of them, however, serve up very tempting opportunities spend lots of money.

While it is great to cruise on a frugal budget and I encourage it... it is all together a different story attempting to cruise if you don't have enough money. There is a mighty big difference between these two. Cruising with not enough money is guaranteed to make your life and voyage extremely miserable.

When choosing your boat. . . THINK SLOW BOAT!

Speed on America's Great Loop is your enemy. You do not need a fast boat, and twin engines (at an average of $4.75 a gallon) will be a real budget buster. Your daylight distance cruising will (for the most part) be restricted by lift bridges, locks and distances to safe anchorages and marinas. Normally, that fast boat that passes me during the day, is at the same marina or anchorage at sunset.

Remember, Frugal Voyaging is a smart, conscious choice you make between spending your hard-earned money and savings on your boat and boat-related expenses, or spending your money on you, doing the things that make you happy, and keep you in your comfort zone.

A $12.29 per day voyage around the Loop

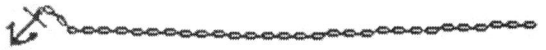

So, how frugal can one be? How much does it take? What is the minimum amount one has to spend to cruise the entire Great Loop?

Would you believe my oldest son and I did it for $12.29 per day? It's true! We did exactly that. The only thing it didn't cover was our food and beverage. It in fact included all our boat, boat related, and marina expenses.

I've had many people over the years tell me that if America's Great Loop had a Missionary – I would be it. I take that as a compliment as long as they realize my compass points toward Christ first. I confess however, in my daily life, it is difficult to avoid conversations about the Great Loop.

Similarly, when the subject turns to the Great Loop, what I keep hearing most often is how expensive everyone believes it is. When I hear someone say "they would do it, if they had the money" well, that's when the missionary in me burns into action.

In addition, my Great Loop website has been on the Internet for more than 20 years. It now has over 4 million readers. As a result, I get the "cost of cruising the Great Loop" question all the time.

So, finally in 2010, not knowing myself how "frugal" it could be; I recruited my oldest son, and we decided to prove just how frugal two people could – safely and comfortably – cruise America's Great Loop.

I had always preferred power boats. So with the help of my oldest son (a very experienced and accomplished sailor), we set off on voyage with a mission.

To do so, we needed a boat two people could life on, with a slick, smooth, full-displacement hull and a small engine. In fact, the more we discussed the requirements, the more obvious it was we needed a small live-aboard size sailboat.

So leaving my newly completed, custom-built 40' power catamaran at home, my son and I took off on a 3,000-mile journey by car – to find just the right vessel, at just the right "frugal price."

We drove from Galveston to the Great Lakes, down the Atlantic coast and back across the Gulf Coast as far as Mobile Bay. We must have looked at 300 boats and climbed in and on at least half of them. We finally agreed that the one we saw in St. Augustine, FL was "the one."

It was a 1969, 27' Albin Vega. She cost $3,000. We sanded and repainted the hull ourselves, and then we had a professional mechanic tune her engine and repair or replace anything else she needed. We spent $300 on three new marine batteries, and paid the mechanic $190 for his parts and labor. We then put her in the water.

While we made a few "sailing" side trips, we motored the entire way around the Great Loop averaging only .4 gallons per hour. Our entire fuel cost was pennies shy of $1,300 for one 5,720 mile trip around the loop.

We spent 372 days on the Loop, but actually cruised only 112 days. We spent 265 nights "on the hook" (anchored out for free) and 107 nights in a marina at a cost of $3,272. We had no mechanical or boat-related problems except for minor glitches we fixed ourselves.

So our 2010-2011 trip around the Great Loop cost us $8,062. Mind you – that included the boat we made the voyage in. Subtract the $3,490 we paid for the boat and getting it in ship shape – and that means one trip for an entire year voyaging around the Loop for two people cost only $4,572.

Folks, that turns out to be $12.29 per day for every day we spent on the Loop. That was the cost of our tiny "motel room" on the water. It included our weekend marina stays, our fuel and all our boat related expenses.

Furthermore, I am sure it wasn't the most frugal trip that's ever been made around the Loop. It does however prove my point: YOU DON'T NEED A BIG EXPENSIVE BOAT OR A BIG BUDGET to cruise around America's Great Loop.

Obviously, what that amount did NOT include was our food, clothes, beverages, ice, entertainment, dining out, souvenirs, or items we purchased for ourselves and others along the way. These things however are personal choices dependent on one's own lifestyle and comfort zone.

As to the Albin Vega? I was amazed! It is a great seaworthy sailboat. In fact, my son and I continued our Great Loop voyage "side trip" into the Caribbean. This small 27' sailboat however worked out wonderful for us, and for what we wanted to do together. . . I agree, it was small. I would have preferred something a bit larger, but it is a great seaworthy boat.

Now of course, I am not at all suggesting anyone do as I do, or as my son and I did. We did this to prove a point while enjoying the time together doing something we both love to do. The point I wish to make, is that you can if you wish, make an economical boat choice, and therefore make an extremely economical voyage around the Loop. Obviously, maintaining your lifestyle and staying within your comfort zone is critical.

For many of us, it is a question of more fun or more fuel? To me, a full-time live-aboard voyager, I can tell you for sure, more fun makes for the most carefree, stress-free, happy boating. The choice is yours to make.

Remember, those that have more will spend more. Those that have less will spend less – and that's the way it should be. I just want to make it clear – whatever the size of your boat or your budget – you will be the happiest of boater, if you can spend the bulk of your budget on fun, rather than fuel.

Your expenses will also depend on the type of boat, size of your boat, condition of your boat, number and size of your engines, maintenance needed along the way, any accidents or emergencies, and a "boat load" of factors possibly neither of us might even be able to imagine.

The very most important factor to being a successful frugal voyager, is to keep in mind that the very moment you select your boat, you have predetermined your long-term, long-distance "boat related" cruising costs. If you plan to cruise on a frugal budget – this one factor alone can be your budget buster. I cannot emphasize this enough. Even with a fully paid-for boat, your boat choice is absolutely critical to "happy cruising" on a budget. If you want to be a happy frugal voyager you have to have a happy frugal boat.

America's Great Loop
Your Great Loop Adventure

I have attempted to provide you all the information you need to make your voyage around America's Great Loop the very best it can be. In doing so, my goal is to insure "ALL" your "unexpected surprises" are of the most wonderful kind.

When planning on your trip – plan on taking your time. Speed in fact will be your enemy, not your friend. True, in a fast boat or a slow one, averaging 50 miles a day (which is what most Loopers do) one could "conceivably" cruise the 5,600 miles of the Great Loop in 110 days. However, there is good reason why most Loopers take a year to complete their voyage. Now having said that, it is better to do it in 5 or 6 months than not at all. It will still be the adventure of your lifetime. It just may leave you wanting more.

Cruising the Great Loop is not a race. For one thing, there is simply too much to see and do along the way. Additionally, in most areas your speed will be greatly limited by 10 mph speed limits, no wakes zones, tides, water conditions, traffic and wait times for bridge or lock openings.

Your primary consideration in determining your day's cruising distance will <u>not</u> be based on how fast your boat <u>can</u> go. Instead, it is determined by how far you need to go in order to reach a particular marina or safe anchorage during daylight. For very, very few exceptions it will not be safe or practical to cruise at night. (I never do.)

Your secondary consideration is whether or not there are any stops, restaurants, or interesting sites along the way you want to visit.

When it comes to cruising the Great Loop at sundown the Tortoise and the Hare most often find themselves at the same marina or safe anchorage. That "fast" boat that passes you during the day will most likely be at the same marina or anchorage you are at night. So remember, regardless of your boat's speed capability, you will do well to average any more than 50 miles a day. Besides, this voyage is all about the journey. It is not a race, and "speed" may at times be your very worst enemy.

Plan on days off and plenty of rest. I know, it sounds silly to plan on "days off" from boating – when you are used to planning days off work to go boating. However, the longer you cruise, the more often you will need (and want) to take a day or two off from cruising. Plan on it!

We plan our days off around what we want to see and do on land. Very seldom are we actually cruising more than 5 days a week, and this works very well, as we have plenty of time to do laundry, buy provisions, and see the local sights. After a day or two, we are always rested and eager to get going again.

Once you have the boat, all the equipment you need, and all your provisions and clothing onboard, you will be feeling really anxious and excited to get under way. You have successfully closed that gap between where you are now, and where you want to be. The dream is about to become reality.

Obviously, since America's Great Loop is a loop, you can start your adventure anywhere along the way.

While the route listed in this book starts on the Atlantic (ICW) obviously, it doesn't matter where you actually start, and after all, it is a "loop." So you can start anywhere on the loop you so choose. Whether you live in New York, Pittsburgh, Nashville, Tulsa, Sioux City, Kansas City, Little Rock, Minneapolis or Memphis, or if you live in any of the more the 25 states along the Great Loop route – you can start from there. The main thing to remember is that in order to enjoy all the best weather, water, and temperature conditions, if at all possible, you want to boat by the seasons (in the very best of weather). So remember:

Spring Up - "Spring Up" the Atlantic ICW in spring.
Shuffle Off - "Shuffle Off" to Buffalo and Chicago in summer.
Fall Down - "Fall Down" the inland rivers in fall.
Winter Across - "Winter Across" the warmer Gulf in winter.

Mid-September is the preferred time to depart Chicago and enter the Illinois Waterway. In most cases the summer heat has passed, and the touch of the Master's hand will be painting the landscape with the brilliant and beautiful colors of autumn as you journey south.

There are two routes from Lake Michigan to the Illinois River. If you can clear an overhead structure of 17', you can take the scenic route, which is right through downtown Chicago. If you cannot clear 17' you will have to cruise about 11 miles south of Chicago and take the Cal-Sag route. In either case, it is less than three miles down river from the junction of these two routes, where you will meet up with that 19'1"bridge you must go under in order to reach the Mississippi River.

That 19′ 1″ Bridge

After you pass under "that bridge" at mile marker 300.5 and then the U.S. Coast Guard's electric Asian Carp barrier field at mile marker 298, you will soon find yourself on your way... voyaging at last, on your own adventure in the wake of Tom Sawyer and Huck Finn on the mighty Mississippi.

Beginning south of the St. Louis Gateway Arch, at the amazing confluence of the Mississippi and Ohio Rivers, it is now decision time.

From Cairo your options are wide open... this "Water World" of America's Heartland connects you with over 24,000 miles of navigable rivers and waterways. So, the question is: Where do you want to go? Louisville? Cincinnati? Pittsburgh? Chattanooga? Knoxville? Nashville? Mobile? Or do you want to take a side trip to Hannibal or even Minneapolis? Or do you want to cruise on down the Lower Mississippi to New Orleans?

If you haven't made your decision by the time you reach Cairo, chances are, your vessel's fuel range will make the decision for you. The farthest distance between fuel on the Tenn-Tom route is only 250 miles for all boats. On the Lower Mississippi route, you need a fuel range of 376 miles for diesel, or 449 miles if you use gasoline.

The difference in fuel range is due to the fact that diesel fuel users have an option of having fuel trucked in to a delivery stop at Cape Girardeau, and Vicksburg. For insurance reasons (they tell us) no one any longer delivers gasoline to boats. (We have more details on fuel range on each river's page.)

Do you want to take the Lower Mississippi to New Orleans route? Or do you want to take the Tenn-Tom route up the Ohio River to the Cumberland River, and pass on into Lake Barkley?

If you choose to take Tenn-Tom, America's Heartland will welcome you much in the same manner as it did the original steamboat settlers. This entire area which includes the Tennessee and Cumberland Rivers, Lake Barkley and Kentucky Lake, in the fall, will absolutely be the most beautiful part of your entire journey.

This is your chance to cruise by and visit the friendly towns they settled, tour the stately mansions they built, and walk on the very battlefields on which they fought. This is where the great rivers opened up America's pioneers to the land of opportunity, and where your own exploration awaits you.

This is the land of red, white and blue-jeans, of rhythm and rivers, of patriotic, interesting and colorful characters, and of boundless beauty. From fish camps and shanties to magnificent mansions and stately plantations, what better way is there to discover it all, than from a slow boat?

In these waters, it won't take you long to discover the refreshing simplicity of life. It is here, cruising through these waters, you will come to understand that true wealth has much more to do with needing less, than it does with having more.

As your heart and mind wraps up what is really important and what really excites and energizes your life, you will discover your "land-loving life" has walked the plank. And it took all of your stress with it leaving you with a much richer life, one not earned by burning your candle at both ends, but given freely by just letting it burn more brightly at the one.

Maybe you want to tour Clarksville before traversing Cheatham Lock to Nashville and cruise past the homes of Reba McEntire, Barbara Mandrell, Martina McBride, and the late Johnny Cash. You may even want to cruise on up to Brad Pitt's little "fly fishing hideaway."

We Loopers are all different. We all have our own set of schedules, time frames, financial situations, and preferred routes we want to take. Yes, it all boils down to your own likes, dislikes, lifestyle, and pocketbook. As a result, there is no one "perfect boat" to cruise the Loop. Likewise, there is no rule that says you have to do it a certain way or within a certain time or take a certain route. While most of us like taking our time and cruising with the seasons, if you're into fast boats or jet skis, go for it!

If your desire is to cruise the Great Loop, you can do it. No matter what your work, retirement, income, or situation is – where there is a will there is a way – and it will be well worth the effort to figure out which way suits you best. For sure, whatever your situation is, it is very likely that someone under similar circumstances has done it already.

Yes! ... You can do this! Furthermore, you can do it "your" way!

America's Great Loop
Living Aboard

It really is a great lifestyle. Living aboard combines serenity, nature, relaxation, and a waterfront view. It is a dream many share and more are achieving every day. This slow-lane lifestyle transcends all economic and social boundaries. Live-aboards can be found on lakes, rivers and oceans, north and south, east and west, in all kinds of climates. Some live in marinas, some live on the hook, some cruise, some stay put, and some do both. What we all hold in common is a fierce independence, and love of freedom. We are a community, (a diverse one) bound by our unique lifestyle and respect for others.

There are basically three kinds or types of live-aboard boaters: The Nowheres –The Weekenders –and The Voyagers

We'll start with the "Nowheres." These are the ones that live on their boat full-time, and as the name implies, go nowhere. Some live on large expensive yachts. Others live on smaller boats, and some live on broken dreams.

Many "Nowheres" act as gatekeepers at the marina… they have lived there so long, they know everyone, every face, and who belongs as well as who doesn't. Most often you will find them to be very friendly and helpful.

"Weekenders" are part-timers and vacationers and are also among the live-aboard community. This group is generally loading up their boat for a weekend cruise and an overnight stay anchored out at a beach or peaceful cove. For the most part, they are party goers who join groups of other boaters and raft off each other for a weekend of fun in the sun.

Then there are the rest of us, "Voyagers." The ones that live on our boats for the purpose of travel. We are the group that is mostly on the go. We cruise from one interesting port to another. We stop long enough to see some sites, maybe take in a movie, eat out at a local restaurant or two, replenish our provisions, and then we are off again on another leg of our journey.

For the "Nowheres" – living aboard in a fully paid for boat can be a very economical and even envied lifestyle. Certainly you can't beat their waterfront view. If you love nature, seafood, and a more relaxed carefree lifestyle – living on a boat can be just what the doctor ordered. You have no gutters to clean, no yard to mow, no snow to plow, and once a year annual maintenance on a "Nowheres boat" is pretty simple indeed.

If you are a "Weekender" or vacationer that lives on your boat part-time, you can enjoy the water by living on your boat instead of owning and having the expense of a boat as well as a Lake House or cabin.

If one likes the water, and wants to live on a boat but doesn't care to go anywhere, it can be a great life. If this is the case, one can purchase a fairly large live-aboard boat with all the comforts of home.

So, if you want to live-aboard and/or retire on your boat, and if you can deal with the lack of space, the lifestyle can be truly terrific. It also offers many, many benefits. The downside is that there is never enough space on your boat, regardless of how big it is.

The good parts of living aboard include the wonderful smell of a clean sea breeze, the solitude of leaving civilization behind, and the freedom of movement and life that surpasses imagination.

The sunsets and sunrises will amaze you. So too will the stars. And if you are one of the lucky ones who can share this experience with the one you love – then I hope you realize how wonderfully blessed you really are.

The list of benefits are as many as the waves upon the ocean. Living aboard and retiring on your boat is ocean-side and waterfront living at its very best and at a mere fraction of the cost for a house on the hill overlooking the Bay.

Despite all the benefits, however, living aboard is not for everyone. For some it is an experience far outside their comfort zone. While many make the decision to retire on a boat for good sound practical reasons... some do it for all the wrong reasons. I have been an eye witness to many "live-aboard" disasters: Most come from those who move on their boats as a result of financial disaster, divorce, job loss, or whatever. I just know that moving onto your boat as a result of financial or relationship problems is not going to improve your situation in life.

The allure of the romance of the sea can also spell disaster. We are constantly presented with it in movies and television. We see the pictures and we dream…but once you are living on your boat, it is no longer a dream, it is reality. The lifestyle has (along with its benefits) an equally amazing number of challenges, surprises, and issues. It is something that must be considered with your eyes wide open.

The practice of safe boating and sailing demands knowledge and experience, not so much for the summer days when the water is calm and the breeze fresh, but for those moments when things are not going as we dreamed. When on the water, safety must always come first. Whether you are boating on an inland lake, cruising America's Great Loop, or voyaging in the Caribbean – the difference between a "beautiful dream experience, and a dreadful, life-threatening nightmare," may be separated only by a few seconds.

There are "issues" living on a boat. Most of these issues are common sense ones that can be easily avoided or fixed. Some, however, are much more complex. The more complex issues are those that come with experience. If not our own, then certainly ones who have sailed these seas before us, and have left behind their words of wisdom for us that follow.

While I have been a live-aboard size boater almost all my life, never have I found the words, the books, the magazines, or any "advice" in any form that explains the subtleties of the essentials of living comfortably (on a frugal budget) on a boat, in the middle of paradise.

So... this is the best my experience can offer, when asked the question:

"Is living aboard really a good thing?"

An emphatic "YES!" "Well, maybe." "It depends." is my answer. It is an adventuresome romantic life, different than the norm, much more economical than life ashore and truly has some amazing benefits. But still, it simply is not for everyone.

"So what does it depend on?"

Well... are you doing this by yourself, or with a mate? If you are doing it with a mate, then it depends on how much your mate wants to do this. In this case, it takes two to tango and in my experience, it has proven time and time again that the unwilling mate is the most significant reason why couples cease the live-aboard lifestyle. I've witnessed many mates walk the plank. I also know an awful lot of very happy live-aboard couples (and even families) that would not give up the life for any mansion on the hill.

It also depends on whether or not the reality of living aboard is an acceptable lifestyle once everyone realizes it is not all romance or always a pleasant adventure. The clothes still need washing, and the deck still needs scrubbing... unless you have a boat that doesn't need maintenance (and who has one of those?) This lifestyle is not entirely about sitting on deck off of a beautiful tropical island with an umbrella drink in your hand.

It also depends on whether or not you can handle the motion of the boat – and that motion is constant. It comes when you are at sea, at bay, at anchor and even in a marina. While much of it is hardly noticed in a marina, I can't even begin to remember the number of times I have had my dinner and drinks thrown off the table by speeding boats in a NO WAKE ZONE.

"So why do I do it?" you might ask. For me, the benefits far outweigh the downside difficulties and lack of space. I love being able to take my home wherever I go. I love boating, fishing, nature, outdoors, sandy beaches, deserted islands, a bit of solitude, meeting people, and making new friends. Above all else, I love the freedom.

The freedom that comes with living on your own <u>paid for</u> boat (even with a limited income) is an astonishingly noticeable <u>absolute</u> freedom. I can stay put, or go where I want – when I want. I just point my bow in the direction I want, and go. Lucky for me, my friends and family live on or near the water.

Living on my boat, I am totally independent in a self-contained environment. I have no need of utility companies, government or government assistance. I have no need for lawyers, salesmen, shopping malls, Walmart, or convenience stores. In fact, I am so removed from all the violence in the news, I sometimes feel I must be on a distant planet.

I have all the amenities of home: central air/heat, TV, stereo, high speed Internet, and a cell phone. I never have "locked up" my boat. I don't even have a lock on the cabin way hatch (door). I have never had a single item stolen off my boat. I have never felt threatened in any way. But it is possible that the bottom line to all the reasons I love living and cruising on my boat, is that I simply could not afford to travel as much or as far as I do, or live as well, if I were living on land –and I do love the travel.

Despite the myths, the imagined and the real dangers, my experience tells me a safe boater is far safer cruising around the world, than driving his car to work – or in these days, possibly even being at work.

For sure, anyone at almost any age in reasonable health can live on a boat and go cruising. Some retirement couples simply find a wonderful cove, drop anchor, and live out the rest of their lives on their boat in paradise. Others plan to cruise and return to the mainland to live on their boats. Some, plan to "stay out" as long as health permits, and then sell the boat and buy a condo. It is truly a matter of what fits your philosophy, pocket book, and lifestyle.

Whether voyaging around the islands of the Caribbean or cruising around America's Great Loop... you will be shocked and amazed at not only the numbers of "senior citizens" doing it, but also the numbers and ages of all people doing it. I am 67 years old, and last year I thought for sure I would be the senior of seniors both cruising the Loop and sailing the Caribbean –was I ever wrong about that!

There are live-aboard sailors "out here" much older than I am, and these retired or semi-retired sailors range in ages from their mid-40's into their 80's. I in fact met one couple in their mid-80's – and they were as active and happy as anybody I know. The fact is that senior citizens are out here, still sailing, still active, and still enjoying every minute of it.

I guess it is a question of how long is long enough? Maybe our physical health will dictate how long we keep sailing, or how long we remain in paradise, or possibly, our mental health will let us know. I simply don't know the answer to this question– at least not yet. Maybe it is just a matter of when we can no longer raise the sails; we drop our anchor for the last time. Whatever it is…I do know this: I am one that will have no end-of-life regrets. I will continue living aboard, feeling blessed, grateful, and happy that my God and my mother gave me the gift of life, and that my Dad taught me how to live it.

Great Loop Musing

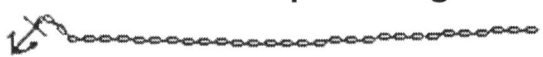

When it comes to boats and boating, for sure, the devil is in the details, and you don't have to look very far behind the devil to find his sidekick, Murphy (and we are all too familiar with Murphy and his Law). For sure, some of the most pleasant and wonderful experiences of our lives came about because we took care to cross our T's and dot our i's. So, now that I have given you some of the glitzy, glimmer, and encouragement, you also need to take time to learn about some of the details.

This book is NOT a cruising guide. It is also NOT a boat safety course. My intention is to inform you about America's Great Loop, not to teach basic boat safety. Truthfully, America's Great Loop is a magnificent journey. Whether you are a novice or an old salt, you can make this journey safely simply by being a safe boater – but learning what you need to learn to be a safe boater is not the intention of this book.

While I have mentioned on several occasions that you don't need a ton of education or experience to cruise the Great Loop safely – I am making the assumption that you are a safe boater, or will be one before you begin your cruise. Knowing the waterway rules of the road, and knowing your vessel, and how to maintain and operate it safely is critical. You don't need a sextant, you don't need to be an expert at navigation, and you don't need a Captain's license. If you can follow the road signs and your GPS directions in your car – you can follow the waterway signs and your GPS around America's Great Loop.

Your Dinghy

Think of the Great Loop as having 5,600 miles of free dinghy docks! Many (if not all) private marinas provide free dinghy docks. Additionally, most (if not all) city docks, city piers, waterfront restaurants, state and national parks, wildlife reserves, historic and tourist sites, small towns, counties and municipal areas provide free dinghy docks. Without a dinghy, in all but a very few cases, you will pay $1.00 a foot (or more in some locations) to dock your boat. So be aware of this before you buy that 60 footer vs. that 30 footer, and in either case, (unless you are doing the loop in a dinghy) you will want a dinghy. Not only is it wonderful to have for fishing and exploring, it is the single most valuable tool you can get for cutting expenses, and cruising on a frugal budget.

While your boat will be your home on the water, your dinghy will be your SUV on the water. It is your taxi, your U-Haul, and your utility vehicle. It will take you to shore anytime for any reason. In fact, a dinghy will save you a thousand dollars or more in dock fees and/or overnight stays at marinas. Additionally, in many areas it will save you a mile or more walk to a local supermarket, movie theater, or discount boat supply store. So often you can get so much closer to these places with your dinghy than the marina is.

While it may seem contradictory to say you need to purchase an optional dinghy to cruise the Great Loop on a frugal budget – the fact is that it will save you much more in docking fees than you will pay for it. It will provide you access to a totally unlimited amount of site seeing, exploring, beautiful beaches, fishing, and shopping opportunities that you would otherwise not be able to reach. In many areas it will mean the difference between walking three miles (and back), or walking three blocks (and back).

When cruising America's Great Loop – you will see all kinds and types, sizes and shapes, of both new and used boats. The bigger "yachts" are the ones that are more for show than go. Most of the ones you see will be at the dock, and they remain at (or near) the docks.

When you think about a boat and budget for actually cruising, you must think in terms of minimal space, with enough room for you to be comfortable and happy. For sure, the boats that are great for overnight or long weekends, simply won't work over the long haul for a cruising couple on the Great Loop. They may suit a "back-packer" type – if rigged properly.

Remember, indeed, the very day you purchase your boat, you <u>predetermine</u> your on-going, fixed, long-term cruising expenses. If you choose the right boat, then your individual choices in lifestyle will be the majority of your cruising cost. This means you can spend the majority of your budget on yourself and on what makes you happy, rather than on your boat, fuel, and boat-related expenses.

Choose the wrong boat, and your vessel could end up a vessel of burden, rather than a vessel of freedom and pleasure. In all areas along the way, we have come across "Looper boats" that are for sale simply because the boat proved too expensive to cruise on, and sadly, they remain unsold for that very same reason.

Questions...WOW! Do I get the questions on my website! More than half of them involve general Loop cruising. The rest are "expense" questions. Since keeping track, I have answered over 6,200 questions.

In the past, I have always been "vague" when it comes to expenses. Of course, the reason being I would hate to mislead anyone in one direction or the other. However, when you consider I now have over 3.5 million visitors a year to our website, I cannot ignore the interest in answering the question of exactly "How much does it cost to cruise the Great Loop?"

It would be nice if I had a simple answer. It would be great if we could all just go out and buy a ticket, and have all our boat and boat-related expenses included, but it just isn't that simple and it doesn't happen that way.

So, for that reason and for the reason of dispelling the myth that one has to be "rich" to buy a boat and cruise the Great Loop, this is one of my main reasons for this book.

For most freedom lovers and frugal voyagers the dream is really all about living aboard and cruising, with the ultimate goal of staying out longer. It is no longer about the boat. In fact, if your dream includes a "dream boat" chances are you will never cruise the Great Loop or even beyond unfamiliar waters. Most of these vessels never do. So, hopefully, (if I've done my job) your Great Loop "Dream Boat" is now a comfortable, safe, seaworthy boat you can live the dream on.

From bums to billionaires, on the water, we are all often at the same marina or the same anchorage, or the same beach sharing the same fish fry, lobster bakes, and barbecues. While our pocketbooks, bank accounts, and boats are not at all the same size or price, what we all have in common is a fierce love of freedom and a great respect for Mother Nature and each other. No one cares who has what boat.

Respect "out here" is earned by being a good, careful, safe, and considerate boater, not from the age, size, or price of your vessel.

On the Great Loop, those voyagers that are in the smallest, simplest, and most humble of boats earn the greatest respect and admiration from everybody. Almost all of the most experienced and accomplished live-aboard and cruising voyagers, have purchased used boats, under 36 feet in length.

According to the latest US Census – over 160,000 US citizens claim a boat as their primary residence. This is an increase (by the way) of almost 30,000 over the previous US census. Obviously the living aboard lifestyle, cruising or not, is getting ever more popular.

For most of us, cruising or not, the main thing that separates the land-lovers from live-aboards is space. If you are addicted to stuff, you are going to need a really, really big boat.

If you need a really, really big boat, you'll never make it as a frugal voyager. One of the basic facts of life about living aboard is that there is never enough space. In addition to space (or I should say lack of it), in order to live-aboard successfully, one has to assume somewhat of a bum mentality. The slow-lane lifestyle of the live-aboard really starts to become appealing shortly after you have moved aboard, and you realize that it just isn't as important that you dress in the height of fashion every day.

In warmer places such as the Gulf states from Texas to Florida and in the Caribbean, it's possible to live the rest of your life with a dozen or so t-shirts, a few pair of shorts, a couple pair of jeans, a sweater or two, a light jacket, and a windbreaker.

Having long ago retired to live and cruise on my boat, my income is a very small fraction of what it used to be, but so too are my expenses. For the first time in my life I am exactly where I always wanted to be – doing exactly what I always wanted to do. Ask me, and

I will tell you, I would not exchange my lifestyle for any mansion on the hill. But living on a boat does have its drawbacks. Yes, I did an about-face and dropped out of the rat race. I am not healthy, wealthy and wise. I am much healthier, happier, and well, maybe a bit wiser.

The key to success (if you plan to go cruising) is NOT to think of your boat as your home, but instead, to think of it as a big suitcase – that just happens to have a bed, a head, and a small galley.

If you are cruising in areas by their preferred boating season, you will spend very little time inside your boat's cabin. If you are living on the hook, or at the marina and not going anywhere, your inside cabin space will be everything.

If you plan to live on your boat and not go anywhere, I suggest you get the biggest boat you can afford. For this, houseboats are about as good as it gets. If you plan to go cruising, your choices will be power or sail. Those staying close to home and cruising in local waters have several options, and a Trawler may be your very best selection as they offer lots of deck and cabin space, as well as great cruising ability and amenities. For those who desire to venture into more long-distance cruising, I strongly suggest you limit your choice of vessel to sail.

The main reason of course, is today's cost (and continually rising cost) of fuel. For those that think living on a boat is a simply a cheap alternative to housing – think again.

While living off the grid in a boat can seem attractive, it takes an awful lot of up-front expense to do this comfortably and successfully. Additionally, once all is said and done, it is probably not nearly as cheap as you think. By far, most everyone who moves onto their boat for negative financial reasons ends up moving back on land within a few months. It can be a wonderful life and lifestyle for those of us that do it for all the right reasons. And going through a divorce or tough financial times are NOT good or successful reasons.

On maps, charts, websites, and dated material: The Great Loop is undoubtedly the safest long-distance voyage any American can make without having to go to sea. But it does have its hazards, and most of those hazards change daily with the winds and the tides.

For sure, knowing the tides (tide changes, ranges, and depth) in the area you are cruising is a must. In addition, cruising on a rising tide is your safest most carefree daily routine. In fact, cruising on a falling tide could lead to total disaster – resulting in the loss of your boat.

Speaking of change... my first cruise around America's Great Loop was totally incident free – I was lucky. It was a non-stop, quick trip around the Loop. My second and third times around were very different, though still incident and accident free. My fourth time around I ran aground for the first time and had some minor mechanical problems.

Now, having completed my fifth cruise around the Loop, I find myself stopping more frequently, I ran aground twice, and discovered more changes along the way than in any trips before.

The point I want to make is, for sure, your journey will be different from all of mine, and unique to everyone else's. Fact is: rivers change their banks, tides wash away the sands, beaches erode, and the current moves the muddy bottom just as effortlessly as the wind moves falling leaves.

When boating around the Great Loop, your route will be basically the same as others, but that is where the similarities stop. Silting occurs, sand dunes form, bridges and wing dams are built, docks, piers, and marinas come and go. So, while I encourage you to learn all you can before making this voyage, I want to direct your attention to some common Looper mistakes:

Caution should be used when reading articles and books (even cruising guide books), and other **dated** material. Don't ever "blindly" expect fuel stops, docks, depths, piers, marinas, safe anchorages, gunk holes, or even a favorite restaurant to be there when you are. Things change, and if there is one thing you can expect cruising the Great Loop, it is that you can expect the unexpected.

For sure, keep your fuel tanks topped off and ample provisions on board.

Paper Charts and Sextants: You don't need either. Thanks to modern technology, I haven't used either since my second time around. I use a medium-priced Lowrance GPS.

Take your time. Cruising the Great Loop is not a race. In most areas your speed will be limited by 10 mph posted speed limits and no wake zones. In other areas, there will be sites to see. Traffic (and often crab traps) may also hinder your safe speed. Whatever the case may be, you are most likely to enjoy the safest incident-free voyage by just going slowly. Not paying attention and not following the rules can ruin your entire day, if not your entire journey.

When it comes to living aboard, be very realistic (cruising or not). Look before you leap. If you don't have your boat yet, spend a lot of time looking at every live-aboard boat you possibly can. Get a solid idea of the type and kind that fits your lifestyle, pocketbook, and purpose. Sure, we all want that big expensive boat we saw at the Boat Show. But the hard, cruel fact is that a dream boat is more often than not, a dream buster.

Be comfortable–Today, cruising or not, refrigeration on a boat is no longer a problem. Neither are other creature comforts such as TV, laptops, Internet, microwave, cell phone, etc. Long-distance voyagers today no longer have to live like cave men. Instead, most boats are more like man caves.

Deal with it (cruising or not). The biggest single difference between spending a weekend on your boat vs. an extended cruise is the things you have to just deal with. These include the size and type of boat that will work best for you, the amount of storage, tolerance, and close quarters. It is far easier to do without some creature comforts for a weekend than it is for months or a year.

Dinghy(especially if cruising)– I've mentioned it before, but I cannot stress it enough – you not only need one, you will wish like crazy you had one before your voyage is over.

Good tools (cruising or not) are a must when you're out here on the water. A new boat warranty won't do you any good. Good tools and few easy to replace spare parts are better than money in the bank.

The weather outside–As my son says, voyaging around America's Great Loop is much like chasing an eternal summer. The weather you will encounter will be, for the most part, very easy to deal with. Obviously you will encounter some heavy rains and some thunderstorms, but the hurricanes and tsunamis are easily avoided.

Other than that, you will need to prepare for boating through all kinds of weather. Cruising around the Great Loop will start with timing your departure so that you are in the cooler north during summer and in the warmer south during winter. So, it is unlikely you will experience any of the extreme weather these seasons have to offer.

Me? I wear mostly shorts and jeans, t-shirts, windbreakers, a few light cotton long sleeve shirts (sun protection), a couple of sweaters, and hooded sweatshirts. That makes up my entire boating wardrobe. Aside from rain gear, cotton and removable layers are the key to keeping comfortable on your cruise around the Great Loop.

You will also need lots of sun and weather protection for your skin. Most people don't realize that you can get just as sunburned from long exposure to the sun's reflection bouncing off the water, as you can get from exposure directly from the sun. So be prepared for this.

A Bimini top is an absolute must. Let me say that again. A Bimini top is an absolute must! The bigger, the stronger, the better! In addition, if your vessel does not have screened windows, hatches and hatchways into your cabin with an inside helm, you will wish it did.

If it doesn't, you will need to install screens or mosquito netting. Preferably, you will have (or can devise) a method of applying mosquito netting in such a way where you can cruise and relax in the cockpit or at the helm with complete protection against mosquitoes, black flies, love bugs, attack bugs, gnats, no-see-ums, Asian carp, and flying alligators (just kidding about flying alligators).

I guarantee you that before your voyage is over all those flying, flesh biting, blood-sucking critters will have their way with you at least once. And if you don't go insane, jumping into the alligator-infested Lake Okeechobee will seem a better alternative than staying on your critter-infested boat.

The conditions inside– On the inside, your vessel needs to have lots of free air circulation. This goes for your cabin, closets, and bilge. Even with air conditioning, plenty of ample outside air flowing through your vessel will keep it smelling fresher and free of mold and mildew. The fewer cabins and enclosed area, the better.

A place for everything–EVERYTHING on your vessel needs to have a place and a useful purpose. There is simply not enough space anywhere for "stuff" you don't need or use. Furthermore, everything needs to have a place and that "place" needs to be determined early in your voyage – then, it needs to stay there. Everything (from fire extinguishers, flashlights, hand-held VHF radios or GPS, binoculars, PFDs, wire cutters to toilet paper) needs to have its rightful place on your vessel.

Shower–While not absolutely necessary, before your voyage is over you will want a self-contained fully-enclosed shower. Showers that wet down the entire head (bathroom) are better than nothing, but not the best for a long-distance, long-term cruise.

Cruising in tidal waters– In many areas on the Atlantic and Gulf ICW tides can change the water depth beneath your boat as much as five feet. This, of course, is not good at all when you are in eight feet of water and the tide is falling. Always cruise these areas on a rising tide. This way, if you do go aground, you simply wait until the rising tide floats your boat again. Going aground on a falling tide, however, can be disastrous.

Anchors aweigh– Your boat is your own special island, with some of the comforts of home. I average spending over five nights a week on the hook while cruising. Many boaters have had bad anchoring experiences cruising unfamiliar waters. It shouldn't happen. So invest in a good heavy-duty anchoring system, and learn how to use it. This will prove to be better for a good night's sleep than any Sleep Number® bed.

Also be careful anchoring in tidal waters. Make sure you know the ebb and flow as well as the low and high tide times and water levels for the immediate area you are cruising in. This information is not only available in chart form; it is also broadcast by the USCG hourly updates on the VHF.

Schedules– There is one thing you will never see on my boat – and that is a schedule. When I'm cruising, I am on CMT – that's "Caribbean Maybe Time." If I say I will be there, I will be there, but it doesn't mean I will be there any time soon. I'm on a boat, not a train or plane. I don't even try to run on a schedule – neither should you. This is what gets most boaters in real trouble. If you like a place, stay longer. If you don't like it, move on. If the weather forecast is good – go! If it is bad – stay put!

Keeping in touch–I keep in touch online. This goes from keeping in touch with family and friends, to banking. I pay for everything I need with a Visa debit card on a dedicated account. I never have more than $20 cash in my pocket. Laptops, Wi-Fi, Internet, and cell phones are wonderful. With Wi-Fi and nation-wide minutes, I am very, very seldom out of cell phone range. Even when anchoring out, I plan my nightly stops to be within Wi-Fi and cell phone coverage.

When to go– If you're waiting for the perfect time to go…like anything and everything else…there will always be reasons, issues, situations, circumstances, and things to overcome. Don't wait until everything is perfect to start your voyage around the Loop – it never will be perfect!

Your lifestyle– It is absolutely essential you (and your mate) remain in your comfort zones and maintain your lifestyle. For me, eating out, an occasional good glass of cool wine, and a daily shower – keeps me happy.

On fishing– If you like to fish, and love seafood – you are in luck. God does provide, and when it comes to Mother Nature's food stamp program, she provides ever so abundantly.

I catch everything from amberjack, tuna, flounder, pompano, sail cat, redfish, sea trout, and sea bass. I also catch more blue crabs than one can possibly eat. In some locations the same is true for netting large schools of shrimp.

On the Gulf ICW and around Florida I dive for scallops and lobsters. On the Great Lakes, I catch salmon, lake trout, and walleye. On the Inland rivers of course, I catch more catfish and bass than I can possibly eat.

More often than not, you will find yourself releasing more fish then you keep. I only keep what I need to make a meal for that day's dinner. Point is, if one likes to fish and has the desire and equipment to do so, it is very possible to have fresh seafood on your plate all the way around the Loop or all the way around the world.

On fishing licenses– I get this question all the time. Obviously, if you are boating through 25 or more states on your route around America's Great Loop, you don't want to buy a fishing license in every state – and fact is, you don't have to. Well, at least not if you plan it correctly.

For example: From Carrabelle to Jacksonville, FL you will be spending a month or more in Florida waters. It's worth buying a temporary license. I always do.

In salt water, Georgia recognizes both the Florida and S. Carolina license. Likewise, N. Carolina recognizes the S. Carolina and Virginia license, and New York recognizes the New Jersey license. So I always travel with a Florida, N. Carolina and New York fishing license. I don't need one in New Jersey as I am never in New Jersey waters long enough to fish. My New York license, however, is good from New Jersey all the way through Lake Erie.

For Lake St. Clair, Lake Huron, and Georgian Bay I use my Canadian fishing license, so I always get one of them.

Down the inland rivers you have a similar situation. Since most all the rivers border the states, you don't need a license for both states. So on the inland rivers I buy a Tennessee license which covers me on the major portion of the Tennessee River and on Kentucky Lake. Once through the Tenn-Tom, I am just a few miles away before my Florida license is good again. So in all I have fishing licenses for four states (Florida, N. Carolina, New York, and Tennessee) and one for all of Canada. Besides, I have never been stopped or asked for my fishing license.

Living large on a small boat and budget– This is exactly what I do, and that's what most live-aboard cruising boater's do. Contrary to belief, it's NOT for the rich and famous. The "secret" to doing this successfully is having a fully-paid-for vessel.

Power or sail– There are advantages to living on a powerboat. There are advantages to living on a sailboat. There are also disadvantages with both.

Powerboats require much, much more fuel, maintenance and expenses. They also provide more inside comfortable living space for their size than a comparable sailboat. However, a small live-aboard size sailboat can be quite comfortable. With a sailboat, while you can motor all around the Great Loop if you so wish or need to, you do have the option of extending your Great Loop voyage deep into the beautiful Caribbean.

Whichever boat you buy or have, the key to long-distance living aboard and cruising is self-sufficiency. You will need at least two deep cell 12-volt marine batteries (I have three), and you will need a good appropriately sized solar panel to keep you batteries fully charged and in ship shape.

Freedom: As soon as you realize you can live comfortably on your boat, totally independent for an extended period of time, that's when you will realize what true freedom really is.

While cruising and living aboard, you will develop an entirely new definition of freedom. In doing so, you will gain an increasingly greater appreciation for it. Soon enough you will realize how really incredible and unbelievable it is that we Americans have unconsciously given up so much of our freedom for some very bad reasons.

So if it's not Bush's fault, whose fault is it? I blame most of the problem on the Jones'. Simply trying to keep up with the Jones' (whoever they are) is 99% of everybody's financial problems. Who are they anyway? We have all lived a life founded on dreams and goals, many of which were really never our own, but of those of someone else holding up their goals in a mirror for us to see.

Many of us have lived a life filled with the best intentions to please others. From our parents, to teachers, pastors, bosses, best friends, and from peer pressure to public approval – we have successfully shackled ourselves from our own freedom. It is no coincidence, I believe, that in the face of certain death for treason, all the signers of our Declaration of Independence had experienced the freedom of crossing the Atlantic Ocean at least once.

Franklin, Jefferson, Adams, and Monroe had crossed it several times. Cruising gives you that kind of freedom. It gives one a time to reflect on the real values of life.

You will in the process of cruising America's Great Loop realize that the true meaning of wealth is not having more, but needing less. You will also discover the richness of the life that God planned for our lives.

So I encourage you to take your time. Don't try to do as I do. Do your own thing instead. Stay within your own comfort zone, philosophy and of course, pocketbook.

Whether or not you cruise in a beautiful Flagship vessel or a most humble of boat, in the end you will discover this voyage is the destination. Regardless of the type, size, cost or shine of your boat, the voyage will excite and energize your life forever.

America's Great Loop

Top Twenty Great Loop Questions - Answered

Q: What is the lowest bridge on the Great Loop I must go under?

A: The lowest bridge you cannot avoid going under on the Great Loop is 19' 1" at mile Mark 300 on the Chicago Ship Canal after the Chicago River and the Calumet Sag Channel join south-west of Chicago. There is no other route around this fixed bridge.

Q: What other low bridges might restrict or affect my route?

A: There is a 15' 6" fixed height bridge on the west end (at Tonawanda) on the Erie Canal. If you can clear 15' 6" you can take any route you choose on the Great Loop, including the full length of the Erie Canal into Lake Eire. If you can't clear 15' 6" but can clear 17', you can take the Champlain Canal north to Lake Champlain, the Chambly Canal, Richelieu River, Saint-Ours Canal and the St. Lawrence River. If you can't clear 17' you must take the Erie Canal to Oswego and into Lake Ontario and on to Toronto and the Welland Canal to enter Lake Erie.

Q: How much does it cost to go through the locks?

A: The NYS Canal System charges a toll based on the length of your boat. In 2012, a 10-day pass for boats over 39 feet was $50.00. In Canada tolls are also based on the length of your vessel and days of use. All Quebec and Ontario Waterways (Includes: Rideau, Trent-Severn, Chambly and Sault St. Marie; Excludes: St. Lawrence Seaway Locks) have 6-day passes for $4.00 a foot. On the St. Lawrence Seaway and the Welland Canal, fees are $20.00 to lock through.

Q: What do you think about taking a gun for protection?

A: It's not a good idea, and certainly not needed. As of this date, the only pirates I have seen have not only been seasonal, they have also been under three feet tall and carrying bags for candy. ALL firearms must be declared before you enter Canada, and only weapons with a legitimate sporting use (in season) are allowed into Canada. All handguns are prohibited. Since it is "almost" impossible not to enter

267

Canadian waters when cruising the Great Lakes, the Thousand Islands or the St. Lawrence, and the penalties can be quite severe, I strongly suggest you leave your weapons at home.

Q: How long is the trip?

A: In terms of miles: All Intracoastal and inland river and lake miles are statute miles. If you are talking in terms of miles, the "shortest" trip can be as short as 5,600 miles. The average is closer to 6,000 miles. If you take all the detours and side trips, you can voyage over 29,000 miles – the average distance of a sailor making a round-the-world circumnavigation.

In terms of time: lengthy side trips, you need to plan on about 110 actual cruising days. To that, you will need to add the days you spend sightseeing, and your non-travel days.

Q: How long does it take to complete the Great Loop?

A: Regardless of how fast your boat is, there are a multitude of speed limits, no wake zones, scheduled bridge openings, locks, water safety, navigational, and weather concerns. A typical Looper will average about 50 miles per day regardless of the speed capabilities of their vessel. So, to determine how long it will take, you need to determine how many days per week you will be actually cruising. Due to the fact that it is extremely dangerous (and nerve racking) to cruise before or after dark, your day cruising will be determined by the nearest safe location of an overnight place to stay put - a safe anchorage or marina.

Q: Is there a certain time to cruise the Great Loop?

A: Yes and No. It all depends on from where you start. You have two critical time constraints. You don't want to arrive at the Erie Canal before it opens. Based on the severity of their winter (ice flows) the Erie Canal generally opens around May 1st. However, they may not open until mid-May, and regardless, you don't want to be an early bird for this one, as the worm is most likely to be in the form of a log, or trash in your props. So, give the winter debris plenty of time to clean out of the canals. I suggest you not arrive before mid-May. Again it depends on how harsh and how long the New York winter has been.

On the other side of the Loop, you want to be off the Chicago River no later than mid-September or October 1 at the latest (depending on weather). When the snow falls and the water begins to freeze, the locks and passage are closed. So you probably don't want to get stuck with your boat on the hard for the winter. Likewise, you don't want to be cruising south on the very lower half of the Tenn-Tom or in the Gulf before the end of hurricane season.

If you follow our guidelines around the Loop, your trip should bless you with 95% good weather.

Q: Can you drink alcohol when cruising the Great Loop?
A: I never drink alcohol when cruising. In Canadian waters alcohol can only be consumed aboard a vessel that has permanent sleeping accommodation, permanent cooking, and sanitary facilities, and only when the boat is at anchor or is secured to the dock or land. In the USA, drinking and boating is by far the number one cause of boat accidents, deaths and drowning. You will be boating through 25 US states, and each state has their own laws regarding alcohol and boating. So you are always safe if you limit your drinking to times you are not cruising.

9. Q: Do I need a Captain's License or any special training to cruise the Great Loop?

A: No! Simply put, you will only need to complete your state's NASBLA approved Boat Safety Course. While completion of a NASBLA approved boat safety course may not (yet) be mandatory in your state, proof you have completed it is required in many others – and is mandatory in Canadian waters. The NASBLA approved course is recognized in all US States that require it, and also in Canada as well as all countries (we know of or have been to) worldwide.

Q: What kind of boating experience do I need to cruise the Great Loop. I've been told it takes years of experience?

A: One thing I learned long ago is that the most difficult part of any voyage or journey into the unknown is the very first step. If you are a "safe" boater you have all the experience you need. Simply go slowly, practice safe boating, and you will learn along the way – there simply isn't any other way to get the experience you need.

Yes, I know there are a few boaters "out here" that make the claim you need years of experience and also need to take a boatload of education and navigation courses. I've even had a few old salts tell me one must have a Captain's license. Fact is, like sailing around the world in your own boat, you do not need a Captain's license, nor do you need years of experience. If you have the right boat, or purchase the right boat and learn or know how to use it safely, and know the rules of the road – you are as good to go as I (and many, many others) was our first time around.

Q: I am 62 years old and planning my retirement. I have always dreamed of living such a life and cruising the Great Loop. I worry now that I am too old. What do you think?

A: I am 67 and still cruising the Loop and sailing the Caribbean in winter. For the most part, notwithstanding a couple of bygone exceptions, I am a solo sailor and only accompanied by friends or family when they are on vacation. Fact is, when you get out here, you will be amazed at the number of us "Baby Boomers" that are living aboard and cruising.

12. Q: I have always been under the impression that living aboard and traveling on a boat was only for the rich and famous. I have read several articles about you through the years and read your book. I want to know if one needs to be rich to do what you do?

A: I am certainly not rich. Fact is, I'm not even sure how "financially" comfortable I am. My books are not on the "Best Seller List" and the market is a slim "niche" market indeed. In fact, if I wasn't so passionate about the subject matter – I wouldn't bother.

Sadly and erroneously many people believe as you do. I too held this belief for too many years and in fact, was scared to death while making my first trip around the Loop simply because I was worried about the money. I was afraid that I totally forgot or had miscalculated something and would run out of money. I was not comfortable with my finances until I was so near the end of my voyage, when it became undeniably obvious I would have money to spare. Indeed, cruising and living aboard your vessel is probably the most inexpensive "respectful and dignified" even "envious" way to live and travel on the face of this earth. If you are not doing it, because you thought it was only for the rich, you are (as I was) very sadly mistaken. The key, however, is the choice of boat you decide to do it in.

13. Q: Not counting the boat itself, what is your best advice for saving money while cruising the Loop?

A: Other than a boat as small and economical as safety and comfort will allow, my best money-saving suggestion is to get a good dinghy, and plan on "anchoring out" as much as possible. All but a very few places allow you to dock your dinghy for free, whereas most places charge a fee to dock your vessel. Anchoring out is free, and with all the free "dinghy docks" you can make all your necessary stops for fuel and provisions you need. A good used dinghy might cost you $500; a good new one might cost you $1,500. Even at $3,000 or more, a good dinghy will save you that much (or more) in marina fees – not to mention, in some cases, miles you otherwise would be walking.

14. Q: What about fuel range? How much fuel does my boat need to carry?

A: For boaters taking the Tenn-Tom route to Mobile, AL your required fuel range (as of now) is 250 miles. This will be between Hoppies Marina on the Upper Mississippi River to Green Turtle Marina or Kentucky Dam Marina, both 25 miles from Paducah, just south of the Tennessee and Cumberland River junction on the Ohio River. If you plan to cruise down the Lower Mississippi River from Cairo to New Orleans, you need a fuel range of at least 450 miles if you burn gas, and 359 miles if you burn diesel. The reason for this difference is there is a "trucked-in fuel stop" service for diesel fuel only.

15. Q: I'm just curious. How "high" can you go when cruising the Great Loop in terms of sea level?

A: WOW! While this is not a frequently asked question, it is an interesting one. The "highest" point above sea level on the main Great Loop route is actually in Buffalo, NY where the Niagara River is 620 feet above sea level – just upstream of Niagara Falls. It is the 52 locks in the Erie Canal that over a 300 mile stretch, lift your boat from sea level at the Hudson River to Buffalo and Lake Erie. If you take a detour up the Ohio River to Pittsburgh, then Pittsburgh wins out with a river elevation of 696 feet.

16. Q: What is the best thing you have purchased for your boat?

A: LOL - my Scooter. While I realize this is not an item anyone or everyone needs, for me, it simply expanded my freedom range on shore. For most cruisers, bicycles will do the same thing. My 50 cc scooter, however, is the best addition I have made to my boat since GPS and Solar panels.

17. Q: What is the very best route to take around America's Great Loop?

A: Even on the "short route," in several areas, you do have choices to make where the overall distance is slight. For example, you can take the Virginia Cut, or you can choose the Dismal Swamp. These choices for the most part, depend on you, your boat, your mood and the weather. In other cases, your route choice might make a big difference. For example, you can take the Canadian Heritage Canals or you can take the Erie Canal. I try to alternate my route.

If someone was to do the Loop only once, however, I would have to suggest the taking the trip to Montreal, then the Trent-Severn to North Bay. Other than that, the only other route I would strongly recommend is it taking the Tenn-Tom route to Mobile Bay vs. the Lower Mississippi route to New Orleans. The Tenn-Tom route is not only much more enjoyable, it simply is beautiful and has dozens of more interesting stops along the way.

18. Q: What is involved with anchoring out? Can one just stop anywhere and drop their anchor?

A: No! You can't just stop and drop your anchor anywhere. For one, it is against the law to anchor in a navigable channel – so you have to find a safe place to anchor away from the channel. In addition, there are other concerns such as underwater cables, water depth, and tide changes. However, there are ample safe anchorages all along your route, with only the Lower Mississippi River being somewhat of an exception. There are waterway guides and navigational aids, such as your GPS navigation system that identify the most popular safe anchorages.

19. Q: Why do you claim that cruising the Great Loop takes 110 days? My boat's cruise speed is 30 mph. Why couldn't I do the Loop in one month? Am I missing something?

A: You are missing something. I don't say you can't do the Loop faster, I'm saying you "should" take 110 cruising days if you want to enjoy the ride and see the sites. If you want to speed your way around it – be my guest, it should be fun. You will not, however, make it in 30 days. You might make it in 60. Just remember, there is almost no cruising at night except in areas of the Great Lakes and crossing the Gulf – it simply is not safe. As a result, the location of safe anchorages and marinas are the controlling factors for one day's cruising distance in daylight. Often the situation is that you can cruise past three marinas or three anchorages in daylight, but not four. This is why the fast boat "hare" and the slow boat "tortoise" end up anchored out or in the same marina at night.

20. Q: I know it's not polite to ask, but can you tell me what it cost you to cruise around the Loop?

A: Yes I can, even though I always have serious reservations about doing it. But let me caution you, I am a very experienced voyager, and I cruise and live on what I believe to be a very frugal budget. The main reason of which, is that I know how – and while I have been a boater all my life, it took me over a decade of boating to figure it out.

In 2011 my son and I spent just pennies short of $6,000 living aboard and cruising the Loop. This included all 0ur boat-related expenses such as boat fuel, oil and maintenance, marina fees. It DID NOT include our individual personal living expense for food, clothing, entertainment, etc.

Making the Dream a Reality

America's Great Loop
Keep The Dream Alive!

What if I told you that I could guarantee you that I can make the dream of living aboard and cruising America's Great Loop come true for you. Starting RIGHT NOW!

Are you interested? Who wouldn't be? So, I've included **5 easy steps**, that (if you follow them) I guarantee they will send you speeding down the path of closing the gap between where you are right now – and where you want your life to be.

What brought you here to this place, with this book in your hand, is certainly part of that magic and power, which surrounds us all. Call it luck, fate or God's design. Whatever you believe, there is a reason, and fact is, someone's dream starts coming true every day – and today can be your turn.

I admit that it is scary to drop the dock lines and set sail off into the unknown – into strange and unfamiliar waters. If cruising America's

Great Loop is nothing else, it is a voyage of exploration into the unknown. During your journey you may run out of fresh water, your favorite beverage or snack, you may run out of fuel, and you may even run out of patience. Who knows? But one thing you will not run out of on the Great Loop is the unknown.

Cost is an unknown, and cost is a concern for all of us. Yet, the currency of our youth is in short supply for us all. While we can choose where and when to spend our last dime, we do not have that luxury when it comes to spending our last moment. The Bible tells us our days on earth are numbered, and truth is, regardless of our age, regardless of your beliefs, we are all in the sniper's scope. I cannot emphasize enough how "putting things off" till later, ends up being the major reason so many never accomplish those things they always wanted to do. Living your dream (no matter what is is) is something that will change your life forever - for the better.

If your dream includes cruising America's Great Loop, I am here to tell you this awesome adventure, especially with the one you love, is simply priceless. How do we count the richness of our life anyway? It's certainly not by adding up all of our debt.

Long ago I discovered the single biggest thing all long-distance voyagers have in common is a positive attitude. Before any of us ever cruised that Great Loop, before we ever sailed the Caribbean, we all did it first in our minds. We did it time and time again, long before we ever did it for real.

For sure, good common sense and being a safe boater, together with a positive attitude and a safe seaworthy vessel can take you around America's Great Loop. If you are one that keeps putting this off because you are afraid of floods, storms, hurricanes, tsunamis, earth quakes, pirates, running aground or sinking your boat – don't be. If Little Red Riding Hood taught us anything, she taught us that the fear in our imagination always makes that big bad wolf far bigger than he really is, and that certainly applies to cruising the Great Loop. Indeed, (and I wouldn't kid you about this) cruising America's Great Loop can be easily and safely accomplished by any safe boater in a safe boat.

So here are the five easy steps to make this dream a reality:

1. **Passion**: Passion is the key to releasing your power to realize your dream. Passion is the most powerful inner resource we have. Doctors and Scientists alike tell us, it even surpasses our brain when it comes to possibilities.

Remember your first love? Remember when nothing this side of high water could keep you and your loved one apart? That's passion!

When we are passionate over someone or something, we are completely focused, all our actions are intentional, and nothing keeps us away or prevents us from reaching our goal. Your passion is your access to the power that motivates, energizes, and excites your daily life. It fills your tomorrows with great expectations. Passion permeates everything else! It is the essential ingredient for releasing the power that gives purpose to our life and makes our dreams come true. If you don't feel passionate over this dream, you are indeed fantasizing.

Dreams: When I speak of dreams, I speak of your most passionate and fervent desire, aspiration, and hope for how you want your life to be. I am NOT speaking of such things as winning the lottery. Winning the lottery, for example, is the most commonly shared fantasy in America. Many people spend a lot of time fantasizing. Fantasies, however, are a means of escaping reality. Dreams on the other hand, are a fact of reality. Our dreams, no matter what they are, always answer the question of "How do we want our life to be?" To that end, we have control over making our dream come true. You must be passionate about making your dream come true. If your dream is cruising the Great Loop – you must be passionate about accomplishing it.

2. **Define and clarify your dream:** This is the most critical component of making your dream a reality. Defining and clarifying your dream accurately and truthfully is necessary to realize what your dream really is. In doing so, you must be true to yourself. Remember, dreams always answer the question: "How do we want our life to be?" A fantasy never answers that question. In order to be successful at closing the gap between your dream and reality; your dream must be defined and clarified in a way that passionately inspires you and gives you control over making it happen. This is the mistake that most people make who never realize their dreams. Why? Because it is what most people omit. If your dream is defined and clarified, and not perceived as something real, specific, and attainable – it is indeed a fantasy and therefore, like winning the lottery, it is something you have absolutely no control over.

When it comes to defining and clarifying your dream, you must be true to yourself and think of yourself as a project.

From birth to death, we are all a project. We are a project of God, our parents, our teachers, and all those that have an influence over our everyday lives. Everyone has attitudes and beliefs about the aspects of their life. Our opinions and philosophy are long-term fully developed parts of who we are today. Whether you are 27 or 67 years old, the decisions and choices you make are all ultimately a result of the attitudes and beliefs you have developed over your lifetime. Our attitudes and beliefs create our thoughts and feelings which in turn influences our choices and (consciously or unconsciously) controls the decisions we make.

If you think of yourself as a project, you can understand why you must base your life on true and accurate information. Above all else, you must be true to yourself! No project can turn out successfully, if it is based on inaccurate, false or tainted information.

So, when you clarify your dream you must be truthful with yourself. Do you dream of a dreamboat? One you already know you could never afford? Or do you dream of the adventure? If you have to win the lottery to afford your dreamboat, than indeed your boat is a fantasy, and has no rightful place in your dream of a cruising adventure. In most cases it is indeed the dreamboat that is the dream buster. Why? Because most dreamers are never honest with themselves over what they can afford. You must define and clarify your dream in order to make it attainable. If not, it will never be a reality.

3. **Talk the Talk**: Once you define and clarify your dream to a point that you are passionate over its attainability. Once you separate the dream from fantasy – the truth from the myth - it then becomes important for you to "talk the talk."

Share your dream with others. Remember: a passionate purpose in life ALWAYS attracts others. The more you speak of your dream, the sooner you will live it. Look for appropriate opportunities to share your dream and tie it into the other aspects of your daily life. In doing so, you will discover that having a passionate purpose in life not only attracts others, but also that these others are key to your success.

You are now on your way to developing a winning team and that winning team will help you make your dream come true. For this, joining the AGLCA - America's Great Loop Cruising Association (for example) will instantly put you in the midst of a winning team. They help keep you informed and stay motivated. The AGLCA makes a great team member!

Remember, to be completely truthful with yourself. Most importantly here, you <u>must</u> also be truthful with ALL others. If your dream is the adventure, and you are working with a frugal budget, then when you speak of buying a boat – be sure to call it a "boat" and not a "yacht." The right word, as opposed to the wrong word, can be as dramatic as the difference between lightning and the lightning bug. This is especially important when talking to someone close to you that may not be so eager to support (or share) your dream.

Once people realize you are passionately determined to reach your goal of cruising America's Great Loop (or any other goal for that matter) your enthusiasm will be all you need. Enthusiasm is one of the most desired and attractive emotions any of us can possess in life. At work or play, regardless of what you do. You must talk the talk of cruising America's Great Loop.

4. **Remove the obstacles:** If you believe it is possible for dreams to come true, yet your dream hasn't come true already, obviously there's a gap between where you are now, and where you want to be. This gap is filled with obstacles. Most of these obstacles are comprised of your own attitudes and beliefs. You must remove all obstacles.

Recognize and trash all the excuses and get started on removing the obstacles. If your dream is the adventure then don't let your dreamboat be your major obstacle. You must simplify the process of living your dream, not complicate it. Sadly, many of the attitudes and beliefs we have, and have grown up with, are based on false information. For example, many believe that living aboard and cruising is only for the rich and famous. Others believe it is only the most accomplished sailors. These beliefs are absolutely not true. Believing them, however, makes them insurmountable obstacles to overcome.

Excuses are obstacles. As with our attitudes and beliefs, most excuses are also based on false information. I hear the same ones over and over again: "I don't have enough money." "I don't have enough time." I am too old." "I don't have the skills or the knowledge." "I don't have enough experience," etc., etc. etc.

All of the above excuses are but sad rationalizations based on false beliefs. Take lack of money for example: when in 2011 my son and I (to prove this very point) bought a $3,000 boat, and cruised the Loop for a total "boat and boat-related" cost for a year less than $15.00 a day - you will never convince me that "I can't afford it" is an obstacle that can't be overcome in short order. Indeed, if "I can't afford it" is your excuse – you're looking at (or have) the wrong boat.

Time is a funny thing, and another popular excuse. Sometimes we feel that it is closing in on us. Yet, when it comes to something we are passionate about, we always manage to take the time to make it happen. Truth is, time is not an excuse. Those that use it as their excuse are simply more committed to other things – and that's fine, as long as they are being truthful about it to themselves. You must remove the obstacles to make your dream become a reality.

5. Commitment: It's required to make your dream a reality. To live your dream you must close that gap between where you are now and where you want to be. To do so requires a passionate commitment. Remember, your passion is the key to your success. Your commitment is key to staying on track. Getting in touch with your passion will always get you out of the rut, and onto higher ground. **You must be committed to making your dream a reality.**

Finally, let me remind you that dreams really do come true. Every day some very ordinary people with an extraordinary dream can be found in the most humble of boats, cruising America's Great Loop. A passionate purpose, a positive attitude, an unstoppable persistence allow anyone to make it happen. It's a lot of work to live your dream. It also requires a lot of personal sacrifice. But the process of making your dream come true will energize and excite your life beyond belief.

Whether you realize it or not, you are already at the helm on the ship of your life. What you put into your mind is your autopilot. With every thought, your mind automatically steers in that direction. The winds of change always turn in the direction of your thoughts. That is why your thoughts are so important – they determine the course of your life.

The possibilities are already there just waiting for you to let them happen. Your passion is your power, and this power will produce extraordinary results to make your life the wonderful experience God meant it to be.

Finally, my prayer is that God blesses you with smooth sailing, in life, on land and sea. That you allow him to show you the way to make this dream a reality, and that he blesses you with a safe and uneventful voyage that will bless, energize and excite your life forever. Amen! Bon Voyage!

Comments & Suggestions

If you have comments you would like to make, or suggestions for additions you would like to see in the next edition of America's Great Loop & Beyond you may email them to:

Captjohn@captainjohn.org

If you like this book, you may also like:

For too many years, mariners turned writers have leading us to believe the voyage is more about them than the journey; that it requires a big expensive yacht, an advanced degree in navigation, and a meteorologist level of weather forecasting ability in order to live this dream. In "Caribbean Island Hopping", Capt. John hangs out the "All Are Welcome" signs for boaters of all experience levels with the dream of voyaging safely and comfortably on an affordable boat and budget. He combines captivating descriptions of the Caribbean with inspiring narratives of the islands and cays that lay in your path along the most beautiful cruising grounds in the world.

For those new to boating, no nautical glossary of sailing terms is needed. Capt. John writes for the dreamers and the novice boaters. His narratives are encouraging, educational, and include the kind of information only experience can provide, to those of us that have little or none.

Capt. John brings a refreshing encouraging down to sea level attitude to living the dream on an affordable boat and budget.

B. A. Ruisi, Ph.D.

ABOUT THE AUTHOR

Capt. John enjoyed a 23-year successful career as a Senior Executive in a Fortune 500 company from which he took an early retirement in 1993. Since then, he spent much of his time building his dreamboat and voyaging. He spends most of his time cruising America's Great Loop and the Caribbean.

A firm believer in God, country, freedom and family. Capt. John has two adult sons and a daughter. He was born and raised on a small farm in Terrell, Texas. He lives on his boat full-time.

Capt. John was the 2012 and 2013 Best Selling author in the nautical market. His best-selling BYOB series also includes "America's Great Loop & Beyond" and "Caribbean Island Hopping." He also maintains one of the most popular Great Loop websites on the Internet.SAA6

A USCG licensed captain, and a card carrying Senior Citizen, Capt. John still cruises the Loop and spends winters in south Florida and the Caribbean. He is a passionate lobbyist active in his efforts to keeping the Great Loop open to navigation. A closure of which, is threatened by proposed remedies to prevent Asian Carp entering the Great Lakes.

America's Great Loop

Talking the Talk

If you are seriously planning to cruise America's Great Loop – someday! Understand it is vitally important to "talk the talk" and stay motivated. If your goal is to lose weight, join Weight Watchers. If your goal is to cruise America's Great Loop, join the AGLCA.

There is no better way to stay "in the Loop" than this. If you believe birds of a feather flock together, then believe the AGLCA is the Loopers' nesting place.

This is a fine organization. Their primary purpose is hard aground on a foundation filled with a passionate purpose for promoting and educating boaters about America's Great Loop.

The AGLCA – **America's Great Loop Cruisers' Association** is full of boaters who share a sense of adventure and a curiosity about America's Great Loop. Their primary purpose is to provide you with information in order to enhance your overall experience of learning about and safely cruising America's Great Loop.

I strongly encourage you should visit their site at:
> www.greatloop.org < and review the many benefits of joining this Association.

Remember, the one thing all us have in common is that fact that we made that voyage over and over in our minds before we ever did it for real.

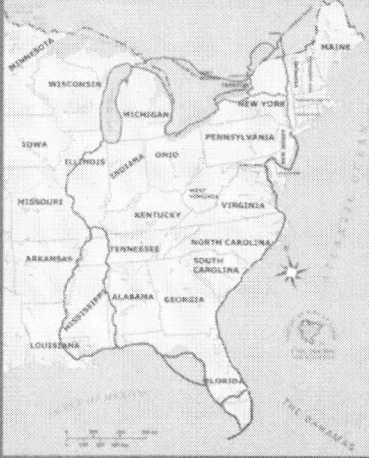

Made in the USA
Lexington, KY
26 October 2014